A TALE OF TWO DIVAS

A TALE OF TWO DIVAS

*The Curious Adventures of
Jean Forsyth and Edith J. Miller
in Canada's Edwardian West*

by Elspeth Cameron with Gail Kreutzer

A Tale of Two Divas
© 2016 Elspeth Cameron

Editor: Doug Whiteway

Cover design by Terry Gallagher/Doowah Design. Cover image from a poster of chanteuse Yvette Guilbert by Ferdinand Bac, published by Affiches-Camis, 1895. Prints & Photographs Division, Library of Congress, LC-USZC4-13940 Author photos by Foley's Imaging Services.

Images on previous page:
(Left) Jean Forsyth in her prime wearing a fashionable turban, "Canadian Women in the Public Eye," *Edmonton Journal*, Sept. 22, 1923. (Right) Edith J. Miller in her glamorous New York gown, publicity shot for the Edith J. Miller Company western tour, *Town Topics*, Oct. 13, 1900.

Printed and bound in Canada.

We acknowledge the financial support of the Manitoba Arts Council and The Canada Council for the Arts for our publishing program.

Library and Archives Canada Cataloguing in Publication

Cameron, Elspeth, 1943–, author
    A tale of two divas : the curious adventures of Jean Forsyth
and Edith J. Miller in Canada's Edwardian West / Elspeth Cameron.

ISBN 978-1-927922-33-0 (paperback)

    1. Forsyth, Jean, -1933. 2. Miller, Edith J. 3. Sopranos (Singers)--
Canada--Biography. 4. Contraltos--Canada--Biography. 5. Animal
rights activists--Manitoba--Winnipeg--Biography. 6. Animal welfare--
Manitoba--Winnipeg--Societies, etc.--History. I. Title.

ML400.C182 2016   782.1092'2   C2016-906857-9 Publication

J. Gordon Shillingford Publishing
P.O. Box 86, RPO Corydon Avenue, Winnipeg, MB Canada R3M 3S3

West to East

It is useless, West is strong, stronger than East.
Here I must stay until God's great feast.
When He will say, "This is best,
Better than East, better than old Ontario,"
[It's] where my heart longs to be.

—Jean Forsyth [1]

CONTENTS

Foreword.....13
List of Illustrations.....9

WINNIPEG

LIST OF ILLUSTRATIONS

Jean Forsyth. "Canadian Women in the Public Eye," *Edmonton Journal*, Sept. 22, 1923.....title page *(left)*

Edith J. Miller. *Town Topics*, Oct. 13, 1900.....title page *(right)*

Winnipeg Downtown in 1893. Notman & Sons, photographer. City of Winnipeg Archives.....15

Jaroslaw de Zielinski. University of Minnesota Immigration History Research Centre Archives.....25

Jean Forsyth oil portrait, *circa* 1817, artist unknown. Property of Elspeth Cameron.....28

Jean Forsyth. *Town Topics*, Oct. 13, 1900.....32

Signor Francesco D'Auria photographed by William Vaisey, *circa* 1887 in Ezra Schabas, *There's Music In These Walls*, (Toronto: Dundurn, 2005).....46 *(left)*

Edith J. Miller. *New York Times* photo, Oct. 23, 1899.....46 *(right)*

Alberto Randegger. Publicity photo, Carlo Rosa Opera Company, *circa* 1879.....60

Jean Forsyth. *Winnipeg Tribune*, July 2, 1904.....61

Mathilde Marchesi *circa* 1895. Photographer, Wilhelm Benque. Bibliothèque nationale de France.....71

Emma Albani, *circa* 1876. Sadie, Stanley, ed. *The New Grove Dictionary of Opera* (London: Macmillan, 1992).....77

Jean Forsyth and her dogs, *Town Topics*, Oct. 13, 1900.....100 *(left)*

Edith J. Miller, *Town Topics*, Oct. 13, 1900.....100 *(right)*

Edith J. Miller, *Town Topics*, July 28, 1900......101

Robert Campbell, *Town Topics*, Oct. 13, 1900.....102 *(left)*

Stanley Adams, *Town Topics*, Oct. 13, 1900.....102 *(right)*

Mrs. R. Percy Barnes. "Women of Edmonton," Gertrude Seton Thompson, *The Canada West*, vol. VII, no. 1 (London: Vanderhoof-Gunn Co. Ltd., Nov., 1909).....154 *(bottom centre)*

Mrs. Richard (Eliza) Hardisty. "Women of Edmonton," Gertrude Seton Thompson, *The Canada West*, vol. VII, no. 1 (London: Vanderhoof-Gunn Co. Ltd., Nov., 1909).....154 *(bottom right)*

Edith J. Miller. *Winnipeg Tribune*, May 1, 1909.....159

Mrs. Arthur (Emily) Murphy. "Women of Edmonton," Gertrude Seton Thompson, *The Canada West*, vol. VII, no. 1 (London: Vanderhoof-Gunn Co. Ltd., Nov., 1909).....174

Miss Katherine Hughes. "Women of Edmonton," Gertrude Seton Thompson, *The Canada West*, vol. VII, no. 1 (London: Vanderhoof-Gunn Co. Ltd., Nov., 1909).....177 *(left)*

Mrs. George Hedley Vicars Bulyea. "Women of Edmonton," Gertrude Seton Thompson, *The Canada West*, vol. VII, no. 1 (London: Vanderhoof-Gunn Co. Ltd., Nov., 1909).....177 *(right)*

Mrs. Joe (Margaret) Morris. "Women of Edmonton," Gertrude Seton Thompson, *The Canada West*, vol. VII, no. 1 (London: Vanderhoof-Gunn Co. Ltd., Nov., 1909).....178

Emma Albani, *circa* 1872. Robert James Manion, Library and Archives Canada, C-003307.....188

The Blue Moon Tea Room, interior, *Maclean's Magazine*, Jan. 1915.....191

Jean de Reszke, 1896. Aimé Dupont, photographer. Library of Congress, LC-USZ62-62697.....199 *(left)*

Jean de Reszke, 1898. Félix Nadar, photographer. Metropolitan Opera Archives.....199 *(right)*

Dame Nellie Melba. *The Victor Book of the Opera: Stories of One Hundred and Ten Operas with Seven Hundred Illustrations and Descriptions of Twelve Hundred Victor Opera Records* (Camden, NJ: Victor Talking Machine Company, 1915).....200 *(left)*

Dame Nellie Melba, *Illustrated London News*, June 25, 1904.....200 *(right)*

Jean Forsyth, *Maclean's Magazine*, Jan., 1915.....204

Edmonton branch, Women's Canadian Club, 111912. City of Edmonton Archives ea-10-2191.....212

FOREWORD

Imagine a world without Internet, television, movies, stereo, radio, automobiles, or even telephones. Imagine that that world was early Winnipeg, then Edmonton before Alberta was a province. Imagine there were only horse-drawn taxis and electric streetcars to get around. What could you go to? What would you do for entertainment?

This is the curious world of this book. A time when Winnipeg and Edmonton were cities of quickly made wealth and aspirations of greatness.

Entertainments were live. Men who could afford it went to their clubs. Women hosted each other at teas, some so large there were dozens of guests. Bridge and euchre parties were popular. Sports associations—tennis, cricket, rowing, curling, hockey, snowshoeing, golf—appealed to many. These associations held annual parties or enormous balls. Associations of all kinds sprang up. Yet the chief entertainments were live performances: vaudeville, skits and plays, music concerts. Music in these fast-growing communities centred on churches. At first it was church choirs that soon sallied into classical oratorios like Handel's *Messiah*. Churches began to hold mid-week concerts of music that had little to do with religion. Concert halls soon became a necessity. Before long, touring singing stars came to town by rail. Everyone read the local newspapers, and they reported everything, every detail.

This book tells the story of two singers who began as soloists in church choirs, but eventually moved on to spectacular careers. Soprano Jean Forsyth and contralto Edith Miller knew each other well. They met when nineteen-year-old Edith studied vocal music with Jean, almost twenty-five years her senior, in Winnipeg in 1894. After that their paths crisscrossed.

This tale of their two voices throws open a window on a world that never stopped changing. Music gradually left religion behind, shifting to romantic subjects, then to the anguish of the Great War. Topics at teas were gossip-fests until temperance and women's suffrage took the floor. Women who had been mere appendages of their husbands began to claim independence. Some succeeded at careers. Jean Forsyth and Edith Miller had careers all along, for singing and other performance arts were some of the few areas a woman could strike out on her own. At first, such women had to fill concert halls with their voices despite breathtaking corsets and Victorian flounces. Over time—especially with the appearance of the bicycle—fashions loosened up, causing many a scandal.

This tale of two voices contrasts the ways in which Jean and Edith achieved success. Edith Miller's path was clear and committed. An only child from Portage la Prairie when there were only about 700 citizens, she forged through to the very top in England, singing in the Proms, at the Festival of Empire to celebrate the coronation of King George V in 1911, and at Covent Garden, before marrying a baronet. Jean Forsyth never married and was drawn to many other interests. What might have been a vocal success story like Edith's was diluted by the compassion for animals that led her to found the Winnipeg Humane Society, her support of various charities, her dabblings as an actress, her journalism, her utter dedication to the many vocal students she launched on careers of their own, and her fulsome enjoyment of many social events. Her delight in society and her remarkable organizational and entrepreneurial skills ultimately led her to open her Blue Moon Tea Room that soon became the hub of Edmonton. It hosted every event imaginable, from dance lessons, to religious meetings, to union meetings, to young people's coming-of-age parties, to Christmas dinners.

Many books have been written about Winnipeg and Edmonton's early years. Yet none has been written about the cultural world of these cities or the daily social life of the women who moved from other places to establish their own ways of life. We know about the history of railways in the West, but the many visits women made to friends and relatives by train have remained vague. So too do their travels after 1880 by ocean liner across the Atlantic. Women in the West actually travelled often by themselves, and were in other ways freer than their eastern Canadian sisters. It is predictable that Emily Murphy, the first female magistrate in the British Empire and a friend of Jean's, would carry out her transformative work there. It's time such women as Jean Forsyth and Edith Miller and the way they led their lives in the Edwardian West came to light.

*

In this biography of Jean Forsyth and Edith Miller I have written a few chapters in fictional form. I have done this to give immediacy to this tale of two voices. These fictional chapters are not completely inventions, however. The content and details remain true to factual accounts that are backed by endnotes. At times the dialogue is fictional; at others it is as quoted in newspapers or other sources. I have taken the liberty of a sigh here, a laugh there, or an outcry of disappointment elsewhere. Yet these are in keeping with the natural reactions of characters I know well from reading so many accounts of their doings. Even settings remain true to photographs or descriptive accounts.

Entire letters or excerpts from newspapers occasionally make up a chapter. These appear as they did in their original sources. I have inserted newspaper headlines and advertisement verbatim in the main text to show the way information was presented in an era long gone.

My own vocabulary in writing the main nonfiction text has often drawn from the words commonly used as the nineteenth century turned into the twentieth century to maintain an aura of the times.

In all these ways I hope to make this book a layered and textured experience for readers.

WINNIPEG

Winnipeg Downtown
as Jean saw it on arriving in 1893.

1

JEAN

I started my enterprise boldly. It was a promising sunlit afternoon. I got Mr. Shakespeare's address at a music store. The house was in a fashionable part of London, near the renowned Langham Hotel. Then, I faltered. I walked around the block, the long skirts of my grey day dress swishing with every step. I crossed the street and back again, before I gathered nerve to ring his doorbell feebly.

An impassive manservant answered the door. The next minute the great William Shakespeare bounced out of a back room. I nearly laughed in his face with relief. He was a jolly little fellow, not the sort of singing master to strike terror into the heart. It must have been the greatness of the name past and present that scared me.

"I'm Miss Jean Forsyth," I said. "From America," I added, extending my gloved hand. "How do you do."

"How do you do," he responded. "I'm going to have to stop taking English pupils this season," he said, shaking his head. "I have so many Americans coming over."

Yet he agreed at once to take me as a pupil. Half an hour, three times a week, for a guinea. Tomorrow is my first lesson.

Waiting to begin next day, seated in his cramped dining room, I studied the life-size oil painting of my new singing master. His manservant had delivered notes for me to peruse before entering his study. The study itself was adorned with photographs of former pupils and musical celebrities, most of them autographed. The piano was a small upright and Mr. Shakespeare handled it with aplomb.

I gained only one idea for my guinea today, and a fine one it is too, if only I can develop it properly. *The inspiratory muscles must control the expiratory; that is, you must press out your sides to prevent the breath from escaping faster than you wish.* To demonstrate, he shoved me across the room, he representing one set of muscles and me the other. It seemed to me a stupid illustration. I suppose the little man is glad of an excuse to stretch his legs.

I had taken a nearby room on Gower Street offering "Board and Residence" instead of an "Apartment." I didn't want to cook and the landlady had a piano I could practise on. She provides breakfast and six o'clock dinner. Lunch I must find outside. This scheme would work well if my landlady were more liberal in her table. I suppose one cannot expect everything for twenty-five shillings a week. I shall have to economize in omnibus fares and lunches if I am to stay three months.

My second lesson repeated my first. Mr. Shakespeare's theory is similar to that propounded by Emil Behnke in his *Voice, Song, and Speech*.[1] It reminds me too of my many experiments at home using Madame Seiler's methods in *The Voice in Singing*.[2] I could see that Behnke insists on abdominal breathing, whereas Shakespeare emphasizes the "hold" of the breath at the waist after inspiration. I was just getting somewhere with this idea when the small voice of the manservant summoned my master, who dashed out of the study to meet a new student. That ended my lesson ten minutes early. I was chagrined.

My dear father once told me, "Go to the very best vocal teacher at the Royal Academy of Music in London."

"Dear little Pussy" (for that was his nickname for me), he used to say. "It will please me more than anything to think of you being over there developing yourself. If you are ever going to sing well enough to earn your living by it, you must have good lessons. I believe in going to the top of the tree at once."

When I expressed my trepidation, my father added, "The best master in London will tell you right away if you are good enough. If he says you cannot do it, why, then you come home again and start to learn typewriting or something of that sort. You seem entirely disinterested in marriage. You have had more than your share of suitors. Yet none seems to please you. We must consider how you will earn your living." As he used to do so often, he kissed my fair curls on both temples.

At my lesson a week after beginning I confronted Mr. Shakespeare. "Do you think it is worth my while taking these lessons? You promised you would not let me waste my money."

"Most decidedly!" was his reply. "Your voice is worth cultivating. It is not a great voice, but a very pretty one. Stay with me to the end of July and you will be greatly improved. Moreover, I'll give you a little note from myself." I thought he said this because I had told him I would rather teach than sing in public.

My lesson today was the same thing over again. I am getting a little nearer to it, though it is the most uninteresting thing I have tried to practise. No strain at the throat. The shoulder muscles relaxed.

"Laugh it out," he said.

Today he told me to get *Pensée d'automne* by Jules Massenet, which he declared was written for me. I walked out of his house with my nose in the air.

I am becoming very friendly with a certain Scotch spinster, Miss Guthrie by name, who boards in this house. She takes painting from one of the best masters here. Years ago she studied singing. She heard that Mr. Shakespeare could teach well if he chose to take the trouble.

"How much should I practise?" I asked the master.

"Just as much as you feel inclined."

"But I don't feel inclined at all."

"Then don't practise. Aren't you tired?" he asked me, with one of those upward looks from the piano stool that he seems to consider extremely fetching.

"No, I'm not."

"Then you can't be breathing right. You should feel tired—very tired round the waist, but not at the throat."

Then he heard me sing halfway through the Massenet song. He did nothing but correct my French accent and there was no English translation I could use.

Miss Guthrie has proposed sharing furnished rooms elsewhere. The breakfasts here are so very unsatisfactory and the piano is woefully out of tune, I've agreed. We have moved to nice rooms further up Gower Street. We'll have enough to take meals outside that we can't cook on a spirit-lamp. I rented a piano and practise comfortably now.

I expected to get the better of Mr. Shakespeare at a lesson not long after we moved. I had written an English translation of the Massenet song above the French lines. I repented when he wasted five precious minutes criticizing my translation. I never get more than twenty minutes' solid teaching. More discouragement! I wish devoutly that Mr. Shakespeare would not so frequently relax in my lesson. He sits on that piano stool and yawns till I feel like suggesting the lounge and a pillow.

When I was passing the Langham Hotel today on my way from my lesson, who shouldn't come out but Bessie Belnap! Her father is making money on lumber, and this is the second trip that she and her mother have made to Europe. Of course, I was glad to see her and she walked all the way here with me, telling me all the news.

Then recently, I attended a lesson of a student of Emil Behnke's that I had met. He is a tone specialist, not a breath specialist like Mr. Shakespeare. *That* was a lesson worth my while. He gave her three solid quarters of an hour for her guinea. She thinks I should switch teachers, but I don't feel I have given my teacher a fair chance. My blood boils when I see all the "smart" young ladies driven to and from his door in the most fashionable of carriages. They do not grudge a guinea [about $155 in today's Canadian dollars] for twenty minutes' amusement and the pleasure of calling themselves Mr. Shakespeare's pupils.

Every pupil I meet thinks I should leave Mr. Shakespeare and take up with her master. One dark-haired girl from Boston simply raved about her Italian *Signor*. "I feel I can do wonders when he accompanies me."

"But what are you like when you are away from him?" I asked.

"I never can sing so well with another accompanist."

"What sort of songs does he give you?"

"Italian, of course. There is no other language for the voice." She lifted her head as if to say that was the last word on the subject.

"I don't know that they would believe that in America."

"Perhaps not. But give me a foreign master and a foreign language. An Englishman would be ashamed to gush over music the way an Italian does. When he is particularly pleased with me he gets so worked up that he actually embraces me." Her face flushed with pleasure.

Her account determines me to make up my own mind about my master.

"You ought to be flattered that he takes you at all," Miss Guthrie said. I took her to a lesson so she could see for herself. She was agreeably surprised. But then, he did not give my hand the friendly squeeze that he thinks makes up for any lack of attention to business. Nor did he yawn. He kept me at work for the full twenty minutes.

"I'm sure he takes an interest in you, Jean," she said. "He can't have missed your clear blue eyes. Why, the way he gazed up at you put me in mind of that speech in the *Heart of Midlothian*, 'Oh, Jeanie, will ye no tak me?'"

"I know he takes an interest in me, but not as a singer."

"Well, you may be thankful he doesn't try to make you fall in love with him, as a lot of them do. They think it's a fine way to improve their own emotional execution. That was what disgusted me with singing masters long ago. To get on at all you either had to be in love with your master or make him think that you were in order to get anything out of him. Dear Miss Forsyth, the yarns I could tell you about the amount of humbug in the profession of teaching singing here in London! In piano-playing and other instruments there are certain standards accepted by all. But when it comes to the voice, every man has his own method. The recent craze is to expose the science behind the art. What happens to the larynx and vocal chords and so on when notes in different registers are sung? Some actually examine their pupils' throats—and their own! Each master starts off on his own hobby horse and drags after him as many poor pupils as will submit to being tied to his stirrups. If he plays our accompaniments sympathetically, gazes up into our eyes, and tells us we have voices like angels, we pay our guinea without a groan."

When Mr. Shakespeare interrupted me halfway through my Massenet song for the third time, I complained bitterly to Miss Guthrie. "I think it an utter waste of time practising these silly English ballads. Even at concerts here they sing nothing but Italian arias or English twaddle. I have worked hard at home for years, studying the songs of Schubert, Brahms, and Franz so I could sing them properly if ever I had the chance of good lessons! I could have cried this afternoon when for the *third* time he heard me sing halfway through that song and told me, 'We'll take the rest next time.' He said today that I must be a contralto because I had no head tones. I begged to differ. He asked me to sing some. I did, and he said, 'Oh yes, so you have; but of course you don't produce them properly.' And then he yawned. I shall be afraid to sing above E for the rest of my life. If people at home only knew all about it, they would not envy me this 'opportunity of a lifetime'!"

At this, Miss Guthrie became suddenly serious. "Don't let *anybody* know that you have been the least bit disappointed in your lessons. There will be plenty of jealous ones ready to say, 'Of course, Mr. Shakespeare would not take any pains with *her*!' You should give yourself out to be his favourite pupil and charge half a guinea a lesson."

"Oh, nonsense! I never could get that price in America. Nonetheless I have decided to take the very next steamer home."

"Be sure to remind him of the 'little note' he promised before you leave."

"I shall not go near him again. He would be sure to talk me into staying. I'll write and tell him I am going home sooner than expected. Don't imagine for a moment that he'll give me that 'little note.'"

I was right. I wrote politely to Mr. Shakespeare and asked for the note. I never heard back.

Once I was back home two months later, Mrs. Morrow, wife of a lumber king, asked me as a great favour if I would give lessons to her two daughters. She had heard that Bessie Belnap had met me in London. She didn't ask me to sing or question me about my terms or my method. I had been a pupil of the great William Shakespeare at the Royal Academy of Music in London, England. That was enough.[3]

EDITH

June 1892

Dearest Mama and Papa,

I am so very happy today that I cannot resist explaining to you the cause.

I have been awarded the Gold Medal at the Toronto Conservatory of Music for making the most progress during this past year. Can you imagine? A girl of eighteen from Portage la Prairie has won the top prize. Your daughter. Your only child. And this award comes with a scholarship for next year. It delights me that you will not carry the burden of my vocal training for that year at least. Papa cannot make much money as postmaster and, Mama, your payments for playing the organ at church cannot amount to much either. Dear Kind Papa, I know you would give anything to help me in my ambition to sing, but you can rest assured I will always do what I can to contribute.

There must be sixty pupils here, and I think there are about a dozen of us studying voice. It is difficult to tell, as we are only four to a class at most, and classes only last an hour. Most of them are sopranos and tenors, and I have always thought a contralto like me could easily be overlooked. I think all my years of practice sight-singing in our Knox Church choir have given me an advantage. And, as you well know, I have continued in the much larger choir at Bloor Street Presbyterian Church here for a small sum. There have also been music classes at school. Though these are quite easy at the Presbyterian Ladies' College where I have been studying the usual school subjects. These are not much different from those at Lansdowne College in Portage la Prairie where I worked so very hard, especially in my Vocal and Instrumental classes. They look after us very well indeed at the Ladies' College. I believe that they are doing their best "to provide a thorough, practical, and liberal education with the goal of matriculation under the safeguard of pure evangelical Christian principles," as we are reminded twice a day.

Oh, Mama! Oh, Papa! I can scarcely contain my excitement today. Some day I hope you will be able to afford to travel here and see for yourselves this place that means so much to me. The Toronto Conservatory of Music occupies the upper two storeys, and there is a convenient music store on the ground level. How blessed I am to be here, thanks to the sacrifices you are making, and how proud I am to have attended this place that has exceeded the merits of all the other music academies in the city in only half a dozen years.

I met Signor D'Auria in the hall on the second floor of our building on Yonge Street and Wilton Avenue yesterday. He was all excitement. Italians are so appassionati. He flailed his arms around and exclaimed in Italian, words that I am only beginning to understand from my language classes, Brava complimenti, glorificare Dio! Sono orgolioso di te. Then, how superb, how manifeek, how excellente. His wide impeccably groomed handlebar moustache fairly bristled with pride. He embraced me warmly, which made me blush. Truly, he has been the most wonderful vocal teacher I could possibly have, coming, as he does, from Italy itself. He assures us that that is the source of all great music. Some think him pompous, and it is rumoured that he makes an impossible amount of money.[1] But, as for me, I admire him beyond measure, and it is his teaching that has inspired me to progress as much as I have this year. He told me that he hopes to find some students for me here, though I can't think I'm capable of teaching. All I want to do is sing on the concert stage like Adelina Patti. My solo in the year's end concert was "Ah! Quell giorno ognar rammento!" from Rossini's Semiramide. Of course, I sang it in Italian. This is God's purpose for me in this life. Did I tell you that Signor D'Auria accompanied Patti, as he calls her, on her last tour of the United States ten years ago? It seems that he has met with all the major performers here and in Europe. It is a privilege to breathe the same air as he does.

May you both enjoy good health and God's blessings,
Love,
Edith

*

July 2, 1892

Dearest Mama and Papa,

The concert I told you about is over. We rehearsed for so many weeks that I believed it would never come to pass. Mr. William H. Sherwood has returned to his post at the American School of Music at Chicago and things will now return to normal here. I am feeling a little let down. Signor D'Auria tells me that this is usual for performers of every kind. He is a real help to me in every way. How blessed I am.

You can imagine I was all excitement in anticipation of the concert. On reaching the YMCA Association Hall nearby where all the important concerts of the Toronto Conservatory of Music are held, I was shaking a little. I could scarcely wait to sing my solo. And as for the great privilege of singing a duet with Madame D'Auria, I trembled in anticipation.

But first Mr. Sherwood's performance must be described. As I wrote to you, he is one of the leading pianists in America. He played Mendelssohn, Chopin, and Rubenstein. Mama, he is brilliant. He's not a very tall man; rather, he is compact and dark-haired. He has a short thick beard and a thick moustache, twisted like Signor D'Auria's, though not so wide. He has a most intense gaze that made me feel uncomfortable. His playing was so elegant, so delicate, so refined.

I sang my solo "I Am in her Boudoir Fair" by Ambroise Thomas from the opera Mignon as well as I could. I feel apprehensive before I sing, but once I am on the stage, that drops away and I feel excited and confident. That solo from Thomas's Mignon is for a male character, but it is sung by either a tenor or a contralto like me. I find this very odd, but I sing what I am given, and the gavotte is so beautiful that I don't think much about what it's presumed to mean.

My duet with Madame D'Auria was exceedingly well received. It was Italian: "Giorno d'orrore" from Semiramide *by Rossini, the same opera I sang my aria from in our year's end concert. I'm supposed to be an Assyrian commander, but the part is sung by contraltos. Madame D'Auria sang the soprano solo from the same opera. I do love Gaetano Rossini's music, even when I don't understand where the arias and the duets fit into the opera. The plots are too complicated for me to understand yet, even though Signor and Madame try their best to explain it all to me. The Toronto papers praised our duet, saying it was sung sweetly and that our voices blended. They mentioned that I was from Portage la Prairie in Manitoba and that I was attending the Conservatory.[2] That is nothing, of course, compared to the praise heaped upon Mr. Sherwood. They said his playing was a musical treat of rare excellence.*

How sorry I am that you were not there to see Mr. Sherwood and hear him play, especially Bach's "Echo" that he played in the manner of a French overture, or so the program noted. I'm uncertain what that meant. I have progressed quite quickly, Signor D'Auria says, even though the voice cannot be pressured too much at once.

I am hoping to return to Manitoba and see you both again at last for the summer break in August. I expect to give concerts in Winnipeg and at Portage la Prairie while I'm there. I'm sure you will hear a great improvement in my voice.

That is only a month away, and although I will have to return to Toronto early in September to continue my studies here, I look forward to it with great eagerness.

May you both enjoy good health and God's blessings,
Love,
Edith

THE FORSYTH FAMILY

A notice in the *Winnipeg Tribune* on July 15, 1893 ran as follows:

> The coming to Winnipeg of Miss Jean Forsyth, the new soprano of Grace Church, will be a decided acquisition to musical circles. Miss Forsyth comes from Detroit, and is very highly recommended as a singer and teacher. Her voice is said to be of beautiful quality, and she sings with great taste and expression. She is also a fine pianist, an efficient accompanist, and a good all-round musician.
>
> Miss Forsyth intends taking a few pupils for vocal instruction, and she will also be open for concert engagements during the fall and winter, of which concert givers should make a note.
>
> Miss Forsyth has a number of friends in Winnipeg, and her coming to our city will be a distinct social as well as musical gain.

At that time, Jean Forsyth was a soloist in the Detroit Harmonic Society, a German-founded group begun in 1849. She was also a soloist in the Detroit Music Society in the Germantown district, which gave sumptuous productions by men's and women's choral groups.[1] The annual highlight was their Masquerade, a lavish production that included historic tableaux of statue-like poses taken by costumed performers. So important was this event to Detroit that by 1891 there was a parade for it and a holiday for workers in the city. She also sang soprano solo for the Beth El Reform synagogue, a community that had split from its orthodox roots in 1861.[2] She also performed as the soprano in a quartet choir for the Central Methodist Church. Here and there in the Detroit newspapers there are brief announcements of some of her performances.[3] During the eight years she lived in Detroit from 1884 to 1892 she boarded at 37 Duffield St. near Germantown, and could easily have travelled to Chatham to visit her family and friends. Her vocal teacher for at least part of that time was Jaroslaw de Zielinski. She aspired to a singing career and had performed in many places in upstate New York, the midwestern U.S. and southern Ontario. The *Kansas City Times* reported, "Miss Forsyth has one of the loveliest voices ever heard here. It possesses a full, rich quality which must be natural if it exists, and further, it is intensely sympathetic."[4] Yet it seems that what looked as if it would be a strong singing career in Detroit had slowed or even stalled. That, or Grace Church had made her a good offer and stability.

Not long before this, the Forsyth family had owned acres and acres along Lake St. Clair. Later this land would become the fabled enclave of the wealthy known as Grosse Pointe. Daniel Forsyth, Jean's father, a thin man with a sculpted face and bushy shoulder-length sideburns, had been born at Grosse Point in 1806.

A sought-after performer in his own right, Jaroslaw de Zielinski was also a piano and vocal teacher whose method was based on the Old Italian School of Singing.

All generations of the family were intensely loyal to the British Crown. Daniel's grandfather, William Forsyth, had landed at Quebec with General Wolfe and fought with him on the Plains of Abraham. Afterwards William moved to Detroit, where he opened the first tavern. Because William helped in establishing a British fort (Fort Dearborn) in Michigan near Detroit, he was awarded 1,200 acres of land on the shore of Lake St. Clair at Grosse Pointe just northeast of Detroit. Later, with his son James, who was only seven when the U.S. Declaration of Independence was signed in 1776, William sold parcels of this land to French Canadian small orchard farmers at great profits.

There was widowing and remarriage that resulted in William's being the stepfather of John Kinzie, well-known as the "Father of Chicago." John Kinzie trained as a silversmith in Quebec before moving back to the mouth of the Chicago River, where he prospered as a fur trader. Memorials to John Kinzie still stand in the city. Kinzie Street is named for him. Today a plaque marks the location of the "Kinzie Mansion" on the north bank of the Chicago River just east of the DuSable–Michigan Avenue Bridge. Kinzie's daughter, Ellen Marion Kinzie, was said to be the first white child born there.[5] Legend has it that John Kinzie also had the dubious reputation of committing the first murder in the city. Before 1812 at Fort Dearborn near the mouth of the river, he is said to have killed Jean Lalime, his partner and an interpreter at the fort, either underhandedly or in self-defence, and seized DuSable property that was not his.

Once the international boundary had been established between the United States of America and Upper Canada in 1796, the Forsyth family, who strongly identified with the country of their birth, moved across the line and took up a farm with other United Empire Loyalists along the Thames River in what is today southwestern Ontario.

In 1832, Daniel left the farm where his father James had settled and arrived at a negligible hamlet called Chatham. Chatham then was nothing but a few shacks circled by forest and poorly drained boggy land next to the Thames River. The famed essayist Anna Jameson described a trip to Chatham five years later. There was no road to speak of. The only crop was "Indian corn" (as opposed to British corn, i.e., wheat). The log houses were surrounded by muddy ground and "dark mysterious woods." Mosquitoes seemed to be everywhere, rattlesnakes were common sights, and oxen were the means of dragging "enormous trunks"—or anything else—about. It was also oxen that pulled the "jolting cart" Anna Jameson was sitting in. It was difficult to see that Chatham saw itself then as embarked on the "busy 1830s."[6]

Daniel Forsyth at age twenty-five did not fancy farming. He wanted to be a builder or something more "urban." He and a friend, William Dolsen, went downriver to Raleigh in 1831 to train with Dr. Dorsey, the cabinetmaker. A year later, Daniel built the first frame house in Chatham for a cousin, Thomas Forsyth. (It later became the first site of the Bank of Canada.) The two friends next built a double frame house on Fourth Street in 1833 for William Dolsen.[7] Hotels and taverns began to appear; for example, the Commercial Hotel, a log building, then near the British Hotel. In 1835 the population was still only 300. By 1837, when the Upper Canada Rebellion broke out, the town had been surveyed and promptly became a military garrison town.

Now the place was filled with squabbling soldiers—militiamen and regulars—and the scarlet uniforms of officers could be seen here and there. Some of the troops who arrived a bit later were "coloured" (all runaway slaves except the officers). This was no novelty, as a "coloured preacher" called Darkie Rhodes (ironically, his name was Steve White) had been one of the most active squatters who camped downriver.[8] Despite the extra manpower, improvements were slow because the soldiers spent most of their time gambling, drinking and fighting. The "garrison" was a "little wooden hut" that featured framed prints of the Queen, Windsor Castle, the Duke of Wellington, and Lord Nelson.[9] One report in 1838 said the roads from London to Chatham were "really awful" and "muddy and full of holes." The town itself was "a sad little hole," even though there was faith among its citizens that someday it would be "a place of great importance." A steamboat called *The Kent* ran regularly up and down the Thames across the border.[10]

By 1841 things had improved a little. Chatham was not yet incorporated, but the military presence was dropping away, while the number of permanent residents grew to roughly 800. Daniel Forsyth was now one of the many merchants and businessmen whose shops and offices lined the main street parallel to the river. Forsyth, who had joined the Kent Militia in the 1837 rebellion as a commissioned officer, set up a general provisions business there. His reward for his service to the Crown was an appointment as Chatham's tax assessor and collector. The taxes he collected (fairly, it was said) were used for town constables, rudimentary road care and education. By the early 1840s there was a glint of civilization.

By 1843, the Anglican Church, St. Paul's, taught a Sunday school of seventy children. Although the Forsyths were Scottish and might have been expected to attend a Protestant church, they attended St. Paul's. This was probably because the Anglican churches attracted British patriots and usually served the elite, regardless of background. Daniel Forsyth was active in church decisions; the record of a vestry meeting on April 13, 1839 lists him as one of the ten men present. The treasurer's report showed that the church was merely breaking even.[11] Building began that same year for St. Joseph's Roman Catholic Church. Given that there was a "strong Scottish element in the population,"[12] it is not surprising that St. Andrew's Methodist Church, known as "the old Kirk," was the first built in 1840. Bagpipes were occasionally heard and kilts swirled from time to time. There were still some "pretty rough scenes" during elections after 1841[13]; the first plowing match in 1874 was as "primitive" as the "methods of the Egyptians"; Jim Taylor's Commercial Hotel held its own as the community meeting place (with drinks) for matters of public interest, such as forming organizations like the Agricultural Club; and the scattered houses on "narrow crooked streets" and slippery clay riverbanks gave the place a "struggling and ragged appearance."[14] Most houses had a sow and piglets in the yard. Dogs roamed free. Common expressions were: "dang gone it," "S'lang," and "Sacre crapeau!"[15] No doubt there were others that were unprintable.

The town grew rapidly on the basis of its business enterprises. By 1841 there was a steam-driven sawmill in south Chatham. On the north side of the Thames River was a water-powered gristmill. There were two breweries to supply the hotels and the four taverns. There was at least one tailor, tanner, gun maker, leather maker and saddler, butcher, lumber supplier, builder, cabinetmaker, lawyer, title conveyancer, hairdresser, steam scourer and dyer, and music supplier. There were two surgeons and two druggists.[16]

A rough social strata had emerged during the 1830s. There were three prominent families in the community: the Dolsens, the McKellars, and the Forsyths. Already a street had been named Forsyth Street in honour of Daniel.[17] A British-style village common was kept free of building at the corner of King, Fourth, Wellington, and Fifth Streets. And events that could be called cultured had begun to take place. A famous singer named Brahman visited in September 1842 and gave a concert, offering tickets at a dollar a person.[18] Dances called "hops" costing two dollars were held in the top-floor ballroom of the Royal Exchange Hotel on the corner of Fifth and King Streets. Once most of the soldiers left, manners in the community noticeably improved. A notable visit from the British Lord Holstead seemed to promise a positive influence, but it did nothing to raise standards of behaviour. The "flashy Lord Boozoo," as the locals called him, put on airs, but managed to steal Henry Eberts's horse and cutter, borrowed money from male admirers that he never returned, and "made love to some of the young ladies."[19]

Daniel Forsyth and his wife Winifred (née Weir) began their family of four daughters (one died in infancy) in 1841 at the end of the "busy 1830s." Sarah was born first, then Mary Alice three years later. After Frances died in 1846 it seemed there would be no more children. Yet five years later, in 1851, the youngest daughter Jean (a.k.a. Jane) was born.

In 1851, the same year Jean Forsyth was born, Chatham was incorporated as a village. Jean's father, Daniel, like others, conducted much business on the "barter-and-trade" system, rather than using money (which was still British currency). Jean would have attended "the public school run by Miss Pratt in her house on Colborne Street." What education she (and her sisters) had after the usual completion of public school is unknown. There is no record of where or exactly when this was, nor the type of education. Jean was an attractive, outgoing child with bright

Jean Forsyth oil portrait, *circa* 1817, artist unknown.

blue eyes and golden ringlets. She was extraordinarily gifted with music, as was her sister Sarah, and even as a child she was taken about to local communities to sing.[20] Soon she would play the piano. Her education—and possibly that of her sisters—must have included music. It is clear that the education Daniel Forsyth's daughters received was thorough and cultured far beyond the basics of public school and far beyond the social life of Chatham in the 1840s and 1850s. They were raised to be "ladies." Certainly Daniel Forsyth as one of the three prominent families in the village and, as a man with the prestigious and lucrative position of tax assessor and collector, would have been able to send his girls anywhere he liked for their schooling.

As for the 1,200 acres at Grosse Pointe, Michigan that the Forsyth family had owned, it developed into a summer playground for wealthy Detroit people and eventually became an exclusive suburb of Detroit, a symbol of American wealth and power with its exclusive clubs for golf, tennis, and yachting. It was such a symbol of this lifestyle—with ornate mansions copied in the early 1900s from several European architectures—that it was called "the Newport of the Midwest" after the exclusive summer resort of New York millionaires in Rhode Island. Many members of the Ford automobile family later lived in Grosse Pointe.[21]

Jean Forsyth, then, grew up in a rough-and-ready pioneer village struggling towards cultured life. Her family was one of Chatham's "elite." By the time she was born in 1851, her father had become quite wealthy through his dry goods business, then as the village's tax assessor and collector. Both parents encouraged education and culture—especially music. Jean read widely and intelligently. She could play the piano with verve. She was equally gifted as a young church singer in Detroit and in concert tours that she performed wherever and whenever she could. She was well-known in Minneapolis–St. Paul, Detroit, Chicago, and many towns in southeast Upper Canada—such as Hamilton, Kingston, London, and Guelph—when suddenly the opportunity for a full-time position opened up in Winnipeg.

Mrs. Verner, soprano soloist in the choir at Winnipeg's Grace Church, was leaving. She was said to be the leading soprano in the West, said also to have a "voice [as] true as steel to the pitch."[22] The solemn, long-faced Mrs. Verner was the wife of Thomas Henry Verner from Montreal, who worked in the Excise Department. James Tees, choirmaster at the church, offered Jean the job. Everyone musical in Winnipeg looked up to Tees. The man with receding dark wavy hair and a droopy moustache was—as someone put it—"one of the undaunted few who, in the face of discouragements, are well and truly laying our musical foundations."[23]

JEAN JOINS THE WINNIPEG MUSIC SCENE, 1893

Jean Forsyth knew little of the young western Canadian city she was moving to. The furthest west she had travelled was by train to Minneapolis–St. Paul to give one of her concerts. She would have had letters from a few friends and relatives there who had succumbed to the lure of the West. James Tees, choirmaster at Grace Church, who had offered her the job of solo soprano, might have heard Jean at one of her eastern concerts or in Minneapolis–St. Paul, as there was a rail route there from Winnipeg.

Even a quick look at Winnipeg's early musical history shows how difficult it was for James Tees, who wanted nothing more than to establish a large choral society. Winnipeg was in many ways a young pioneering community much like the Chatham Jean had known. Yet it was much further advanced in most ways. The backwoods village of 1866, with its scratchy fiddlers and folksongs, had ballooned into a city of about 7,000 ten years later. And a decade after that, in 1888, once the CPR drew wave after wave of newcomers from Eastern Canada, it had become home to some 10,000 citizens. Those newcomers were not the skilled tradesmen—like William Forbes Alloway (tobacconist, and freighter with up to 6,000 oxcarts) or Alexander Brown and his partner Rutherford (Brown & Rutherford planing mill) or James Ashdown (wholesale hardware), who parlayed early Winnipeg into a manufacturing town and then parlayed their success into more thousands by investing in real estate. These were businessmen from prosperous firms in the East, seeking to expand their wealth, such as John Galt (son of central Canadian capitalist A. T. Galt) and his cousin George F. Galt (wholesale groceries), Frederick Brydges and his brother-in-law William Rae Allan (Vulcan Iron Works, then the financial firm Allan, Brydges & Co.), and the three Drewry brothers E. L., George and Fred, who revived the defunct brewery (Redwood, then Drewry's). Winnipeg was by now the third largest city in Canada with a convenient link to St. Paul and Minneapolis through the St. Paul, Minneapolis & Manitoba Railway that had been functioning for ten years. These men and their families knew what civilized culture—opera, music, drama, literature, architecture—was like, and they hastened to replicate what they knew from the East in this "gateway city" of wide sidewalks, an electric street railway system, efficient sewers for the minority who could afford water closet plumbing, and a good water supply.

By the time Jean Forsyth arrived at Winnipeg in late August 1893, the privileged had built mansions in Armstrong's Point and elsewhere that were as elaborate and imposing as those found in any exclusive district of any city in Canada. Businessmen like Fred Stobart, who sold dry goods, and James Ashdown, who owned a hardware business, each had assets of roughly $250,000.[1]

Music had developed in a tangled web of popular "rot" (like ragtime and "nigger music"), military bands, "smoking concerts" for men enjoying expensive Havana cigars and playing cards to the accompaniment of banjo and ragtime music, church choirs with their choral concerts, and sincere attempts to initiate and sustain classical music and opera. There had been a piano business in the city since 1872, and every home that could afford one, had one. Reed organs and other organs thrived in both churches and homes. A fledgling Philharmonic Society had appeared in 1881. The wooden, brick-veneered Princess Opera House (renamed the Bijou Opera House/Theatre in 1890)—with stores at street level and a concert-dance-hall above—opened two years later. At the same time, Victoria Hall (later the Winnipeg Theatre and Opera House) offered concerts and shows. In 1884 the Winnipeg Operatic Society formed, hoping to imitate the various opera companies, or simply their prima donnas, whose tours from abroad or from America were entertainment highlights.

Another strand of the web of music in 1880s Winnipeg was the Apollo Club, put together as a branch of Apollo Clubs in America by thirty-five amateur musicians. Among these was the peripatetic Paul Henneberg, the well-tutored German-born flautist of the Mendelssohn Quintet in Boston. For Henneberg, who played several instruments and was an accomplished conductor, Winnipeg offered an opportunity to "pioneer" music, to develop classical music from the ground up. This impeccably dressed, precise man with rimless glasses soon became indispensable and remained so for many years.

As early as 1882, Henneberg was offering three concerts a season at the Bijou Opera House and playing violin solos in them himself. He had quickly established his reputation as "skillful, judicious, and indefatigable." Through patient and painstaking discipline, he was seen as rescuing Winnipeg's amateur musicians from "a sea of mediocrity."

In ten years, under various conductors, this group had grown to an orchestra of thirty-five players and a chorus of thirty singers, mainly drawn from Winnipeg churches. They played light, bright popular or classical music at first. The 1892 program shows a taste for exotic subjects: "Overture to *L'Africaine*," "The Persian Peasant," "Gavotte from *Mignon*," and "The Turkish Patrol," for example. Yet the Apollo Club was even then busy preparing two much more serious operas: Carl Maria von Weber's *Der Freischütz* and Mozart's *The Magic Flute*, for the following season.[2] Paul Henneberg was determined to raise the level of classical music in the city and Jean Forsyth would be part of his plan.

As in other major British and colonial cities, men set up various clubs at which they could relax away from home, do business, smoke, and drink, as well as discuss news of the day with their colleagues. In Winnipeg there were soon several such clubs. First in rank was the Manitoba Club. Then followed the St. Charles Country Club, the Pine Ridge Club, the Winnipeg Golf Club, the Carleton Club, and the Lakewood Country Club. The members of these clubs had the power, through various rules, to exclude others. Most of them were Anglican and British, either in origin or by ancestry. There were many, many other clubs, largely formed around activities such as sports or other pastimes.

Jean Forsyth, soprano and *accompaniste,*
Edith J. Miller Company, western tour,
Town Topics, Oct. 13, 1900.

None was more popular than the Rowing Club. Their competitions were fun to watch, reminiscent of England's elite Henley races. Their annual balls drew most of the wealthy citizens of Winnipeg, especially those with daughters and sons of marriageable age. There was no debutante ritual of "coming out," as there was in Toronto, but it lay just beneath the surface of many social events held by the wealthy.

On October 20, 1893, a scant two months after Jean's arrival in the city, the Rowing Club Ball was held at the recently built Manitoba Hotel. That hotel represented the social, economic, and architectural aspirations of a city in a hurry to achieve status. The seven-storey flatiron building was built by the Northern Pacific railway (that linked Winnipeg and St. Paul, Minnesota) only two years before, in 1891. It could accommodate 400 guests, and was said to be the finest Canadian hotel west of Montreal.

*

The Rowing Club Ball was the first ball of the season. The next day, the *Winnipeg Tribune* gave a long description of this major social event.[3] The well-waxed floor was "perfect"; the ballroom looked "lovely," the lights softened by many-coloured shades. Paul Henneberg's orchestra provided the music. Palms, ferns, and flowering plants flanked the "pretty fireplace" at the end of the room. Sitting rooms offered "cozy nooks" for private chats. All in all, it was an "enchanting" scene.

Like all social columns of the day, this notice paid tribute to the elaborate dresses worn by women then, roughly in order of status. "I am sure all who attended the ball last evening will join with me in deciding that never had our Winnipeg ladies looked more charming. Powder and patches are certainly becoming."

Mrs. Brydges, whose husband was the secretary of the Manitoba and Northwest Railway Co., headed the list of forty-one ladies whose "lovely gowns" were described. She was wearing "a handsome dress of cream brocaded satin and diamond ornaments." Her daughter was also wearing "cream duchesse satin" adorned with pink roses." Next was Mrs. George Galt, also wearing cream satin and diamond ornaments. (Her husband was a businessman and athlete who held various civic offices.) Mrs. Angus Kirkland, whose husband was manager of the Bank of Montreal, was wearing an "exquisite" dress of "blue grosse grain silk with pink trimmings." Mrs. G. W. Girdlestone, whose husband was an insurance agent representing five international companies, wore black silk and lace with pink ostrich feathers. Her daughter, like Mrs. Brydges's daughter, wore the debutante cream or white (in this case white) gown signifying virginity. Miss Girdlestone's satin dress was trimmed with black ostrich tips.

At midnight the supper rooms were thrown open to reveal tables almost covered with flowers, ferns, and fruit, "intermingled with fairy lights of different colours." Though some found the dances a little hurried, with not quite enough breathing space between, and though some found the attendance of more than 300 not quite what it should be, the ball was declared successful.

Among those in attendance, along with the best of Winnipeg society and a bevy of marriageable girls, was Jean Forsyth. She had already performed at a tea. Next month she would give her first concert—also the city's first concert of the season—at the Bijou Theatre.

5

"I don't know why I was nervous," Jean said to young Katie Holmes.

The two women were having tea in Jean's drawing room, as yet only partly decorated. It was the afternoon of November 30, 1893, and Jean was reading the review of her first public concert in the *Manitoba Free Press*. Katie had been her accompanist at the Bijou Theatre. Katie smiled her dimpled smile and protested that her new friend had not seemed nervous at all.

Jean ignored Katie's words. She was exasperated.

"I sang so beautifully at Mrs. Hespeler's tea a month ago. That was my real debut, the very first time I sang in Winnipeg." Those thirty guests hearing her for the first time were, she knew, deciding whether she lived up to her reputation or not.

"I was not one bit intimidated knowing that the son of Sir John A. Macdonald was in the small audience. Not one bit!"

As Jean recalled, lawyer and Conservative MP Hugh J. Macdonald and his wife had been quiet and courteous. He gave no indication of his exploits suppressing the second Riel rebellion.

The rest had been from Winnipeg's wealthy elite, if a city can be said to have an elite after only two or three generations: the Drewrys, already "old Winnipeg," Mr. George W. Girdlestone, insurance agent for three British and three Canadian companies, and his wife, Mrs. George Galt, Mrs. F. W. Alloway, another "old" Winnipeg name, Mrs. Angus Kirkland, whose husband managed Winnipeg's branch of the Bank of Montreal, Mrs. Brydges, whose husband Fred was manager of the Manitoba & Northwest Railway company, and their daughter. And, of course, Mrs. Hespeler, whose accomplished German husband William was the manager of the Manitoba Land Company, and Mrs. Holmes, wife of Lieutenant-Colonel Holmes, were there too. Holmes had just taken up the deputy adjutant-general's office at C Battery of the Canadian Artillery, having been transferred to Winnipeg from Victoria.

"You were a superb accompanist," Jean said, looking at Katie over the edge of her teacup. Jean's thoughts went directly to what had been her second private performance: a small musicale Mrs. Henry Fisher had given, again with Katie as accompanist. Henry was an accountant and auditor on Main Street. "Not only at the Hespelers' but at the Fishers' as well," Jean added.

Katie smiled.

"I met Stanley Adams and his two daughters there," she went on. "He's too handsome by far, and he knows it. His baritone voice is warm and appealing, but he needs some tutoring and discipline to refine it."

Katie blushed. She took a quick sip of tea, then said quickly, "He does so very much for the arts here. He is secretary to the Winnipeg Opera Society. He's a moving force in Winnipeg's drama too. Did you know he writes plays, and he and his wife both act in them?"

Jean thought for a moment, then said, "I can see he would be a good bluff as a comedian. The way he spoke to me was most amusing. Yet he is altogether too charming." She paused. "The other half dozen," she continued lightly, "were new to me, all most receptive, though hardly experts in music. One asked me if I was a contralto!

"But *this*! *This*!" A shaft of sun lit up the section of the review that troubled her so. "And it was the first concert of the season, by the Apollo Club at the Bijou Theatre! Everyone was there. Oh dear!"

Katie passed her a plate of biscuits.

"The section that pained me most," Jean said, taking a biscuit, "began by praising my rendition of 'Doris' as full of 'sweetness of expression.' It was my 'Angels Ever Bright and Fair' by Handel that was objectionable."

"I don't understand it," Katie responded. "You came in on time. Your voice soared. It was a pleasure to accompany you."

"It doesn't matter that they said that I displayed 'a highly cultivated method and strong voice.'" Jean pouted. She held the newspaper up. "They took exception to 'the strained effort,' which attended my high notes. The only thing they really liked was my encore, 'Barbara Allan.' What nonsense! That's a slight piece, an easy Scottish ballad. Anyone can sing *that*." Jean turned her eyes to the newspaper, though she had reread it over and over.

"Perhaps they didn't like all that shepherd folderol in 'Doris.' I suppose no one here has even heard of the recent American composer Ethelbert Nevin. But Handel's solo is a solid soprano solo. Difficult, yes, but *real* concert music. And as for my being at a loss for an encore. That's nonsense too. Rubbish! I can sing any number of encores. But I had no further music for you to play. I did not expect more than one encore."

"Oh, well," Katie said, offering Jean another biscuit. "Perhaps the reviewer was in a sour mood. He complained that the concert began twenty minutes late. He complained about the stragglers that came in late." She took the paper from Jean to take another look. "Here," she pointed at the page. "He said Mr. Henneberg's orchestra 'suffered from insufficient practice.' The first number, Rossini's overture to *Semiramide*, was the 'worst rendered' on the program. The cellos were 'grating.' The violins 'lacked fire.' Schubert's minuet was not played as well as Handel's. 'Glaring flaws' intruded everywhere."

Katie set down the *Manitoba Free Press*, hoping Jean's mood had lightened. Then she noticed the *Winnipeg Tribune* waiting on the table. Jean anxiously picked it up.

"Oh, *no*!" she said. "This one damns me with faint praise. 'Doris' is 'beyond the reach of an ordinary singer and requires careful study to properly interpret it.' I sang it in an 'accurate manner.' Nothing about my artistry or interpretation or strength. Only that I have 'a high soprano voice with a mezzo quality.' That insinuates that I really should take mezzo soprano parts and stop aspiring to the higher register. My encore 'Barbara Allan' was sadly 'out of place' because it was a love song following an oratorio selection."

Jean read on. "Now, we're told, the *horns* were not in tune with the *strings*. Otto Henneberg is Paul Henneberg's brother—or some relation. He and Mr. Downard's horn and flute concerto by Anton Emil Titl was a 'disappointment as the flute and the French horn did not blend well together.'"[1]

Jean put down the paper decisively and looked directly at Katie. "But you know, Katie, those reviewers were right. There couldn't be *two* reviewers in a bad mood. I must admit it and do something about it. My voice *was* pinched on the high notes. I was nervous. It might have been those two awkward pillars on either side of the stage, or, perhaps, it was the way that drop curtain came down with such a thump after each act. I must practise, get to know my audience here and their tastes. I know I can do it. And I shall!"

JEAN FOUNDS THE WINNIPEG HUMANE SOCIETY, 1894

"But that's atrocious!" said Jean, her two white-spotted terriers lying peacefully at her feet. She was speaking to Katie Holmes as they enjoyed a cup of tea after rehearsing Jean's songs for the next concert. "You mean there's no Humane Society in Winnipeg? None at all?"

"No," Katie replied. "It pains my heart to see the way animals are treated here. You'd think it was still pioneer days and men desperate to survive. Horses, especially. The day before yesterday, as I was going to Nunn's to purchase some music, I saw a driver hop down from his cart and angrily whip his poor lame horse into motion."

"Well!" said Jean. "Animals are our little brothers and sisters, just as sensible of pain and distress as we are. I intend to do something about this sorry situation. At once!"

By mid-February—only six months after she had arrived in Winnipeg—she had urged the *Tribune* in person to print a second call for signatures in support of a local Humane Society. The first call for supporters, starting with her relations and few friends, had gathered several signatures, but the matter remained stagnant for weeks. She knew people at the newspapers. They had been running her advertisement every month:

MISS JEAN FORSYTH, SOPRANO,

pupil of the Academy of Music, London,

Eng., will receive pupils for vocal instruction.

For terms apply at Nunn's Music Store.

Open for concert engagements.

The Society for the Prevention of Cruelty to Animals had begun in England, started by Richard "Humanity Dick" Martin, a member of parliament in 1824. His first case championed a little overladen donkey covered in sores. This provided great amusement, not sympathy, among Martin's political colleagues, who were astonished that newspapers would feature such trivial news. Such was the attitude of most Winnipeg citizens in 1894. Instances of flagrant cruelty to animals—and to people, for that matter—escaped serious notice. But it was often said of Jean Forsyth, "A love of dumb creatures is one of the first characteristics a stranger, could the average person screw up sufficient effrontery to loiter around her, would notice in meeting her."[1]

By early June, Jean Forsyth's fierce canvassing had resulted in a meeting to draft a constitution and bylaws, and elect officers to a fledgling Humane Society. The *Tribune* announced on June 4 that the proposed society would present their report on the 22nd in the committee room of City Hall at 3:00 p.m. All who had signed the petition were reminded to attend and anyone else was welcome. All would have the right to vote for officers.[2]

A lengthy positive report on that "little gathering" appeared in the *Manitoba Morning Free Press* the next day. The society "with noble purposes" that was "rapidly assuming shape" would "keep pace with the growth of the community." The chair was an ardent Methodist and Grace Church co-founder, Thomas Ryan, known as the "Shoe King" due to his successful business. Eventually he would become Winnipeg's tenth mayor. Charles N. Bell, an active mason and member of most of the city's elite clubs, who had reported on the distressing decline of the buffalo herds twenty years earlier, acted as secretary. A lengthy draft constitution with the usual sections was presented. It was adopted. Now, to determine the best method to secure a larger meeting next time. An eleven-member committee to prepare for that meeting, firm up the organization, and elect its officers convened. In addition to Thomas Ryan, there were seven men and four women on that committee. Jean Forsyth and Mrs. J. H. Gardner, both deeply involved in Grace Church, were among them.

The new society would need to be incorporated, and Jean Forsyth was sent on August 20 to appeal to the Hon. J. D. Cameron, provincial secretary, to grant the incorporation before the legislature sat, even though that was unusual. The next meeting a few days later, complete with elected officers, was the first official meeting of the Winnipeg Humane Society. Alex Smith, a former Montrealer in charge of provincial immigration at the CPR station, chaired the meeting, and T. A. Gamble, a real estate agent, had been elected secretary-treasurer. Jean had persuaded Katie Holmes to take part. For the first time, members of the clergy—the white-bearded Rev. Canon Matheson of Holy Trinity Church and the Rev. R. G. MacBeth, a prolific historian of Western Canada—took part. Dr. Amelia Yeomans was a remarkable and valuable member of the society. She and her daughter were the first women doctors in Winnipeg and would be early suffragettes. It was understandable that the clergy and doctors should take an interest in the Humane Society, because—in these early stages—the society dealt with cases of children, as well as animals, in misery. Dr. Yeomans, Canon Matheson, Rev. MacBeth, and Alfred J. Andrews, a lawyer and currently an alderman, formed a committee to draft bylaws and finalize the constitution. Mrs. W. B. Scarth, whose Scottish husband was a director of the North-West Land Company and a Conservative member of parliament, was one of the directors.

Gamble was directed to interview the Hon. J. D. Cameron again to discover how the society might acquire the necessary powers to enforce damages. The public must be informed through any of its members or the press of any cases of cruelty.

Finally, anyone having papers or funds of the society must hand them over to Gamble, who was to open a bank account in the society's name.

By the end of 1894, the Winnipeg Humane Society was firmly established.[3] Five committees had been formed: Membership and Finance; Cruelty; Humane Education and Bands of Mercy; Prosecution, Laws and Legislation; and Literature and Publishing. Jean Forsyth was on the two committees that mattered most to her, Membership and Finance, and—above all—Cruelty. Her fellow members on the Cruelty Committee were Dr. Amelia Yeomans (chairman), Mrs. J. H. Gardner, and secretary Gamble. Jean wasted no time in pursuing cruelty to animals and, along with her Grace Church friend Mrs. J. H. Gardner, started by investigating the condition of her "little brothers and sisters"[4] at the local dog pound.

After visiting Winnipeg's dog pound twice, they were appalled. The pound keeper was away hunting for the first visit. They found the dogs in "a very thin state and very hungry and thirsty." So they provided drinking vessels, water, and food. On the second visit, they reported to the city's Licence and Health Committee, "The pound keeper was very gruff and loud talking." They requested that he receive a reprimand, be warned to treat visitors respectfully and look after the animals properly. They strongly suggested finding a "kind and respectable person" to take over the position. And they asked that the pound be relocated nearer the streetcars, as they intended to make frequent visits in future.[5]

The Society was acting quickly in other ways too. A membership fee was set at one dollar; for young members it was ten cents. Katie Holmes and another member convinced the editors of city papers to run a continuing free notice asking the public to notify the society through the secretary, T. A. Gamble, or any other member of the society of any acts of cruelty they saw or heard about. The Committee on Education was to approach public schools to incorporate humane education into their classes. The Committee on Prosecution, Laws and Legislation were off to the attorney general to define the pertinent codes of law and ask for powers of arrest, like that enjoyed by Humane Societies in the East. This committee, a crucial one, enlisted John MacBeth, nephew of Rev. R. G. MacBeth, a lawyer and former MLA; Alfred J. Andrews, another prominent member of the city's legal community, who would become Winnipeg's seventeenth mayor; W. F. Henderson, a prosperous wholesale grocery merchant; Capt. Michell (a.k.a. Capt. Mitchell), in charge of C Company of the 90th Battalion under Col. Holmes and secretary of the Manitoba Rifle Association; and Dr. W. J. Hinman, a veterinarian and one of the most active members of the Manitoba Turf Club (horse racing).[6] Dr. Hinman would soon make an official inspection of the dairies in the area that discovered tuberculosis among the cows supplying Winnipeg with milk.[7]

Already, the first reports of cruelty to animals from around the city were beginning to trickle in. Objections were made to the way chickens in overcrowded cages were brought into the city for slaughter and kept in "wretchedly filthy places." Another later complaint, in which an inebriated man was fined for cruelty, gives a startling example of why a Humane Society was much needed in the city. Edward Ching separated two fighting dogs on Rupert Street, a collie and a bull terrier pup. When the pup scratched his hand, "he seized the little dog, which did not know enough to run away, and swinging it high over his head brought it down with terrible force upon the sidewalk. Not satisfied with this he struck it upon the curb a second time." The pup had to be destroyed and Ching was fined five dollars.[8]

CHARLES WHEELER

The music critic who had so nettled Jean Forsyth about her debut concert was Charles H. Wheeler. Like so many others shaping Winnipeg, he had come from Great Britain. Lured by an enticing account of opportunities in the Canadian prairies, the forty-three-year-old architect had arrived from Coventry with his wife and six children in 1882.

He had apprenticed in most of the building trades, including metal patterning. For twenty years he had worked various architectural assignments: churches, mansions, and bridges. He had worked for the well-known firm of Martin and Chamberlain in Birmingham. An adventurer, he supervised construction of a jail in Shanghai for two years. Wheeler, assisted by two of his sons, was to become Winnipeg's preeminent architect, designing many civic buildings in the city and in nearby communities. Now a local museum and heritage site, Dalnavert House, originally an exquisite Romanesque Revival home for Sir John A. Macdonald's son Hugh J. Macdonald, was his most famous building.

Yet Wheeler first attracted notice not as an architect but as a singer. A mere two months after his arrival, this large, "long haired Oscar Wilde"[1] was bass soloist and soon choirmaster at Holy Trinity Anglican Church. Soon after he became choirmaster at Zion Methodist Church. Two years later, Wheeler designed the new Holy Trinity church, based on early thirteenth-century Gothic churches in England. By 1885, he had followed the music to Knox Presbyterian Church, where he became choirmaster after helping that congregation resolve claims against its building contractor.

Before leaving Coventry, Wheeler had signalled his keen interest in music by writing music columns for several London weekly papers. Once in Winnipeg, he quickly latched onto the turbulent development of music—and drama—in the city. Amateur performances and variety shows were making way for slightly more artistic melodrama. An amateur performance of *Romeo and Juliet* in 1891 at the Bijou Theatre, for example, featured a specially imported English Romeo, Laurence Cautley, who butchered his lines. When he forgot his lines altogether in the fifth act, he closed his eyes and pretended to faint. He was dragged off-stage and a stand-in took over his part. The fraud Cautley was immediately dispatched back to England, fare paid.[2] An extreme example, but one that shows how far theatre had to go to become professional.

Serious music (that is, music by classical composers) could be found only in touring companies from abroad or the United States or in the local churches like Grace Church, where Jean Forsyth was soprano soloist and Annie Pullar was contralto soloist, were main centres of music. Each choir had soloists in each of the four vocal registers: two women and two men. Charles Wheeler began as bass soloist in Holy Trinity Anglican Church, then soon changed to Knox Presbyterian Church, where he was soloist as well as choirmaster. Some city churches imported salaried organists from central Canada and installed new pipe organs as soon as they could afford it. Some had reasonably large, active choirs.

The division between low-brow and high-brow music at the time was relatively clear. In the theatres, vulgar vaudeville and inept amateur performances in questionable taste appealed to popular audiences, while the liturgical music—such as oratorios—by composers such as Bach, Handel, and Mozart were the province of the churches. Strenuous efforts were being made by the time Jean Forsyth (herself recruited from the East) arrived in 1893 to find a middle ground where the secular classics, especially opera, could be performed in theatres and various public halls, such as the Thistle Rink. Often a compromise was found by holding such concerts and recitals in the churches as mid-week events independent of services. By the mid-1890s it was not possible to tell which faith or church a performer belonged to by the venue in which they sang or played. Jean herself had already performed in Methodist and Jewish institutions and would eventually sing in churches of many faiths.

No one had a clearer vision of the necessity of bringing quality music—vocal and instrumental—before the Winnipeg public than the rather beautiful Charles Wheeler with his dark curls, wide moustache and tiny, twisty goatee. His experience of concerts and plays in Great Britain made him certain that he could be a constructive force in bringing this about. He saw himself as a highly trained cosmopolitan person with a calling to import sophistication and dignity to the performing arts in Winnipeg. Since 1883, he had been writing columns about music and theatre for various Winnipeg newspapers, just as he had done for London newspapers in England.

But Winnipeg was not London. In bringing culture to the Canadian West, Wheeler undoubtedly raised standards for music. Yet his searing criticisms of musicians he thought were "overblown" could be discouraging and wounding as much as they were instructive.

Typically, he blasted the first matinee at the Manitoba Hotel's grand dining room.[3] The music, he wrote in his review, was not "inordinately severe" or "incomprehensibly classical." It was "bright, light, and tuneful"—a somewhat backhanded compliment. The acoustics were bad, largely because the makeshift platform was placed at the end of the long, rectangular room. In future, he more or less dictated, it must be placed halfway down one side. Jean Forsyth, David Ross, and William Young, the vocalists, were "evidently battling with the acoustic difficulties," though he thought Jean sang Leonardo Mascheroni's "For All Eternity" with remarkable expression. Ross, who sang "Bedouin Love Song," lacked "the method to charm the audience" and must "shake himself free of florid delivery." Young had chosen "a colourless ballad." Worst of all, something was "radically wrong" with the pitch of the piano. Even Paul Henneberg, whom Wheeler usually supported uncritically, came in for negative comments. His flute playing was "not as perfect" as his violin work; his melody in Rubenstein's "Melodie in F" lacked the essential rhythm. Only Schubert's "Serenade" with Mr. Johnson playing the cornet solo deserved an encore, according to Wheeler.

It comes as a surprise at the end of the review when he calls the event "altogether delightful" and hopes its success will be repeated.

EDITH EXCELS AT THE TORONTO CONSERVATORY OF MUSIC, 1894

Two small notices in June 1894 carried news of Edith Miller. The first, in the *Winnipeg Tribune*, reported that Miss Miller "of the Portage" was now connected with the teaching staff of the Toronto Conservatory of Music. This position, which she had held for two years,[1] owed much to her outstanding success in her study of piano, organ, and voice. Francesco D'Auria, her vocal instructor, no doubt recommended her with his unmistakable Italian enthusiasm. In late May, the conservatory music hall had been filled with an audience eager to hear the first recital given by her pupils, who were "frequently applauded."

The second notice in the *Winnipeg Tribune*[2] announced that she would be leaving Toronto to spend the summer and winter in Winnipeg instructing pupils. After a year's residence in Manitoba, she intended to further her studies in New York and Europe. These notices suggest that Edith Miller needed employment to sustain her training. Just as she had taken the position as contralto soloist in Bloor Street Presbyterian Church, she had earned money teaching in some connection other than being a staff member with the Toronto Conservatory of Music. Her scholarship would have helped, but if she were to continue on to New York and Europe, she would need a year to earn enough money in Winnipeg and Portage la Prairie.

No doubt she would have resumed performing in nearby locations, just as she had done before leaving the West for Toronto. Back then she had sung in Neepawa;[3] sung "The Quaker's Daughter" in a series of tableaux (scenes in which costumed people assumed and held positions from history or exotic locations) and musical entertainments in St. Mary's Church in Portage la Prairie;[4] and sung "Somebody's Pride" at a reception for the Farmers' Institute at Lansdowne College in Portage la Prairie where she was a student that year[5] before leaving for Toronto.

Her admirers in the West had kept in close touch with her progress in Toronto. Her performance as one of the advanced pupils at the Conservatory of Music was singled out. "Miss Edith Miller's beautiful contralto voice was heard to good advantage in her selection, 'The Garden of Sleep,' and the ballad she sang as an encore was even more appreciated." This "evidenced the future musical prospects of this talented young lady."[6] After she graduated from the conservatory, she returned in the summer to make her first appearance in Winnipeg at the Scottish concert on a civic holiday. The *Winnipeg Tribune* noted that her voice had a "timbre that is resonant and full, the lower register being particularly rich."[7] Now, after finishing her year of teaching for the conservatory, Edith Miller rested at her parents' home in Portage la Prairie for a month or so, taking the train to Winnipeg for further vocal lessons from Jean Forsyth. In Portage la Prairie, she started to canvas for her own students.

*

While nineteen-year-old Edith Miller was saying her goodbyes in Toronto, a complimentary concert to Paul Henneberg was being given to an audience of a few hundred at the Thistle Rink in Winnipeg on June 14, 1894. Lieutenant Governor John Schultz, his wife, and their party entered to the robust strains of "God Save the Queen." The concert opened with a march composed by Henneberg, who conducted his orchestra of what were now forty-five musicians. In his *Winnipeg Free Press* review the next day, Charles Wheeler complained that the basses were "too much in evidence" in that opening piece. Yet he praised Henneberg's training of his orchestra, especially their precision. Jean Forsyth took part in a trio, "better in its ensemble than its solos." The duet she sang with John Forslund from Mozart's *Marriage of Figaro* "developed in a remarkable degree the tuneful range of the soprano." Wheeler saved his best praise for Otto Henneberg's French horn solo, assisted by violins. "He delivered a masterpiece of Bach with a perfection of tone and execution greatly relished." Wheeler's most damning criticism was aimed at the Thistle Rink: "it is not, and can never be made, of any value as a concert hall." The *Winnipeg Tribune* review was gentler and only slightly critical, ending with congratulations to Paul Henneberg on his second annual concert. A week later, the *Tribune* praised Jean Forsyth, saying she "sings in a thoroughly artistic way, with a strongly marked musical temperament which gives much pleasure to connissieurs [sic]."[8]

It was not a year since Jean arrived in Winnipeg. Yet she had soon become a highly visible part of the community. "Winnipeg is certainly a great place for afternoon teas," one journalist proclaimed,

> and the popularity of this form of society recreation seems to be on the increase. I never was in a place where there were so many teas and so much trouble taken in the way of adornment and accessories to make them successful and entertaining; they are a good thing and I hope they will grow in favour.[9]

Winnipeg teas were not small informal gatherings, though those were also enjoyed by women whose husbands could afford to provide them with maids or housekeepers or cooks. One, hosted by Mrs. Frank Hall Mathewson, whose husband was manager of the Bank of Commerce, in mid-February at her Assiniboine Avenue home, was typical. Seventy ladies—often mothers with their daughters—arrived that afternoon to find decorations throughout the house had been done "with much thought and taste. At the centre of the tea table stood a huge silver bowl filled with ferns, while smilax was twined in and out among the dainty dishes." The hostess received her guests in black silk and cut jet. Names of many of the Winnipeg elite were among those listed in the news report: Girdlestone, Macdonald, Galt, Scarth, Killam, Perdu, Brydges, Hespeler, Fortin, Champion, and Gouin. Jean had the honour of pouring tea.[10]

Mrs. Holmes, Katie's mother, had held a similar tea for fifty-six ladies at her home on Edmonton Street. She had decorated with tulips and hyacinths and offered a tea table "laden with delicacies." Her guests were not the same as those

Signor Francesco D'Auria, Edith's flamboyant music teacher at the Toronto Conservatory of Music, 1892. He later became one of the first teachers at the Winnipeg Conservatory of Music in 1894.

Edith J. Miller in a *New York Times* photo, Oct. 23, 1899.

at Mrs. Mathewson's. There were fewer elites and more music lovers. Four were from out of town (Edinburgh, Toronto, Portage la Prairie); the tea was held for Mrs. Irving of Victoria. At social gatherings of all kinds there were often visitors from out of town, as it was customary for ladies to travel back and forth by train to spend a few days or weeks visiting family or friends. Jean and Annie Pullar, the contralto soloist from her church, sang for entertainment.[11]

Mrs. Holmes also held a small musicale one evening for a dozen people in mid-May. Paul Henneberg and Katie Holmes gave instrumental performances and Jean Forsyth and Alfred J. Tuckwell, a Yorkshireman educated at Leeds and Oxford, sang. He was now organist and choirmaster at Holy Trinity Church. Another much more formal *musicale* for the elite was given by Mrs. Kirkland, wife of Angus Kirkland, manager at the Bank of Montreal. Again, the display of flowers was praised. Again, some of the ladies' long, elaborate dresses were singled out. The hostess wore black silk trimmed with white satin, and cut jet. Mrs. L. A. Hamilton, a popular soprano whose husband was land commissioner and had been one of those to survey the 49th parallel, was in pink silk with black lace. Mrs. Stobart's dress was pale blue silk. Jean Forsyth wore pearl grey and white satin. Again, those present included Mrs. Killam, Archdeacon and Mrs. Fortin, the Brydges and one of their daughters, Mrs. Alloway, wife of William Alloway. W.R. Allan and his father Andrew from Montreal, founder of the world-renowned Allan Line Steamship Company and a financier, were there.[12]

There were other kinds of entertainments Jean either attended or performed at, too: a "bonnet hop" (originally a dance aboard ship at which ladies kept their hats on) for the Snowshoe Club; and a dinner at Mrs. J. G. Moore's after the annual tennis tournament.[13] Mrs. Perdue held a tea for twenty-five at her "cosy" (read "small") residence on Carlton Street where guests played whist and Pedro (game in which all points go to the holders of certain cards, the "Pedro" or five of trumps worth five points) and later danced and had a midnight supper.[14] Some were formal performances, like the charity concert at the Bijou Theatre for St. Vincent de Paul on St. Patrick's Day;[15] another charity concert for Holy Trinity Church, attended by Lieutenant Governor and Mrs. Schultz, at which Canon Coombes played a violin piece and Jean Forsyth sang "Dreams of Yesterday."[16] Naturally, there were concerts at Grace Church to celebrate Easter. On Good Friday, the choir presented John Stainer's recent oratorio *The Crucifixion*, in which Jean Forsyth sang the soprano solos and Annie Pullar the contralto ones. Jean also sang the beautiful "Rose of Sharon" (Song of Solomon 2:11).[17] At the end of April, Jean was in nearby Brandon, as accompanist at a secular concert. In the heat of August she spent a week at Lake of the Woods with a group of half a dozen friends, including one of the Brydges's two daughters.[18]

Two events at the end of November 1894 show clearly the contrast between traditional entertainments such as these, and new ways of socializing that had just begun to emerge in a city where it was much simpler to slide out from under custom than in the eastern cities where traditions were deeply entrenched.

Nothing could have been more traditional than the Boys' Brigade concert at the Bijou on November 20[19] and the dance a couple of days later[20] given by the Fort Osborne Club at the officers' mess at the barracks of Fort Osborne. Yet nothing could have heralded a more casual "modern" way of entertaining than the first dance of the Bread and Butter (B & B) Club.[21]

The Boys' Brigade was a military organization begun by the Free Church in Glasgow, Scotland, two years before. The Free Church was the strictest sect of Presbyterians and the aim of this group was the advancement of Christ's kingdom among the boys. Within those two years, 200 companies of Boys' Brigades formed in Great Britain and Canada with 30,000 members. The concert in Winnipeg with Companies No. 1 (Zion Church) and No. 2 (Holy Trinity) demonstrated various types of military drills: rifle manual, bayonet drill, and physical drill. Then came horizontal bar exercises and East Indian club swinging. Opening the concert, Col. Holmes extolled the value of drilling for boys. This was followed by a selection from the Royal Dragoons' band. It seems almost incongruous that this hearty drilling and an intermission, in which Rev. C. Owen from Zion Church recounted the history of the organization, was followed by a musical performance by nine of the city's best musicians, including Paul Henneberg, Mrs. L. A. Hamilton, Katie Holmes, and Jean Forsyth. Even Mrs. Verner, who had stepped back from public singing, offered a solo, possibly because it was such a traditional occasion.

The military ball at Fort Osborne was a formal one. Mrs. Holmes received the more than one hundred guests, who passed into the wide hall and mess room that had a bright coal fire blazing. Opposite the mess room was the supper room;

the table on which the supper was arranged was "very elaborately decorated with ferns, chrysanthemums and palms, beautiful specimens of the latter being placed at every available point throughout the rooms." The billiard room upstairs was available. Music was provided, not by Paul Henneberg's orchestra, but by the band at the barracks. Again, there is the description of various ladies' dresses, this one lengthier than usual. Many also carried flowers. Mrs. Holmes in a "handsome" black dress carried white chrysanthemums. Mrs. Killam wore a pale pink gown covered with tulle and trimmed with moss green velvet. Mrs. Hamilton's dress was old rose brocade; her sister's, from Vancouver, was white *crêpon* trimmed with pearl *passimenterie* (elaborate trimmings, such as embroidery, braid, or tassels). Jean Forsyth, carrying yellow chrysanthemums, wore yellow silk tulle with finishings of black velvet and brown. The guest list included the wealthy of Winnipeg: the H. T. Champions, the W. F. Alloways, the Hugh J. Macdonalds, the G. W. Allans and the W. R. Allans, and several military officers.

In contrast to these celebrations of British customs and manners, a much more "modern" dance was held by the B & B Club in the Cauchon Block, a popular residential quarter downtown, where "several parties of young ladies well known in Winnipeg society lived in suites. The report afterwards in the *Winnipeg Tribune* referred to the last issue of a New York magazine, the *Century*, before going on to describe the dance. In it was a novelette, "The Bachelor Maid," by a Mrs. Burton Harrison. Two bachelor maids in New York discuss the propriety of receiving evening calls from gentlemen without a chaperone present. "This question, if debatable in New York, has been settled affirmatively at the Cauchon," writes the journalist covering the event.

In fact, there was a chaperone—Mrs. H. D. Tulloch—at the party. But the ingenious arrangements by the hostesses, Maggie Holmes (Katie's younger sister) and Nellie Gouin, who, along with Mrs. Tulloch, lived in the Cauchon, were anything but traditional. The Bread and Butter Club itself was a mild rebellion against convention. It stood for Bread and Butter (perhaps cake) and coffee, all that was served at their social events, not the expensive and elaborately prepared "dainties" or full dinners that must have needed days of preparation by maids. In the absence of a grand house, the party was divided up among the apartments of the Cauchon. The Cauchon, built in the Greek style in 1882, had been turned into apartments instead of a residence for former lieutenant governor J. E. Cauchon. It had several expensive stores on the ground floor at Main and York Streets. It was the first apartment block in the city and, starting in 1885, rented "very well indeed" mostly to young men. Now, eight years later, several couples and "bachelor maids" lived there.

These "bachelor maids" included Jean Forsyth (then thirty-three) and Katie and Maggie Holmes, Nellie Gouin, Emma Buchan (a.k.a. *Winnipeg Tribune* columnist "Dixi")[22] and Miss Eagles. Other young, unmarried members of the B & B Club included George Montegu Black, later grandfather of Conrad Black, Lord Black of Crossharbour, newspaper publisher, author, and columnist. Katie and Maggie Holmes shared the role of hostess for the forty or so guests. Rooms of Miss Buchan and Mrs. Tulloch on the third floor became the ladies' dressing (cloak) room. The men's dressing room was Howard Wright's room on the second floor. The large reception room, later the dance room decorated with Union Jacks, was Nellie Gouin's room. The sitting rooms were the combined apartments of Miss Eagles, the two Holmes girls and Jean Forsyth. These were all decorated, especially Jean Forsyth's. Her "rooms looked very pretty and in the subdued coloured light the many cushioned seats and corners looked very tempting." The Holmes sisters had filled their rooms with flowers: roses, chrysanthemums, and ferns. One of the rooms in their suite was converted into the supper room. The modest fare was so simple it did not merit a comment in the newspaper.[23]

Yet the occasion was traditional enough, for the report in the *Winnipeg Tribune* described the ladies' dresses in the conventional way. It is true that dresses of the era—especially ball gowns—were spectacular, draped and wrapped over pinching corsets like gifts in the most expensive materials, imported laces, feathers, and *passimenteries* of various kinds. The list included hostesses Katie (in black silk with buttercup ribbon), and Maggie (in white China silk and pale blue.) The chaperone, Mrs. H. D. Tulloch, wore "a pale pink costume, trimmed with bands of black velvet ribbon." Jean Forsyth was boldly dressed in scarlet *crêpon* with black velvet.

The B & B Club dance for young unmarried Winnipeggers was unconventional. It showed that hosts need not be a couple. And a spacious house in a good neighbourhood was not the only venue. Nor was an elaborate dinner necessary. Yet, if social conventions were truly to be broken, women would no longer be known by their husbands' names. Corsets would have to go, along with fantastic, expensive dresses and arrangements of long hair supplemented with switches and pin-on curls that hampered freedoms of all kinds. No matter how modern their notions, women did not appear socially until after noon, so time-consuming was their grooming and dressing.

ESTABLISHING THE WINNIPEG CONSERVATORY OF MUSIC, 1894

It was late August 1894 and establishing a Winnipeg Conservatory of Music had been underway since June. A notice in the *Winnipeg Tribune* assesses Jean Forsyth's career:

> Miss Jean Forsythe, a soprano vocalist of acknowledged merit, and leading soprano in Grace Church choir, also received her initial training in a noted London college.

> Since her appearance in America, Miss Forsythe has filled numerous concert engagements with great success. Her reputation as an artistic singer is growing, requiring only that larger scope for her undoubted powers which the establishment of the conservatory will do much to develop.

> Miss Forsythe has had considerable experience of conservatory work, and is quite a versatile as well as an accomplished teacher.[1]

The "e" added to "Forsyth" was a sort of compliment. For people who were or thought themselves cultured, the Frenchifying of words signified sophistication. "Quartet" became "quartette," "musical" became "musicale," "artist" became "artiste," "clarinet" became "clarinette." Often French terms were scattered into English sentences, words such as *thé dansant, petite, soirée,* and *passimenterie.*

Considering that the early meetings chaired by William Hespeler had begun in June, it was a prodigious feat of organizational efficiency that the conservatory opened three months later in mid-September. Models were the Toronto Conservatory of Music, the Toronto College of Music, where Edith Miller had taught, and the Northwestern Conservatory of Minneapolis. The school's objectives? Good teaching in the science of music and all its branches with proper apparatus and appliances; powers to lease, buy, build, etc. as determined by the shareholders; and the best educational methods at moderate cost to students.

According to Charles Wheeler, who was "elated," the early committee was "heart and soul into the matter," "unselfishly desirous of affording every possible aid, and sinking all personalities in giving a high class musical education at reasonable cost." He was thrilled that Paul Henneberg was named the musical director. Henneberg was to travel to other conservatories to ensure up-to-date policies. Application for incorporation was immediately submitted. Appeals were made for public donations. A month later, a building had been located, a two-storey brick place with eight or nine rooms on Notre Dame East (another column says Thistle Street) near the electric car system. Alterations and repairs were contracted and quickly underway.[2]

"The Winnipeg Conservatory is now an established fact," ran a notice in the *Winnipeg Tribune* on August 18.[3] Articles in the newspapers exuded sky-high enthusiasm. There were long descriptions of why a conservatory would promote good music in the city. These included the conviction that group study of music (rather than private lessons) inspired all who took part and the importance of establishing a musical culture. The "harmonious sentiments," "irrepressible energies," the "do-or-die" grit of the committee was compared to "stopping rivers in their courses."

Fees were advertised at the same time; ten-week terms varied from $7.50 to $40 "so that all classes of the community may share in the manifest advantages of the conservatory system." Staff was announced. The director Paul Henneberg would teach harmony, flute, violin, piano, orchestra, and theory. Katie Holmes, Miss Semple, Mrs. Dobson ("modest" but "skilled"), and Miss Cowley, a pupil of Henneberg's, would teach piano to junior students. Katie would also teach the organ. Mr. Scott, also Henneberg's pupil, would teach violin. Otto Henneberg offered instruction in violoncello and brass instruments. Brass instruments would also be taught by Mr. J. Johnson, bandmaster of the 90th Rifles. Mr. Williams, a retired army band clarinetist, was to teach "clarinette." There would be a mandolin and guitar instructor—still not chosen.

Singing, termed "Voice Culture," would be offered by two women: Edith J. Miller and Jean Forsyth.[4]

Edith J. Miller (she would use her middle initial for "Jane" from now on) had secured the position of contralto soloist at Westminster Church. This new, young singer was highly recommended by Charles Wheeler:

> Vocalists of Winnipeg would do well to take advantage of Miss Miller's engagement as vocal teacher in the conservatory of music. The Italian schools' method of breathing is superbly illustrated, and voice and style alike good.

> In this instance the mistress practices what she teaches, no small advantage to the pupil.

As for Jean Forsyth, she is almost an afterthought. "In Miss Forsyth the conservatory has secured the services of another valuable vocal teacher, with much experience in conservatory work."[5] A later report in the *Winnipeg Tribune* was more balanced. Even so, Edith J. Miller had pride of place; the column mentioned her "long conservatory training in Toronto, under one of the best vocal teachers in Canada, Signor D'Auria" and said that her "unrivalled method of voice culture will prove of inestimable benefit to pupils who desire vocal fame."[6]

The general exuberance of those involved in the new conservatory meant a special concert—"a feast of music"[7]—by its staff on September 13 to show the public the excellent quality in store for pupils. Any acoustic problems resulting from the poor positioning of the platform in the grand dining room of the Manitoba Hotel had been rectified. Five or six hundred of Winnipeg's leading citizens ("a brilliant assemblage") attended, proving—according to Charles Wheeler in the *Winnipeg Tribune*—that "music forms a prime basis of social society." He went on to say,

"At a future period, not long prolonged either, Winnipeg also may boast, and with pride, that it possesses the finest musical college on the American continent."

The program of music was classical—neither bright nor light, but not so heavy as to tax the audience: a piano and string quartet by Schumann; an *andante* from a sonata by Beethoven; "Spring Song" by Mendelssohn; a selection from Wagner's *Lohengrin*.

Edith J. Miller, who had just moved to Winnipeg, took the enviable spot as first vocalist after the overture by Gerhard von Lentner. She sang "Could I?" by contemporary composer Paolo Tosti and the gavotte ("I am in her Boudoir Fair") from *Mignon* by Ambroise Thomas. Jean Forsyth sang the "florid" aria "Robert le Diable" by Giacomo Meyerbeer. In the buoyant review the next day, Charles Wheeler wrote, "Each in her own style, contralto and soprano, Miss Edith J. Miller and Miss Jean Forsythe sang almost faultlessly."[8] Nothing in this "feast of music" was religious; it was an entirely secular evening. This suggests that the highly trained, sophisticated musicians in Winnipeg who were on the conservatory staff thought that concert programs in the city needed to break—at least in part—with church music.

Two days after the concert, Charles Wheeler wrote confidently, "Winnipeg now possesses soprano and contralto vocalists of whom every city might feel proud, and the vocal portions of the Conservatory concert were none the less enjoyable because they were made up mostly of ballads; but even ballads, when they are as exquisitely sung as they were by Miss Miller and Miss Jean Forsythe, possess a charm and a power over audiences, which the classical elements cannot hope to gain." He went on to compare the two: Edith Miller has "a lovely quality of tone, full and resonant, almost without a break in its entire register, adapting readily to the legato requirements of the music, no wonder the audience were delighted; then again its flexibility was tested by the gavotte from *Mignon*, charmingly sung. In quite a different style came Miss Forsythe's song 'O, That We Two Were Maying' interpreted in a beautiful manner."[9]

Wheeler went on to say what might have been on many musical minds in the city. "There cannot possibly be any rivalry between the two ladies, their styles being so different. Comparison is wholly out of the question, and it is folly to attempt it; one might as well compare the cornet with the alto horn, the bassoon with the saxophone, the oboe with the clarinet."[10]

The lieutenant governor and Mrs. Schultz were unable to attend that opening concert because their train from Lake Winnipeg was late. So a second concert was arranged at a time when Lord and Lady Aberdeen were visiting Winnipeg and could attend too. This second concert was held on October 1. The next day Charles Wheeler wrote, "Miss Edith J. Miller's singing was the vocal treat of the evening."[11]

Meanwhile, Charles Wheeler and his wife held their own celebratory musicale for forty guests at their home on Donald Street on September 22. It was said to be one of the principal inaugural events of the season. He himself gave a recitation—a popular form of entertainment that often accompanied music programs. Most of the staff of the new conservatory performed, except Jean Forsyth and Miss Cowley, who were simply guests. Johnson and Williams were not present. Edith

Miller sang twice. Her mother, Mrs. W. W. Miller, who occasionally came into the city for major social events, was present, along with the cream of Winnipeg society. Wheeler's choice of singers, especially since Edith sang twice and Jean did not sing at all, indicated clearly that he favoured Edith. From then on, as before, he did whatever he could to further Edith's career.

Coincidentally, six wealthy women started their own Women's Musical Club of Winnipeg that same year: Constance Hamilton, wife of the land commissioner for the CPR, Laughlan A. Hamilton; Mrs. Angus Kirkland, Mrs. Frank H. Mathewson, whose husband was manager of the local Bank of Ottawa (and later the Canadian Bank of Commerce); Margaret Stobart, whose husband Fred ran a wholesale dry goods business; Mrs. Gerald Brophy, whose husband was a lawyer, and Annie Higginson, wife of Dr. Henry A. Higginson, who was on the staff of the Winnipeg General Hospital. These ladies must also have felt the time was right to have an annual recital series of the highest standard of music. They met at each other's homes to discuss music and to sing themselves.[12]

But it was the opening doors of the Winnipeg Conservatory of Music to nearly a hundred pupils on September 24, 1894 that was a pivotal moment in the city's culture. Now children from most income levels in Winnipeg could study music with the best musicians—many highly trained abroad—that the city could muster.

JEAN NOTICES EDITH

Jean was feeling slightly out of breath. She had danced the last three dances, a waltz, a schottische, then another waltz. There was quite a crush on the dance floor, but what a delight it was to dance to Johnston's orchestra. It was only half past ten, but there were so many guests already that Mr. Denison, the floor manager at the Manitoba Hotel, had ushered them into the spacious dining room, now ballroom, just before ten o'clock. As she walked through the tinted light from the coloured lamps towards one of the seats to wait out a dance or two, she could hear Charles Wheeler's clipped English accent behind her. He was speaking to William Scarth, whose musical Scottish voice she recognized at once. His wife, Helen, was on the Humane Society committee with her. Even a Canadian wife had not flattened William's accent. She caught only the last bit of what Charles was saying.

"...largest affair of its kind since the opening of the Manitoba. I should say there are upwards of 500 expected. The Rowers' Club always produces a top-rate show. They are quite the most popular club in the city. I believe the executive committee has worked hard indeed to make it such a success. William Allan is the chairman, I believe."

"Aye, but surely some of the fairer sex lent a hand. There are no five bachelors alive who could see to this fascinating scene."

"Indeed, half a dozen of our dear ladies worked just as hard as the rower bachelors. They rented the extra furniture from Scott's and from Leslie Bros. I believe the flowers came from Mr. Braxton's and Mr. Alston's greenhouses, no doubt arranged by the ladies as well. It's my daughter Lily's first ball. That's her over there to the left with the other debutantes. She's the one in pale blue silk with natural flowers. How time flies."

"Aye," responded William. "So many pretty faces and pretty figures...aye, and manly forms too. 'Tis the flower of Winnipeg youth, that it be."

Just then, Katie Holmes stepped up to Jean's side. "Katie!" Jean said. "I was looking round for you, but there is such a mass of people here. I thought to escape it for a few moments off the dance floor, but it is every bit as crowded here as it is there. Even the seats are all taken. Don't you look splendid in your black silk with those delicate little white bows around the top of your hem ruffle."

Katie smiled.

"And here I am in my pure white grosgrain silk with lace collar. It is Honiton lace. My dressmaker managed to get some from Devon a few weeks ago. I am especially fond of the pattern of birds and leaves. As we stand here, the two of us, we look like black and white piano keys!"

Katie laughed, her dimple deepening in a charming way. "Yes, indeed we do. Did you see the flowers on that petite woman?"

"No."

"She's here just on my right. Don't stare. She'll know we're speaking of her. In the white dress with a huge cascade of red roses."

"Oh, yes, I see," said Jean without moving her head, which was coiffed to perfection with a fringe of bangs, the rest of her fair hair swept up most becomingly. "Those roses! Why they are simply splendid. She's not from here, is she?"

"No, she lives in Ottawa. She's visiting her friend, Mrs. Dickins, for a week. There's someone here from Woodstock and someone from Chicago too. I can't see her.

"Oh, yes, there she is in the far corner. She might be a debutante. She's wearing white satin with white chrysanthemums. Just there." Katie nodded her head slightly.

"No, I can't. There are just so many people here, and more arriving by the minute. I rather pity Mrs. Alloway and Mrs. Galt receiving so many guests in such rapid succession. Their gowns and jewellery are enviable though. Mrs. Alloway's cream brocade with lace and velvet is extraordinarily becoming. And Mrs. Galt almost outdoes her in her lovely white *duchesse* satin with pearl *passimenterie* looping all over the bodice and pearl ornaments. I don't see how a ball in Toronto or even London could outdo this and I have attended balls in both cities. Ah! Mr. Denison has thrown open the doors of the supper room. Shall we enter?"

Katie nodded and the two friends, arm in arm, proceeded slowly among the crowd in a sea of gauzy dresses of white, cream, black, and delicate pastels in the direction of the supper room. They passed the palms, ferns, and huge flower arrangements that—as William Scarth had surmised—the ladies had arranged so tastefully that the place looked like a fairyland.

Glancing over this crowd chattering to each other in a layered mixture of various old country and American and Canadian accents from points east, Jean recognized many of those she had known now for a mere year and a half.

"There's Stanley Adams's daughter, Ethel, in white silk net trimmed with satin ribbons down each sleeve. And beside her, Mrs. Hugh Macdonald, looking charming, as always, in her white satin and diamonds. Mrs. Hamilton shows well in black satin and lace draped over it and drawn into fullness—almost a bustle—at the back below her tiny waist. She's whispering something to her sister, Miss Boddington, who's wearing a most elaborate gown of mauve silk embroidered with pansies and covered with black silk net. Who's that in the latest puff sleeves—and in heliotrope too? I think it's Mrs. Black, though I don't know her at all well. Ah, there's the Archdeacon's daughter, Rachel Fortin. She did come after all, and how pretty she looks in her white and pink. She's such a sweet girl, and I'm glad she lives at the Cauchon Block. Maggie Strang is looking especially well in creamy yellow *crêpon*. She is chatting with Edith Kirkland, dressed in pale blue silk and draped over all with black lace," not Honiton, Jean noted, "and her husband Angus."

Everywhere, ladies and girls alike were carrying flowers: pale chrysanthemums, roses, spring flowers.

Jean's shoes had begun to pinch, and the lace bows on them were scratching her instep. She took one last glance over the animated crowd before pressing Katie to hurry in to the various dainties and fruits that would surely be artistically laid out on decorated tables.

"Who's that in brilliant yellow at the very edge of the crowd? Petite, with frizzed bangs, her thick dark curls elaborately arranged like wings with a feather arching back over one shoulder? Why, of course! It's my student, or rather my former student, Edith Miller. She's with Stanley Adams and his wife, discussing music no doubt.'"

THE WINNIPEG HUMANE SOCIETY'S FIRST YEAR, 1895

It was the first Winnipeg Humane Society meeting of real consequence. There had been twenty-one meetings during the past year, but these had mainly set up committees and bylaws to consolidate the new society. All that remained was legislative approval for their constitution and the bylaws defining cruelty so that they would have power to act. This would have to wait until the legislature resumed. Now, on January 9, 1895, in the committee room of city hall at 4:00 p.m., their work had begun. That work concerned neglected and abused children as well as animals, for separate societies on behalf of children, such as the Children's Aid Society, had not yet been established.[1]

Because of the short term—only half a year—in 1894, it was agreed that all officers should be re-elected, but that this was not to set a precedent. It was a formidable group, with representatives from church and state: doctors, a veterinarian, an alderman, women of culture, and men of business. William Whyte, general superintendent of the CPR, was president. T. A. Gamble, as from the outset, was secretary-treasurer. He reported that there were now 115 members of the society, two of them juveniles. That meant $86.83 in the bank, after expenses were deducted. There were three vice-presidents, one for each electoral district in the city: W. F. Henderson, the wealthy wholesale grocer, for Winnipeg South; Thomas "The Shoe King" Ryan for Winnipeg Centre; and H. S. Crotty, owner of Winnipeg's first real estate firm and vice-president of his electoral district, for Winnipeg North.

Jean Forsyth was one of the five women on the executive committee, along with Katie Holmes, Dr. Amelia Yeomans, Mrs. J. H. Gardner, and Jessie Scarth. The ten men on the committee included veterinarian Dr. Willett J. Hinman, Rev. R. G. MacBeth, Canon Matheson, Capt. Coulson N. Michell, Alderman Alfred J. Andrews, the lawyer and avid golfer who would later become "the Boy Mayor," lawyer John MacBeth, Fred Stobart, Charles N. Bell, Alex Smith, and George Hague.

There were also a number of members present, each having paid one dollar to join the society, and possibly some juvenile members (at ten cents).

There were ten cases of cruelty to animals already dealt with and two cases underway involving children. In that era, before cars, horses were the usual means of carrying goods. Portage Avenue, with its electric streetcars (the Winnipeg Electrical Rail Company) that required space for double rails in each direction, was exceptionally wide, as were the boardwalks on either side. Between the rails and the boardwalks a whole street width accommodated various horse-drawn carts. Especially in the poorer northwest part of the city, horses were neglected, maltreated, or abandoned. Older horses were being turned out to linger and die. Efforts had been made to locate owners and punish them. Excessive whipping was common. Two men, James Surtry, wood contractor, and George River, hay presser, and their servant, Albert Howard, from the Beausejour area were prosecuted for "terribly" maltreating horses and oxen by beating and stabbing them with pitchforks. Several complaints had come in from around Portland Avenue and Notre Dame Street about the brutality and "vile language" of Montana horse trainers. Visits from officers of the society had stopped this. A farmer from St. Andrews was forced to stop driving his heavily laden lame horse until the animal recovered. Another case involved a horse left standing in the cold for far too long.

Dogs, of course, were a central focus of the society. One who was on fire had had to be killed to end its suffering. The investigation was inconclusive. Someone reported a small dog left out every night in the piercing cold. The dog was seized and given a new home. The two reports on the state of dogs at the city pound and the rudeness of the pound owner made by Jean Forsyth and Mrs. Garner were raised. The two ladies had filed a complaint after their visits to the pound with the Health and Licence department, and the poundkeeper, Hans Jessen, was given a reprimand. He was warned to treat all visitors respectably [sic] and look after the animals properly, as he was well paid for it. Jean Forsyth asked again that he be replaced with a "kind and respectable person," and that the location of the pound be relocated near the streetcars.[2]

A clear success for the society resulted from complaining about the "greasy pig chase" that had occurred as a "sport" every Dominion Day. The event was struck from the program.

The committee on Humane Education and Bands of Mercy had made some progress with the school board that represented the fifteen public schools in the city. Dr. Amelia Yeomans had looked into what was taught in the French schools in her native province of Quebec. They had an active humane education program, and Dr. Yeomans reported that their French Humane Society confirmed the "most valuable results of such a teaching especially on children who have not good homes." She had learned that the subject was an option in one Winnipeg School already. The society wanted it taught systematically, and Dr. Yeomans suggested a rotation of pairs of Society members going to the schools every month. The school boards were not ready for this "at present." She distributed two books to all present at the meeting: *Twelve Lessons on Kindness to Animals* by George T. Angell,[3] and *Band of Mercy Melodies* by the same author along with Rev. Thomas Timmins.[4] These two men founded the "Band of Mercy" for animals in Boston in 1882, more than ten years before Jean Forsyth initiated the Winnipeg Humane Society.

The two cases involving children were painful. One, which would eventually alter laws in the province, concerned a blind fifteen-year-old. He had "watery eyes" when he was young and whatever was put in them resulted in terrible pain and loss of vision. His "intemperate" father died when he was eight; his half-breed mother, a "hopeless drunk," was put in the Home for Incurables in Portage la Prairie. Neither his sister in Tacoma, Washington, nor his brother in St. John, North Dakota, wanted anything to do with him. Application to the same institution his mother was in was declined. All they could do was find him a temporary bed in St. Boniface Hospital, where he was born. Visits there reassured the society that he was being well treated by the sisters. That did nothing to solve the problem of what this young man, who had no education, was to do with the rest of his life.

A three-year-old girl was brutally abused by her aunt and uncle, who were raising her. The society intervened and arranged to send her to her father at Langenburg, Saskatchewan, but kept her for two weeks to let the "black and bruised parts" heal before she was sent.

There was no doubt that a Humane Society was sorely needed in Winnipeg, and it must have pleased Jean beyond measure that her efforts had begun—finally—to pay off.

TWO FAREWELLS, A CONCERT DEBUT, A MARRIAGE, AND A FAMOUS SOPRANO

An announcement of a concert to be given for Edith J. Miller in Westminster Church on May 15, 1895, included this statement, "Miss Miller leaves very shortly for London, England, for a course of training."[1] Several musicians were taking part in this tribute concert. Jean Forsyth was not among them. In early August Edith would leave behind her position as contralto soloist in the Portage la Prairie Knox Church choir, her vocal students in Portage la Prairie, and her position as vocal teacher at the new Winnipeg Conservatory of Music in pursuit of an international career. What Charles Wheeler called "her rich, powerful, resonant tones"[2] would no longer be heard in the Canadian West, at least for the time being. In a later column, he wrote, "There can be no question that the absence of Miss Edith Miller will be severely felt not only by the church but in musical circles generally, and to fill the void thus caused will prove uphill work even to a more talented singer."[3]

Edith was to study with Alberto Randegger, an Italian musician and composer who had moved to England in 1854. This short, portly, balding man with neatly trimmed sideburns extending almost to his round chin was an even-tempered, indefatigable worker. His tasteful compositions were not outstanding, but his vocal teaching was. When Edith arrived to study with him, he was on the staff of the Royal Academy of Music, where Jean Forsyth had encountered William Shakespeare. He was also conducting Italian opera for Sir Augustus Harris, as well as many choral concerts. Within a year of Edith's arrival he would become a teacher at the Royal College of Music, adding to an already taxing schedule. His specialty was oratorio, and he would train Edith in the contralto solos in a number of such works. Most of them were religious, like the *Messiah*.

The last performances Edith gave in Canada before leaving were a series of concerts with Jean Forsyth in Regina during the last week of July. They would each sing some of their "favourite solos" and also several duets.[4] During the previous months, the two of them had sung in many performances, but seldom together. Edith had starred in the opening of the Portage Club in her hometown; Jean was not there.[5] Nor was she a performer in another concert in Portage la Prairie, which Charles Wheeler claimed had "the best talent from Winnipeg." Edith was one of the singers at the opening of the new St. Andrew's church with Lieutenant Governor Schultz in attendance in early February, not Jean.[6]

There were a few events at which Jean performed where Edith was not among the singers. This was especially true as the time drew near for Edith to leave for England. Jean took part in a benefit for the German Lutheran Church (contralto Annie Pullar sang one of Edith's favourites, "Could I?"), a celebration of the tin (tenth) wedding anniversary of the Reverend Coombes and his wife in June, the

Alberto Randegger, Edith's teacher of religious music at the Royal Academy of Music, London, England, 1894. Publicity photo, Carlo Rosa Opera Company, *circa* 1879.

conference of Christian Endeavor group, a sports event to celebrate the 24th of May, a lecture by James Tees called "Men in Music" (ironically, women singers were used to illustrate his points), a contrasting lecture "Women in Politics" by Dr. Yeomans, a vaudeville-like talent concert at the Bijou in aid of Holy Trinity Church, and concerts at Grace Church. Jean also appeared at social events that Edith did not attend, such as Mrs. Frank Phippen's euchre party and the annual Fort Osborne ball.

As instructors, both singers performed in the second recital of the Winnipeg Conservatory of Music. And they both performed in the year's most ambitious presentation, the oratorio *Athalie* by Mendelssohn. It is questionable whether Holy Trinity's choirmaster, A. J. Tuckwell, made a suitable choice for the Winnipeg audience. *Athalie*—based on Racine's play—was rarely performed. The subject—the revenge murder of Queen Athalie for turning her worship from Judah to Baal (the evil demon of fertility)—was both obscure and dark. Tuckwell amassed a huge (for the times) chorus of seventy singers from Winnipeg churches for the concert that appeared, with much advance billing, on Tuesday and Thursday, April 23 and 25. The female soloists were Mrs. Verner (who was now back on the music scene) and Jean Forsyth, sopranos, and Edith Miller, contralto. In the review that followed, these three were praised for their trio "Promised Joys." And Jean and Mrs. Verner were praised for their duet "Ever Blessed Child Rejoice," though Mrs. Verner was criticized for "the acuteness of her vocal pitch." The tenor and baritone soloists "were not up to pitch either." Katie Holmes accompanied on the organ, as usual, and was highly praised. Rev. Cecil C. Owen had the "ungrateful task" of reading the spoken parts of *Athalie*. The reviewer wrote that the oratorio—far from Mendelssohn's best—"will be better understood on a second hearing." A "very large audience" attended the first performance; he expected even more at the second.[7]

Tuckwell may have been endeavouring to raise the musical level of his church after Charles Wheeler wrote that Holy Trinity was obviously "a little behind hand in musical matters to at least three other churches one could name."[8] That might have been the reason Tuckwell included the "Eia Mater" chorus from Dvořák's *Stabat Mater*, in which the Mother Mary stands agonized at the foot of the cross as her son dies. Music by Dvořák was performed over and over at Winnipeg concerts during

Jean Forsyth as vocal
teacher, *Winnipeg
Tribune*, July 2, 1904.

MISS FORSYTH

Talented local Teacher and
accompanist, who has conducted a successful season's work.

this period. It signalled "modern" or "contemporary" as well as "seriously classical." His music was often played—here and elsewhere—to show that Winnipeg
was up-to-date. Tuckwell also included a third piece based on a passage in Isaiah:
"Wilderness" by S. S. Wesley. This anthem, featuring a quartet, portrays the wilderness as a place of fertility, miracles, and delight. As the reviewer notes, the three
composers are "utterly unlike each other:" *Athalie* being a stately oratorio on a heroic
(and uncomfortable) subject; "Eia Mater" an expression of the most intense grief
possible; and "Wilderness" being a jubilant celebration of God's benevolent power.[9]
It would have been a disjointed concert.

Things in Winnipeg's music world shifted dramatically that fall of 1895. Jean
took over Edith Miller's students in Portage la Prairie, travelling the hour by train
on Tuesdays and returning Wednesdays. Annie Pullar, Grace Church's contralto
soloist, would take Edith Miller's place at the usual concerts and other musical
performances around the city. She would also replace Edith as vocal teacher at
the Winnipeg Conservatory of Music. James Tees, "that sterling friend of music," retired from the concert scene. Music had advanced significantly in the city.
Charles Wheeler could now say with confidence that "circus methods are out of
place" in concerts.[10] Katie Holmes, Jean's friend and favourite accompanist, married the outstanding young tenor Holmes M. Cowper, one of Jean's students, who
would go on to an international career. Much was made of both having the name
"Holmes." Jean would replace Katie as accompanist in many musical events. As
Charles Wheeler wrote in the *Winnipeg Tribune*,

Accompanying is a fine art. It is an accomplishment in itself. Mrs. Cowper, née Miss Holmes, possesses this gift to a high degree.

But of late Miss Jean Forsyth has been showing such unusual excellence in this department as warrants a belief that when Mrs. Cowper leaves the city her mantle will have fallen gracefully over the shoulders of Miss Forsyth.[11]

Wheeler also praised her as a teacher.

Miss Forsyth is a great acquisition to our musical world, and it can readily be understood how much her services in the Grace Church choir are appreciated. Her thorough knowledge of the teachings of singing should be of great value to the limited number of pupils who are placing themselves under her direction.[12]

A farewell concert by the choir and friends of Grace Church for Katie Holmes was held mid-November at the church. The reviewer found the opening number, "Praise God from Whom All Blessings Flow," odd. "Is this in regret or disguised happiness at the talented organist's departure?" he quipped. The music was all religious. Jean Forsyth sang one of her favourites, "There Is a Green Hill Far Away" by Gounod, a solemn devotional hymn about the crucifixion. Annie Pullar sang a solo by Saint-Saëns. The baritone George Bailey sang a selection from the *Messiah*. Katie herself played four organ solos. Jean was singled out for praise in the review.

Miss Jean Forsyth is excelled by no vocalist in this city as a church choir singer. Her solo at the farewell concert in Grace Church...was an admirable example of pure unadulterated vocalism, free from tricks or mannerisms, sung in an artistic as well as true devotional style.[13]

A week later, Jean, along with Paul Henneberg and several others, headed off on the Great Northern Railway for five days in St. Paul to hear the famous Australian soprano Nellie Melba.[14] Melba had made her debut in 1884 in Melbourne, and since then had studied with the celebrated vocal teacher Madame Marchesi in Paris. Usurping the aging top soprano Adelina Patti this very year, 1895, she had been busy "winning her way into the hearts of the American public" through her "brilliant singing and extraordinary technical gifts."[15]

"Surely," Jean would have thought eagerly, "there is much for me to learn from her. And I shall."

A DEVASTATING FIRE, 1895

It was only a few days since Jean returned from hearing Melba's concert in St. Paul. Her head was filled with ideas about ways she could improve her own concert singing. She must refine her high notes, flying up to them and perching on them like a cat gracefully leaping onto a table, not sliding up fearfully from underneath. She must also work on gliding from one register into another imperceptibly. Then there was tone. Interpretation. So much she needed to work on. She was more than ready.

Those thoughts were probably still swirling about in her head as she waltzed in the swirling kaleidoscope of vivid dresses on the dance floor to the melodies of Paul Henneberg's twelve-piece orchestra. It was the annual Rowing Club Ball in the dining room of the Manitoba Hotel on December 6, 1895. Her gown, white silk with large blue satin bows on each shoulder and a blue ribbon around the hem, was most becoming. The blue matched her eyes exactly. It made her feel girlish. There was a new lieutenant governor now: the Irishman James Colebrooke Patterson. He had left his post as Conservative cabinet minister to come to Manitoba. He was tall and imposing, more majestic than Sir John Schultz from Ontario. His wife was wearing a dramatic black silk dress with white silk sleeves. Very stylish. The startling innovation of having a bugle call announce each dance that night was deemed "novel and acceptable." Certainly, for once, everyone was acutely aware of the start of each dance: the waltzes, the lancers (a quadrille with four couples in a square), the two-step, polkas, and schottisches (an old Bohemian couples dance).

Ten days later she was dreaming about stretching to find something that was just out of reach when she suddenly awoke. It was dark. Half asleep, she thought she heard voices and loud crashings in the hallway outside the apartment she shared with Anna Fortin, the archdeacon's daughter, in the elegant Cauchon Block. She called Anna, then remembered she was away, visiting relatives in Chicago. Again, there was a crash in the hall, this time right outside her door.

Then she smelled smoke.

She took the clothes she was wearing the day before off the chair and got them on quickly. Now she could hear screaming, shouting, people scrambling about calling names and pounding on doors. She opened her door and tasted the smoke that surged in. In the dark she could see the brilliant orange glare reflected from the Hudson's Bay windows. The Cauchon Block was on fire.[1]

Jean's room on the second floor was near the fire escape on Main Street. "*This way out!*" she shouted in a voice made loud by years of practice. "*This way out! At the end of the hall! Here! This way out!*" A few figures, some half-dressed, some in nightclothes and caps, emerged from the deafening confusion of the crowd, stumbling over the heaps of plaster that had fallen from the ceiling, out of the darkening roils of smoke. The

Simpsons from the apartment next hers had already raced out onto the fire escape—a wooden stairway that led down to the roof of one of the lean-tos. Jean took her friend Mrs. Georgen's elbow and guided her to the escape. Then Joseph Martin and his family appeared, Mrs. Martin crying out that her daughter had been suffering from asthma for a long time.

"She must get away from this smoke!" she shrieked, as she followed Mrs. Georgen out onto the fire escape. The Earls, the Simpsons, the Martins, with bits of clothing over their mouths, were running towards her. Now, she realized she must go down the fire escape herself. It was freezing and the wind was blowing hard towards her and over the roof. That means the smoke and flames will be going towards York Avenue, she thought.

"*Oh, no!*" she exclaimed. "What about those coming after me?"

Her skirt snagged something on the stair. She felt dizzy. Those below her had reached the lean-to where another wooden fire escape led to the street. She could hear the cries of horror and shouts from the crowd desperate for relatives and friends gathered on Main Street below. She heard the fire engine pull up to her left along the galvanized steel wall on Main Street.

Then, shivering and shaken, she set both feet on the frozen ground in the vacant lot behind the building. The whole south end of Main Street on her right was lit up, though it was still dark. Someone wrapped her in a blanket and moved her away towards one of the little houses past the vacant lot on the east side of the Cauchon.

"Thank God!" she cried out, seeing some of the others being hurried away in the same direction. Looking back, she gasped. She could see Mr. and Mrs. Baby throwing their two little children out a back window to waiting arms holding a blanket three storeys below. Then they themselves jumped onto the pile of clothes and bedding piled on the lean-to below. Jean could tell from their screams that they were badly hurt. Above them the yellow flames blown out over York Avenue were terrifying. The smoke coming out the windows swirled black in the frigid wind. She heard a series of crashes from York Avenue.

"Oh, no! That must be part of the wall collapsing! I hope they all got out!" she shouted above the noise before stumbling through the crowd gathered behind the building now belching fire in every direction. As she skidded past she heard someone telling a reporter, "Thank God for the lady, whoever she was, who stood at the end of the hall leading to the fire escape and called 'This way out, this way out.'" She could hear an ambulance siren. Then she almost fell into the open door of one of the little houses behind the building, where, amid the chaos, Dr. Simpson from the maternity ward of the General Hospital was tending to Mrs. Calder's face burns. She was moaning about the terror of descending the iron bars set into the brick wall at the end of the York wing. "They were loose. They were loose. Some of them were coming nearly out of the wall. They were loose," she kept saying.

That same day's evening edition of the *Winnipeg Tribune* gave a thorough account of the fire. It had begun in the furnace room just after 6:30 a.m., leapt up the central staircase off York Avenue and the elevator shaft beside it and "rushed up it like a volcano" until it burst through the elevator cap on the roof before any of the alarms from different quarters had sounded.

The Cauchon had two iron firewalls with iron doors, one in each side of the L-shaped building. In an earlier fire these doors had effectively saved the two wings—though not the squared-off corner at Main and York—in April 1885. There were thirty-two residential tenants then, although the handsome, luxurious building was originally intended to be an office building in 1882. Its galvanized iron front imitated a famous block in Paris. It had been named after former Lieutenant Governor Joseph Édouard Cauchon. He failed to realize even a quarter of the $40,000 in rents he expected because of the "hard times" that set in almost immediately after it opened. In 1884, the Cauchon was sold and turned into an apartment house that rented quickly "mainly to young men, though a number of families and a dancing school," were also occupants. At once the Cauchon Block acquired a reputation as a "high class" address. The impoverished scowling Cauchon was given a free apartment. That earlier 1885 fire started on an April afternoon. All thirty-two of the tenants—among them a lawyer, a banker, a real estate agent, a music teacher, and a future MP—were saved. One journalist reported that the fire was so exciting, "for a time all thoughts of the Riel rebellion were banished from the minds of the citizens." Thanks to the solid brick firewall, most of the building was saved and damages were only $10,000.[2]

This fire was far more serious. By now, the building was owned by E. J. Prine in Quebec. There were forty-four suites and 124 tenants. The ground-level stores on Main and York were: Grundy pianos, Manitoba Plumbing, Lacey Carpets, and spice merchants Williams & Hilton. One commercial space was the Lantham dining room, where many of the residents took their meals, and another was a kindergarten school for which Jean had raised money by giving charity concerts. The York Avenue wing was almost destroyed; the outer walls supported by two large chimneys collapsed a few weeks later. One firefighter died a few days after the fire. The Baby family was taken off to the St. Boniface Hospital by ambulance where Mr. Charles Baby remained for three weeks. Damages were triple the amount of the 1885 fire.

Worst of all were the deaths of Major J.F.B. Morice and his wife. According to Mr. Christopher E. Buckley, who had roused the major from his third-floor room in the York Avenue wing next to and *inside* one of the fire doors, "He rushed out to see to the safety of his daughter whose room was in the south end of the building near the billiard room. He had to go about 100 feet from his own room to hers. ... This terrible exposure to heat and smoke were too much for the Major."

The crowd in front of the building began to scream and turn away in horror as two firemen carried out the major between them. They made their way to Burke's livery stable across Main Street where Dr. Ferguson was busy with injuries, especially architect George Browne's previously sprained ankle that had hindered his exit from the burning building. Fortunately, Mrs. Lait, wife of William B. Lait, an architect, was close to the York wing fire escape, for she had just recovered from an attack of quinsy (a rare and serious complication of tonsillitis in which an abscess forms on the tonsils). The major never regained consciousness. The "horribly burned and disfigured" body of his wife was found later by the firemen among the debris near the northwest angle of the hall. It was put in a coffin and quickly taken away. It seemed she was trying to find her husband. Joseph Aldritt, the caretaker of the Cauchon Block, died a month later of complications from smoke inhalation.

More than one hundred surviving tenants had lost everything but their clothes, apart from Mr. Christopher Buckley, who had managed to save his banjo and two cups he won snowshoeing. Jean was one of about a dozen tenants who had pianos in their suites, except for those in the music store on the ground floor. All were destroyed, either burnt or ruined by smoke, heat, and water. Furniture, pictures, clothes, other belongings—some precious—were reduced to ashes, even though a few managed to carry furnishings down the Main wing fire escape.

All the tenants, insured or not, had to find temporary lodgings, some in hotels and others with friends. Jean Forsyth was taken in at the mansion of her friend, soprano Mrs. L.A. (Constance) Hamilton.

The architect who restored the building, which was renamed the Assiniboine Block, as a modern tenement—with wider halls, better exits, and a two-storey brick wing on York Avenue—was Charles Wheeler.

CHARLES WHEELER'S CHRISTMAS GREETINGS TO MUSICIANS, 1895

As a Christmas greeting to all Winnipeg musicians, Charles Wheeler wrote a fanciful tribute in the *Winnipeg Tribune* for the December 21, 1895 edition. He quoted passages or phrases by authors or composers that he thought appropriate for each musician:

COMPLIMENTS TO MUSICIANS

Vocalists, Instrumentalists and Lovers of the Art Hit Off in Appropriate

Quotations From the Works of the Master Spirits of the Ages.

For Jean Forsyth he quoted from Wordsworth's poem "A Morning Exercise": "Bright gem, instinct with music, vocal spark." The poetic compliment to Edith Miller was: "What fairy-like music steals over the sea, / Entrancing our senses with charmed melody" from lyricist Mrs. C. B. Miller's "What Fairy Like Music."

Since Charles Wheeler would follow closely the careers of both singers, this characterization reveals his early impressions. To his well-trained ear Jean Forsyth was all "spark," an intuitive singer with a "bright" voice; Edith Miller was "entrancing," a "charmer" resembling an otherworldly fairy.

Of orchestra leader Paul Henneberg, Wheeler cited seventeenth-century essayist Isaak Walton: "Lord, what music hast thou provided for thy saints in heaven when thou affordest bad men such music on earth!"

In another entry, by Walt Whitman, Henneberg is praised: "The tempest, waters, winds, operas, chants, marches and dances, / Utter pour in, for I would take them all."

Otto Henneberg, Paul's brother, who played the French horn, trumpet, and other instruments, earned a quote from the seventeenth-century poet the Earl of Roscommon: "Charmed by these strings, trees starting from the ground / Have followed with delight the powerful sound."

His tribute to Signor D'Auria came from Longfellow's "The Day is Done": "And the night shall be filled with music, / And the cares that infest the day / Shall fold their tents like the Arabs, / And as silently steal away."

Tenor Jackson Hanby, destined for an international career, seemed to Wheeler like Mozart's "A man of superior talents" who "deteriorates if he always remains in one place."

Wheeler thought Stanley Adams, who dabbled in drama and music without strong direction, needed advice: "A man with fine capabilities has the absolute duty imposed on him of becoming something really superior."

James Tees, the choirmaster at Grace Church who had invited Jean Forsyth to take the position of lead soprano, was given several lines of poetry by American poet George W. Curtis that suggest Tees's fervour about religious music:

Near heaven's gate
I thought I stood unconscious of all sin;
With a sweet soulful ecstasy within,
A golden sea in the celestial choir,
Where harps, cherubic voices oft begin;
With angel and archangel's trembling lyre,
In choral fraught with a resounding holy fire.

Wheeler also offered quotations for groups such as The City Organists, The Bands of the City, The St. Andrew's Society and the Clans, The St. Patrick's Society, and The Pianists' Club. For The Conservatory of Music he quoted Robert Schumann: "Good teachers turn out not pupils, but artists, who become teachers in their turn." He did not mention the Women's Musical Club.

Wheeler finished his Christmas good wishes with a cheeky Shakespearean quotation for Frederick William Sprado, the manager of the Manitoba Hotel, where so many musical events took place: "The Prince of Caterers; / A jolly good fellow; / Courteous to all, mesdames and messieurs."

EDITH'S PROGRESS TO PARIS AND MADAME MATHILDE MARCHESI

The *Manitoba Morning Free Press* announced on May 11, 1896 that Mrs. W. W. Miller had returned to Portage la Prairie from Winnipeg,

> ...where she had the pleasure of meeting Mr. Watkin-Mills, the English singer, who spoke flatteringly of the progress Miss Edith Miller is making in her musical studies in London. She is expected to leave about this time to take up a course of instruction under Madame Marchesi, of Paris.[1]

Robert Watkin-Mills, a handsome, well-known baritone, had travelled to America two years before on a tour that included Indianapolis, Chicago, Minneapolis, Boston, and Carnegie Hall in New York. He had trained in England and Milan. The stout, genial Mills also gave tours in Great Britain, Australia, and Canada (where he eventually settled, in Winnipeg, in 1914). That he would have heard of Mrs. Miller's daughter Edith spoke of the rapid progress she had made with Alberto Randegger and the concerts she had given in London. No doubt her ambitious mother, who had welcomed her back for a short holiday in May, was delighted. By the time Mrs. Miller got the "flattering report" from Watkin-Mills, Edith had already sailed for Paris.[2]

At this time the best vocal training was believed to be in Paris. And the best professors of singing—at least for women—were themselves women. The most successful of them all was undoubtedly Mme Mathilde Marchesi. This German-born mezzo-soprano had given up her own singing career quite early, supposedly because she felt a tremendous drive to teach. From Cologne and Vienna, she had moved to Paris at the height of her fame as a vocal teacher to a small cottage on rue Jouffroy in the seventeenth arrondissement in the northwest part of the city.

It seems that Mme Marchesi became passionate about teaching because her own teacher was Manuel Garcia from Madrid. The gaunt, elegant Garcia had also left the stage early for the occupation he claimed to love: teaching. She was his student in London at the Royal Academy of Music, where he taught for fifty years. Garcia was widely believed to have revolutionized vocal teaching, taking it from an intuitive and imitative trial-and-error approach to a system that was scientifically based. He had served in a military hospital at age twenty-five just before the first Carlist (Civil) war in Spain, and there he had studied the careful anatomical analysis learned by medical students. He augmented this with special courses in the physiology of everything to do with the voice and the larynx (a.k.a. "voice box"). His sister (later a famous composer and mezzo-soprano) recalls that his obsession with the way voice functions knew no limits.

What do you think he brought [home]? You would never guess. The throttles of several types of animals—chickens, sheep, and cows. You would imagine that these would have disgusted me. But it was not so. He would give me a pair of bellows, which I would insert in these windpipes, one after another, and blow hard! What extraordinary sounds they used to emit. The chickens' throttles would cluck, the sheep's would bleat, and the bulls' would roar, almost like life.[3]

Garcia's curiosity about the mechanical means by which voice is produced led him to attempt to examine his students' throats—when silent and in speech and song. Finally, in 1854, he found a way to watch his own speech organs in action: a double mirror.

He went straight to Charrière, the surgical instrument maker, asked whether they happened to possess a small mirror with a long handle, and was at once supplied with a dentist's mirror, which had been one of the failures of the London Exhibition of 1851. He bought it for six francs.

Returning home, he placed against [his] uvula this little piece of glass, which he had heated with warm water and carefully dried. Then with a hand mirror he flashed onto its surface a ray of sunlight. ...There before his eyes appeared the glottis, wide open and so fully exposed that he could see a portion of the trachea.[4]

After recovering from his amazement, Garcia gazed at all the changes to be seen in his throat as he voiced different tones. He then wrote a description that would transform the teaching of singing. The "laryngoscope" was invented.

Mme Marchesi worked closely with Garcia, whom she dubbed the "Columbus of the Larynx," for thirty years to evolve her own system of teaching. As she put it when she looked back over her career at age eighty-seven with the help of her large intimidating daughter Mme Blanche Marchesi, "I know I improved on what Garcia taught me."

Mme Marchesi was not modest. She thought modesty was "useless." She was convinced that her mathematical refinements on Garcia's "glorious discovery" of manipulating the vocal organs to improve the voice had produced *the one* method by which the voice should be trained. "There ought to be all over the world an understanding like there is in medicine and surgery, that only one method should be taught—the one that makes, saves, and preserves the voice." In fact, there were so many vocal teachers in Europe and America, so many theories of vocal training, and so many books written to illustrate them, usually by singers who had found personal success, that no one method was likely to be universally accepted. Mme Marchesi dismissed most of these as "atrocious."

What Mme Marchesi sought, above all, with her exclusively female pupils, was "the divine quality." Some were born with it, and those made the greatest singers; in others it had to be cultivated. "In art, whether it be painting, sculpture, or music, love of beautiful things, love of human beings, and love of God is perceptible in the work exhibited and elevates it to the highest realms."[5]

This belief raises questions about the difference between a singer like Edith Miller, who was steeped in the Presbyterianism of Portage la Prairie, and a more

Mathilde Marchesi *circa* 1895.

sophisticated, more secular singer like Jean Forsyth, who nowhere expresses conviction in any particular faith. Her Anglican upbringing had developed her social manners more than her spirituality.

Mme Marchesi loftily outlined the qualities of a good vocal teacher like herself. She must be born with a general musical talent; she must have a genius for singing; she must be able to "grasp composition" in order to teach "style"; she must have psychical insight, love of imparting, complete literary historical and musical historical education, an impeccable "ear," and "complete mastery" of at least four languages. (She herself could speak German, Italian, English, French, Spanish, and some Russian.) Most important was the somewhat mystical "inborn quality" of fitness to be a teacher along with "patience *à outrance*," the principal teaching virtue. This was a staggering list of what was necessary to teach, impossible for any human being to achieve. And, for a theory purporting to be "scientific," it contained many vague imponderables. It made absolutely clear how dedicated to her profession Mme Marchesi was. "I have given my life to my students," she said.

She went on to offer advice to singing pupils. How to find a good teacher, for instance, and the "delicate topic" of how pupils must guard against jealousy of other singers. "I regret that...singers who have already achieved success rarely welcome other voices of the same type entering the same field." She recounted the case of a singer she trained who became very famous, and sang opera for thirty years. "She conceived the curious idea of trying to induce me never to train another light soprano in a similar manner. In other words, she not only wanted her own field for her own lifetime but wanted to lease it for all time to come. It never occurred to her that no other singer would ever be born with a voice, mind, and ambition exactly the same."[6]

Mme Marchesi believed that the best evidence of good teaching was the outcome. "It is only fair that the teacher should be judged by the best voices she turns out."

With such opinions, Mme Marchesi did not accept every student who applied to her. In choosing Mme Marchesi, Edith Miller signalled several things. At twenty-one she was sure enough of herself after her experience as a pupil of Randegger in London and the concerts she gave around England to feel she was worth the best vocal teacher in the world. She was moving away from the mainly religious stream of oratorio towards more secular music. Mme Marchesi's selections for her pupils were free-ranging. These were summed up as "whatever is good of its kind irrespective of nationality or date."

Edith had managed to save enough money from her teaching in Portage la Prairie and her performances in England—plus whatever her parents were able to contribute—to pay Mme Marchesi's high fees. She was ready to travel outside her English-speaking milieu into the foreign environment of Paris in the 1890s. Even if only for six weeks, Edith would not only see Paris, board there, build on the French she knew from various songs and language courses, but she would also meet French artists and writers, for Mme Marchesi held occasional *salons* to introduce her pupils to arts other than music.

A LETTER FROM EDITH IN PARIS TO CHARLES WHEELER IN WINNIPEG, 1896

Mr. Charles Wheeler
The Winnipeg Tribune
Winnipeg, Manitoba

May 17, 1896

Dear Charles,

I am so very happy today that I cannot resist explaining to you the cause.[1]

I arrived in Paris last week with a letter of introduction from Signor Randegger, of London, to Madame Marchesi. After settling down in lodgings I wrote to this lady to appoint a time for an interview, enclosing Mr. Randegger's letter.

I hardly dared expect a reply for some days, knowing well what a busy woman Madame was, and how much besieged with letters of inquiry as well. But to my delight I received a note the following morning asking me to call this morning at 11 o'clock.

You can imagine I was all excitement in anticipation of meeting the great authority on singing, for one hears such alarming accounts of her eccentricities: even Mr. Randegger dreaded to have me go.

I had a drive of about half an hour to her house, through the Place de la Concorde, with its imposing statues and graceful fountains, along the Tuileries Garden and Champs-Élysées. The morning was perfect, the trees and flowers being at their very best.

On reaching Madame's home I was shown into a charmingly arranged room, where a musician could be interested for hours in examining photos and autographs of nearly all the celebrities in the world of music and art.

I had waited only a few minutes when Madame Marchesi came in, and the very first impression I got of her appearance and manner was reassuring. She made me feel entirely at ease. Took a chair beside me, and said: "Now please tell me all about yourself; what you desire to do, for I am already much interested in you from Mr. Randegger's letter."

After talking a short time she requested me to go to the other end of the large room and sing for her, first tones, then scales, and then songs, only one verse of the latter. She then told me that I had an excellent voice, of beautiful quality, and sang with great taste and feeling.

I was so amazed at such praise from her that I could not resist telling her how happy she had made me, to which she replied, "Nonsense, child, how could I say anything else but the truth? If your voice was not satisfactory, I should be quite as outspoken in telling you of it."

I explained that I owed my solid foundation to the wonderful gentleman Signor D'Auria, who trained me, as you know, at the Toronto Conservatory of Music and more recently at the new conservatory in Winnipeg.

Madame really seemed genuinely pleased, and thinks that if I could return to her again next year she could bring me out in Paris. As it is I can only have six weeks' lessons now, after which her holidays commence.

Before leaving, Madame took me to see her studio—a large room, with good acoustic properties, and with about twenty seats at one end, where the students remain for about three hours each day listening to other lessons being given. In this room were some beautiful cut flowers, which Madame Melba had sent her.

As I am to take three lessons a week, besides learning French and German, it will keep me intensely busy during my stay in Paris, so that I shall have little time for sight-seeing.

I told Madame that I was charmed with Paris. "Ah, yes," she replied. "It is the beginning of Paradise." I replied, "Paris may be lovely, but I shall always love dear old London best. It is something desperate crossing the busy thoroughfares here; no system whatever, and policemen pay no attention at all. In London things go like clockwork."

Yours sincerely,
Edith J. Miller

MADAME EMMA ALBANI'S
FIRST WINNIPEG CONCERT, 1897

The musical and social highlight of 1897 in Winnipeg was Madame Emma Albani's concert in January and the reception for her at Government House that preceded it. The petite brunette soprano from the musical Catholic Lajeunesse family in Chambly, Quebec was the first Canadian singer to become an international star. By the time her career was over in 1911, she would have sung forty-three roles in forty operas (from *Lucia di Lammermoor* to *Rigoletto* to *Lohengrin* to *The Marriage of Figaro*) in any one of the four languages she spoke. She had trained mainly in Italy, and there changed her name from Lajeunesse to the more European-sounding Albani. Everywhere she sang, she was "loaded with flowers, presents and poetry." She was a favourite of Queen Victoria, who began summoning her to Windsor Castle in 1874 for private concerts. She had just finished three brilliant, breathtaking seasons at Covent Garden in London when she undertook a Canadian tour from Halifax to Vancouver in November 1896. She emoted about Canada's western landscapes. She found the north shore of Lake Superior "all finely wooded, with undulating land and high hills, most lovely bays, and small lakes lying reposefully in their midst; and the light here seems so soft, and the colouring so tender, that even under winter snows the scenery is most beautiful."[1] Sometime during 1897, while her concert tour unfolded she (and Paderewski) was awarded the Royal Philharmonic Gold Medal (a.k.a. the Beethoven Medal). It would be the first of many, many honours showered on her.[2]

The two-hour reception for her at Government House on Wednesday, January 20 called forth the *crème de la crème* of Winnipeg—more than 600 guests.[3] At the entrance to the east wing the *aide-de-camp* announced their names as they arrived to be received by Manitoba lieutenant governor James Patterson and North-West Territories lieutenant governor Charles Mackintosh and their wives. Mrs. Kirchoffer's "superb" gown made news: "a most handsome yellow satin brocade in which the enwoven roses seemed to stand out ready to be plucked, fine Honiton lace was the effective trimming, the sleeves being made entirely of box pleats of the webby mesh, and some rare diamonds studded the corsage and glittered among the puffs of hair." Guests were then presented to Mme Albani herself. Her appearance was even more spectacular. "Rich thick white satin brocade was the exquisite material and made very simply. Diamond buckles fastened the shoulder straps and girdle, and diamond stars finished the *berthe* [a capelike collar of lace worn over a low neckline] while a necklet of the same rare stones lent additional lustre."

The *Winnipeg Tribune* report of this event focused on "the awful crush" and criticized Government House as being "awkwardly arranged for large receptions."

There is only one front stairway, which instead of facing the door so that guests can safely reach the dressing rooms without displaying thick Dolges [heavy overcoats like those tailored for New York's elite by German furrier Alfred Dolge] and heavy wraps, is at the end of the square and a detour has to be made, where from every drawing room the bundled figures may be seen as they work their way up the none too wide staircase and mingle with or dodge, yes dodge, the coming down guests who have already passed unscathed through that part of the fray. It is a very awkward process and spoils the evening before the reception room is reached.

The "massive" crowd affected every aspect of the occasion. People could be viewed only "in bunches and rooms full," not as individuals; even hands seemed anonymous, since all were gloved. From above, "nothing could be distinguished save the back of a striped gown or puffs of fair hair." The supper table was "lovely to behold, with its masses of tulips, daffodils, hyacinths, and violets, but it took time and trouble to gain even a glimpse." For a reporter expected to single out guests—especially ladies and their dresses—it must have been a frustrating two hours from 9:00 to 11:00. Nonetheless, he managed to describe what more than sixty of the ladies were wearing, including Jean Forsyth in her white satin with shoulder straps of wide opalescent *passimenterie*.

Mme Albani's concert was held at the 90th Battery Drill Hall on Broadway Street two days after the reception. There were three thousand people in the audience. The headlines in the *Winnipeg Tribune* the next day implied a staggering success.[4]

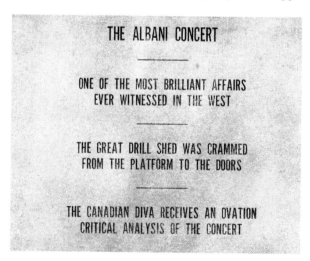

THE ALBANI CONCERT

ONE OF THE MOST BRILLIANT AFFAIRS EVER WITNESSED IN THE WEST

THE GREAT DRILL SHED WAS CRAMMED FROM THE PLATFORM TO THE DOORS

THE CANADIAN DIVA RECEIVES AN OVATION CRITICAL ANALYSIS OF THE CONCERT

Charles Wheeler, the reviewer, excuses his long column on the concert because "visits of great vocalists to this city are so few and far between." The concert was offered in two parts: first, a selection of miscellaneous solos by the members of Albani's company; then, more important, the third and fifth acts of Gounod's opera *Faust*. The musicians with Mme Albani were Miss Beverley Robinson,

First Canadian soprano star Emma Albani as Elisabeth
in *Tannhäuser*, Covent Garden, London, *circa* 1876.

mezzo-soprano; Mr. Braxton Smith, tenor; Mr. Lemprière Pringle, bass; and Miss Beatrice Langley, solo violin, with Signor Armando Seppilil as pianist and musical director.

Wheeler praises *Faust* as "perhaps the most famous opera of modern times" with its "melodious music," "languorous beauty," and "power." He highlights that "divine quality" that Mme Marchesi claimed was essential to great singing: its "augmented expression" echoes "what every person with a soul attuned to sweet sounds feels." He offers a little history of the opera ("a quasi failure" in Paris at first, then bought "by accident" by a London publisher).

Albani portrayed the simple German girl Marguerite, the major soprano role. After seeing her at her spinning wheel, Faust desires her so much he sells his soul to the devil, Méphistophélès, in exchange for her love.

Wheeler points out that "nearly the whole" of *Faust* has already been performed in Winnipeg with "competent vocal exponents and an efficient orchestra." Though this may seem defensive, it could simply signal the immense progress classical music had made in Winnipeg over the previous five years or so. The audience, he speculates, is likely to find only the two acts in Albani's performance "unsatisfying." Even less satisfying is the performance itself. Mme Albani, he wrote, did not fully come up to the "standard of bygone days." Although he found "the same old dramatic fervour, the same powers of expression ripened by years of experience, the same grand voice with the old-time ringing clarion tones" in her voice, the huge audience seemed indifferent. Their diffident response was a far cry from the "wild enthusiasm" of audiences in the past. Famous arias—the "Flower Song" and the "Jewel Song"—were not applauded. Only the climactic final aria in *Faust*, where Marguerite invokes heaven's aid, showed Albani at her best and stirred the audience to applause.

Nor did he find the rest of Albani's supporting cast in *Faust* good enough, given the occasion. Robinson as Martha had a "thin voice and crude style"; Smith as Faust either forced or slipped into falsetto on his high notes and he missed some of his cues in the duets. "Mr. Smith's *forte* is not the operatic stage," Wheeler declared. Pringle as Méphistophélès interpreted his role as "a more vigorous devil than a subtle one," but Wheeler concedes that "his picturesque appearance and big voice" had a "great effect."

Compared to what Wheeler clearly saw as an inadequate performance of *Faust*, he found the solos in the first half of the concert praiseworthy, but only at times. He comments again on Braxton Smith's "limited range" and "his resorting to *mezzo voce* and falsetto to extend it" in his "well-worn ballad "Good Bye" by Blumenthal. Beverley Robinson's "Nobil Signor" from *The Huguenots* by Giacomo Meyerbeer was "above her vocal powers to compass"; nonetheless, she received an encore and a bouquet of flowers. Lemprière Pringle sang the "Toreador's Song" from *Carmen* and his encore "In Cellar Cool," a German drinking song, in a fine tenor voice. Yet, Wheeler found that, although his voice was "rich, big, and resonant," the downwards run of the scale in his encore "developed a weakness." Furthermore, whereas the British tenor Watkin-Mills, who had also performed in Winnipeg, slid down two full scales, Pringle accomplished only one.

As for Albani herself, she began brilliantly with the coloratura aria "Ah fors e lui" from *La Traviata* with "clearness and facility, the final cadenza and a long trill" (both features of the "coloratura" and the popular *bel canto* tradition) being "an admirable bit of vocalization." An ovation followed, along with four or five huge bunches of flowers. Her encore was the sentimental "Home Sweet Home," which Wheeler found "tame, tedious, and monotonous before it was sung half way through." In fact, he thought Mme Albani now seemed tired. Halfway through a second encore, "Angels Ever Bright and Fair" (a popular solo, and one sung by Jean Forsyth), she displayed "a distinct fall from the true pitch." Even so, another ovation and more flowers followed.

It is possible that, after her three seasons at Covent Garden, Albani was either too exhausted to undertake a continental Canadian tour or had entered a stage of her career that was a falling-away from its heights.

Wheeler's choice of his favourite piece of music in the concert was almost an insult. Although the performances were essentially vocal, he thought "the very best numbers" were those played by the violinist, Miss Beatrice Langley, and the violin and piano duet by Edvard Grieg that was "exceedingly well played by Miss Beatrice Langley and Signor Sephilli."

All told, Wheeler concluded, "as a social function the Albani concert was a success; as a financial speculation it was a success; and musically it was successful to a moderate degree, although there are a good many people who will talk of nothing but Albani for years to come."

EDITH RETURNS TO CANADA, THEN LEAVES FOR NEW YORK, 1897

In the spring of 1897, as soon as Edith Miller returned from her training with Mme Marchesi in Paris, she performed in a series of excellent concerts in Eastern Canada. One of these was her debut at the luxurious Massey Hall, a large Toronto theatre that had only been open for three years. Then she returned to the West where she offered a major concert in Portage la Prairie. By then the Winnipeg Conservatory of Music had collapsed. Its demise had been ordered at a meeting in the Manitoba Hotel on January 10, 1896 by the same shareholders that had greeted its beginnings with such enthusiasm. There had been a combination of circumstances to pull it down: the situation of Winnipeg as a rising but still small city; a lack of knowledge among administrators of the way eastern music schools managed affairs; and there had been too much work for its one director, Paul Henneberg.[1]

Edith was not back in time, either, to hear the famed French-Canadian Mme Albani's January concert.[2] Mme Albani had declared Winnipeg "a rapidly growing town, fast becoming a great commercial centre."[3] Albani's patron, Lieutenant Governor Patterson, also provided handsome financial support for Edith's homecoming performance on April 8.

That evening, rain drizzled down under a "dull leaden-hued sky." That did not prevent the lieutenant governor and a large audience of "many hundreds of this talented young lady's admirers" and "many ladies well-known in society circles" from filling Selkirk Hall.[4]

Apart from a few minor criticisms—both of the composers and the singer—of the eleven songs, airs, and ballads Edith sang, the review the next day was filled with excitement and hope:

> One thing is sure. Our young (22-year-old) contralto has returned with her superb voice unimpaired, her pleasant manners as heretofore, and her style of singing as easy and skillful as of old, and as these are the vital features of vocalism it may be taken for granted that the impressions made upon the minds of the audience last night were very pleasurable, judging by the applause and frequent recalls.

She sang arias by Handel ("beautifully sung"), Brahms's famous lullaby "Cradle Song" ("exquisitely warbled"), and a couple of Irish songs.

Her accompanist was Jean Forsyth. She efficiently "followed the moods and fancies of the fair vocalist in an artistic manner." Yet she did not escape criticism for her "too frequent use of the loud pedal."

The concert, as was customary, included other artists. Lawyer Isaac Pitblado's wife gave a reading of "The Bridgekeeper's Story," a sentimental tale of a child in peril saved by its mother. Her encore was "The Circus Has Come to Town." The Mandolin and Guitar Club, led by Mr. Bouche, also offered some "in time, crisp, bright and enjoyable tunes."

The review concludes by anticipating further song recitals by Edith Miller in which any faults no longer exist.

Edith Miller was back indeed. In the six months that followed, she was to be heard everywhere: a superb Easter concert at Westminster Church at which Charles Wheeler provided the *recitatif*[5] and a ballad concert at Knox Church in Portage la Prairie[6] and performances around both cities. She even managed two performances—one at St. Andrew's Church and a recital at the Manitoba Hotel—with a broken rib caused by a fall from a handcar she and another vocalist rode down a mountain in the Kootenay district.[7]

Edith's agent, Frank Yeigh, in Toronto, had arranged an autumn concert tour for her through southwest Manitoba. She and Jean Forsyth set off for points along the Minneapolis and Northwestern Railway in late September, leaving the "teas galore" behind, to return on November 2. On one of these occasions at Glenboro, where Edith Miller had performed before, she was heralded as "the nightingale of the wild and woolly west." Her concert disappointed, however. Far from being a representative of the wild and woolly west, her "educational tour in England" had raised her taste from popular to classical music. "She did not arouse much enthusiasm in her first selection," a review in the *Glenboro Gazette* on October 15 said, "probably because the audience came more for entertainment than the study of art." Later selections "held the crowd as in a vice," however. Every selection was enthusiastically encored.

At each concert, Jean Forsyth was Edith's accompanist.

This tour was Edith Miller's last in Canada before she left for New York. She was off again in mid-November to pursue "the study of art," this time with the inimitable voice coach, George Sweet, in New York City.

Once again, Jean Forsyth would fill in for her, not only teaching her students in Portage la Prairie, but also replacing her as choir leader at Knox Church. Once again, Annie Pullar would fill in for her where a contralto was needed.

George Sweet had studied in Italy, but primarily in New York with the Cuban vocal teacher Signor Emilio Agramonte. He sang major roles in operas such as the comic *Dinorah* by Giacamo Meyerbeer with the Max Strakosch Italian Opera Co., where he was the only non-Italian in the troupe. He was as enthusiastic about Italy and Italian music as Signor D'Auria, and eventually he would return to Florence. Meanwhile, he lent his "clear and agreeable baritone"[8] to his audiences and pupils in New York.

Sweet was enjoyed by his pupils, with whom he mixed quite spontaneously. He was bent on displacing the hold German opera had on the city with an all-American grand opera company singing in English. Appealing to the wealthy and artistic communities in the city, he eventually accomplished this. In 1886, he was one of three baritones in the first season's program "Opera Sung by Americans" that performed arias from works by such composers as Wagner, Rossini, Gounod, Mozart, and Gluck. The program was a success, though Sweet himself never quite overcame his one flaw: a voice unable to fill an operatic stage. At his first appearance in 1881, where he appeared in Mendelssohn's *Ruy Blas* (based on a Victor Hugo novel) and Donizetti's *La Favorita*, he was praised for having "a voice admirably trained, flexible, rich, and sympathetic, and acting that showed dramatic talent," but, the reviewer continued, "his voice is not powerful enough to fill a large theatre." He was, however, an ideal singing teacher. His advertisements in various papers and music magazines in 1891 were clear:

GEORGE SWEET

At the request of many of his former pupils and others, Mr. Sweet has returned to New York and opened a Vocal Studio at No. 57 & 59 West 42nd Street, NY where he is ready to give instruction in the art of singing, and prepare pupils for the operatic or concert stage.[9]

George Sweet was greatly sought after as a teacher, even though the competition for vocal students at the time was keen, judging from the number of other advertisements for vocal lessons in the same journals. (Some ads emphasized the "safety" of a particular teacher's method, implying that some methods damaged rather than improved voices.) He followed the Lamperti method, a method devised by Francesco Lamperti based on his father's theories and the older Italian traditions that emphasized above all clarity, pronunciation, and *legato* (the smooth transition from one note to the next). Of his many books on vocal training, *The Technics of Bel Canto*, which outlined his theories and teaching methods, would appear in 1905.[10] This was his most influential. Definitions of this vocal style that flourished in the eighteenth and nineteenth centuries were many and varied. Lamperti's repeated injuncture to singers was "Quality, quality, quality." By this he meant utter purity of tone. Diaphragmatic breathing, placement of tone, and enunciation were simply segments that produced a voice whose soul and vitality are "quality." Often he worked with a pupil for a whole year on one aria: "If you can sing one, you can sing all, provided that once your voice is placed in purity of tone."[11]

Despite many definitions over the centuries, since *bel canto* referred to the ethereal voices of falsetto singers (Italian *castrati*) in the Middle Ages, an audience in the late nineteenth century would expect vocal fireworks such as trills, runs, leaps from a low note to a much higher one, and other ornamentations. The singers were mainly sopranos, and often coloraturas like Jean Forsyth who specialized in what was called "artistic" or "dramatic" renderings.[12]

Whereas Manuel Garcia, "Columbus of the Larynx," moved vocal methods into a scientific sphere, Lamperti (and his father before him) reflected the old historical Italian methods taught by much more vague and flexible methods depending on the pupil. George Sweet seems to have tended to the *bel canto* method, connecting with his individual pupils rather than analyzing the vocal organs to improve voice quality.

Edith Miller was soon said to be his favourite pupil.[13]

ADVICE TO SINGERS

The following was reprinted in the *Winnipeg Tribune*, December 31, 1897, by Charles Wheeler. It is a leaflet of advice to singers by Mr. J. H. Wheeler (no relation), the well-known vocal teacher, now of New York.

1. "Avoid singing in the open air at night."

Doubtless applying to those idiots who make the nights hideous with their alleged songs when on their way home from evening parties.

2. "Do not sing with the piano against the wall."

Good. Prop the instrument up in the centre of the room, then circle around it gracefully until you can focus your voice. Or better still, shove the piano into the hallway, and follow it yourself. This is a capital method to produce tonal effects.

3. "Never sing in a room filled with furniture, draperies or bric-a-brac. A carpet deadens the sound."

This idea is not wholly original; however, it is commended to those persons possessed of limited incomes, who have not as yet completed their house furnishing. Besides, a room denuded of its furniture makes a splendid dance apartment.

4. "Do not keep late hours. The singer needs rest and sleep."

Again, good. The usual supper after a concert, so dear to the ears of most professional vocalists, is here to be dispensed with. It comes cheaper too, and that may be a consideration with some people.

Then snoozle in bed until twelve o'clock the next morning; never mind callers, they must wait.

5. "When smoking causes expectoration it dries the pharynx and throat, therefore it impairs the voice."

Moral: Smoke as much as you like but do not spit. Spitting is injurious, smoking is not. How about chewing?

6. "Never drink spirituous liquors. Never drink water just before singing."

Always drink champagne, it is more expensive than rum, whiskey or brandy.

Then there are many fine brands of ale and porter. No need to mention water to musicians, it is carefully abstained from as rigidly as can be desired.

7. "When singing never wear anything tight about the neck."

Dudish singers take note of this and leave off those attempts at suicide by means of high collars. Those red-faced efforts at strangulation on the concert platform are not pleasant to look at.

8. "Never contract the waist by tight dressing."

Ladies never do? This advice seems superfluous, for sopranos and contraltos were never known—or at least hardly ever—to tighten up the breathing cavity.

A well-shaped corset, they say, produces a pretty figure, but you will never get a woman to confess to any compression.

9. "Never sing long at one time."

Most singers like to sing as long as they possibly can at concerts judging from the encores they so anxiously await.

A long-suffering public heartily subscribes to the rule, but to get the consent of the performer is another matter.

10. "Never sing just after eating, wait an hour, if possible."

This maxim hardly fits in with number four. Vocalists usually eat and drink well of the best, hence the nice little suppers after the concert, and late hours.

A hungry singer gives forth a hollow tone. A full one means resonancy of voice but if possible, wait an hour as above. Famous men and women have been known to fill up upon a hearty meal ten minutes before being called upon for heavy operatic duties, and to have had refreshers between whiles.

11. "Do not constantly clear the throat; it is a habit."

Quite true. Take a drink of porter, if a male; champagne, if a female. This should clear the throat of all impediments and warm the whole system for the evening's work.

For certain it is a vocalist cannot sing until the throat is unobstructed.

JEAN FOLLOWS EDITH TO NEW YORK TO STUDY WITH GEORGE SWEET, 1898

Four months after Edith Miller left for New York, where George Sweet coached her voice, Jean Forsyth left Winnipeg, with her bags, on the Northern Pacific train for a series of sessions with George Sweet. She was not seeking to improve her concert singing, as Edith had done. She wanted to learn from this popular vocal teacher how to improve her own teaching.[1]

By this time, Jean—now forty-six—had produced students that were themselves taking professional singing positions. Holmes Cowper was by far her best student. His tenor voice was exceptional. It was "of the English type, not particularly powerful, but rich in quality and ample in tone."[2] With support from Jean and from James Tees, he left behind his job as a bank clerk for the much more lucrative singing career ($300 a performance for solo oratorio performances) in Canada and the United States. Eventually he taught students and was a university administrator, ending with an appointment as dean of the College of Fine Arts, Drake University, Iowa. He remained in Winnipeg for the time being and sang as tenor soloist at Grace Church. Others also stayed in Winnipeg, like Minnie Pace, who would replace Jean as an accompanist while she was away.[3]

Over the past year, Jean had given several concerts for her students. These were not insignificant occasions. Jean had them perform in the same venues as professional singers, usually the dining room of the Manitoba Hotel. More and more, Jean was highly praised as a teacher. At one of her recitals in late February, patronized by Lieutenant Governor Patterson, whose arrival was greeted by the national anthem, ten students—one violin, two piano, the others voice—performed an impressive two-part program to a "well-filled" room. One star student was the irrepressible Stanley Adams, who had finally decided to take lessons to tame his voice. He sang three songs. Others were Miss Clara Bull, Minnie Pace, and Maud Lane, who all gave two performances. Most of the songs were typically Victorian, sentimental and coy, with titles like "Souls Awakening" (Clara Bull), "Fairy's Cradle Song" (Winnie Parker), and "When Night Winds Are Sighing" (Stanley Adams). The most difficult piece was "Dove Sono" from Mozart's *The Marriage of Figaro* sung by soprano Minnie Pace. Maud Lane sang "Norwegian Song," a choice that might have reflected Jean's awareness of the Scandinavian community quickly gathering and becoming noticeable in the West. The write-up next day singled out Stanley Adams ("among the most enjoyable") and Miss Perkins, who sang "Valse Carmena" by Wilson H. Lane, an American composer. Piano solos by Cyril Dickson—"Valse Fantaisie" by Austrian pianist and composer Hugo Reinhold and "Mazurka" by Czech contemporary composer Erwin Schulhoff—were excellent.

Most of these students had studied with Jean Forsyth and would continue to train with her. "No other vocal teacher in the city," ran the review of her pupils' concert, "has made so excellent a showing as has Miss Forsyth, several of those whom she has trained being now the occupants of enviable positions in the vocal world.⁴

Teaching and accompanying singers was emerging as Jean's primary work in music. There were times, such as the Good Friday concert at Westminster Church in 1897, where she was not part of the program, as she once had been. Particularly in performances that featured Edith Miller, she found herself as an accompanist, not a singer.

Once Edith left the city in November 1897, Jean and Annie Pullar would perform on occasions that might have centred on her. It must have been a disappointment to the Presbyterian congregation of Portage la Prairie, and especially Edith's mother and father, that she was away for the opening of the "handsome and elegant" new Presbyterian church there at the beginning of 1898. Jean took Edith's place as choir master and Annie Pullar replaced Edith as contralto soloist at a special dedication service conducted by Rev. Principal King of the Manitoba College of Music. All of this was mentioned in the news write-up in the *Winnipeg Tribune* on January 9, where the music—despite Edith's absence—was described as "simply superb."

A small news item in 1898 announced that Jean Forsyth "has been offered a remunerative choir position in one of the largest churches of New York."⁵ She would leave behind all the teas, the balls, the euchre evenings, and her position as solo soprano in the choir at Grace Church—even her pupils—for the chance to work with George Sweet to improve her teaching methods, methods that were already the best in Winnipeg.

EDITH FINDS A POSITION IN NEW YORK, 1900

Jean's expectation of a lucrative choir position in New York never materialized. However, a telegram on February 22, 1898 brought news of a stunning event in Edith Miller's career. It announced:

> Miss Edith J. Miller, formerly of this place, out of over one hundred applicants, has secured the position of contralto soloist in St. Bartholomew's church, New York, at a salary of over $1,000 a year.[1]

Edith assumed her new position on May 1. Now Edith's photo and a series of write-ups would appear in *The New York Times*. A picture of her showed her seated, three-quarters profile, wearing a gauzy light dress with puff sleeves and a ruffled bodice, one hand leaning on a table, the other holding a small bouquet of long-stemmed roses. Her dark hair is swept up, small bangs fringing her forehead. She was hailed as "coming from Canada, where she had already become famous." Since she was joining a church choir, the review emphasized her oratorio training with Alberto Randegger in London. "She has a soulful and melodious voice, and sings with refinement and musical intelligence."[2] It seemed that her coaching from George Sweet (with whom she parted ways and accepted Harry Luxtone, a New York vocal instructor, as her coach) had prepared her also for the concert stage. She was to make her concert debut in the fall of 1898 as well.

Already, before her appointment to St. Bartholomew's, she had replaced the contralto Katherine Bloodgood "in a fashionable New York church,"[3] an engagement that might have provided her with a reference for the competition she won. Certainly, she would have had a reference from Mme Marchesi. She had also met Colonel James Henry Mapleson in New York and he had referred her for the position.

The colonel was an English opera impresario who was credited with leading the way in opera production and the promotion of the careers of singers he thought promising in London and New York City in the second half of the nineteenth century.

The rakish Colonel Mapleson was a sort of Barnum and Bailey agent for classical singers. Today, he would be a promoter of talent or even a media guru. He is best known today for his early scratchy experiments with recordings known as the "Mapleson Cylinders." In 1856 the tall, military-looking man (he had served in the army) had founded the first musical agency in London after his own career in Verona, Italy (under the stage name of Enrico Mariani) failed due to throat problems. In London, he managed the Lyceum Theatre and, later, Her Majesty's Theatre. When Her Majesty's burned down, Mapleson moved to the Theatre Royal, Drury

Lane, where he managed a collaboration with Covent Garden. Financial scandals followed him everywhere. In 1885, he tried to finagle the use of the Academy of Music for productions of Italian operas he had organized. That, predictably, resulted in conflict. He was involved in an apparent scam producing opera in New York in 1879, returning after a season he produced in London's off-season with $50,000, leaving the Royal Academy of Music in the red for $3,000. In 1884 he left his guarantors to pay his overdrafts. He brought a splendid company to New York City in 1887 and made tours of U.S. cities. Yet he soon went bankrupt in the late 1880s, and wrote his reminiscences *The Mapleson Memoirs, 1848–1888*. Yet he continued to wheel and deal in the classical and opera music fields as a freelance entrepreneur. In 1896 he brought two opera singers—Signor de Marchi and Mme Darciée—from Milan to New York to join his New Imperial Opera Company. They were never paid the balance owing on their contracts: 13,000 francs for Mme Darciée and 7,000 francs to Signor de Marchi. Mapleson maintained they had been paid. Realizing their contracts had been violated, the two returned to Europe. Mapleson was not easy to pin down. A chronic liar, he was given to lying low, or fleeing the country, to avoid financial consequences. For Edith to have his support no doubt introduced her to an unpleasantly sophisticated world of music, but also to profitable opportunities in the U.S. and Britain from then on.[4]

✳

St. Bartholomew's was a historic Episcopal church at the southwest corner of Madison Avenue and 44th Street in Manhattan (relocated in 1918 at Park Avenue between 50th and 51st Streets). Its style, designed by James Renwick, the architect of St. Patrick's Cathedral), was impressive, if not intimidating: Lombardic style (seventh-to-ninth-century northern Italy, with a high central hall). It stood majestically on one acre of land sold to the church by William H. Vanderbilt, father of the wealthy financier Cornelius Vanderbilt II.[5]

Edith wrote home to explain that she would not be returning to the Canadian West that summer. Instead, she took a position at Chautauqua Lake's summer educational and cultural gathering as one of the few entertainers, as well as giving concerts in the eastern U.S.[6] Occasional news of her "progress" away from home filtered back to Winnipeg papers. One item described her new circulars advertising her openness for concert and oratorio engagements and song recitals. She has secured W. W. Thomas of Carnegie Hall as her manager. The circular lists her "partial" repertoire: 29 oratorios, 81 important arias and songs, as well as countless "ordinary" songs, all in original languages of English, French, German, and Italian. "How much hard work does this tremendous list represent?" asked a journalist for *Town Topics* in Winnipeg.[7]

Edith made the most of her Christmas vacation from St. Bart's. She gave a solo performance in the *Messiah* with the Mozart Club in Pittsburg, performed a "very fashionable concert in the Fifth Avenue Lotus Club," took part in a Christmas concert in the New York Produce Exchange, appeared in Carnegie Hall with the New York Symphony, and appeared in Toronto, Montreal, and Quebec.[8] "Wherever she sings," *Town Topics* reported, "a re-engagement nearly always follows."[9]

Two months after Edith resumed her position for the second year at St. Bart's (as it was commonly called) in May 1899 she resigned. Her salary was high there, but she found an even more remunerative position as contralto soloist at Tompkins Avenue Congregational Church in Brooklyn. This church at 480 Tompkins at the corner of McDonough Street did not have the same cachet as St. Bart's, but its religious orientation was probably more suited to Edith's Presbyterian beliefs.

Even so, St. Bart's must have missed her, for they hired her (at what was probably a large sum) to sing again as contralto soloist for the lavish funeral of Cornelius Vanderbilt II. It was described in *The New York Times* as a "simple service," though it was anything but. The fifty-five-year-old socialite and businessman had inherited five million dollars from his grandfather, also Cornelius (a.k.a. The Commodore), who had died the richest man in America. He had made his many millions in the railroad and shipping businesses. Cornelius II had also inherited $70 million from his father, William Henry "Billy" Vanderbilt. In his time Cornelius II succeeded as head of the New York Central Railroad and other related railroad lines in 1885. St. Bartholomew's Church was familiarly known as the "Vanderbilt Church."

Many of the hundreds attending Cornelius II's funeral were top executives, managers, directors, and staff of these railroad systems. Others were eminent financiers, the chancellor of the University of New York, the president of the YMCA, the president of the American Museum of Natural History, the president of Trinity College, the superintendent of St. Luke's Hospital, representatives of the Seamen's Society and the Home for Incurables, the president of the American Express Company, members of the New York Press Club, the American Institute of Christian Philosophy, the New York Eye and Ear Infirmary, the New York Home for Incurable, the New York Society for the Ruptured and Crippled, the Sloan Maternity Hospital, the Provident Loan Society, the American Geographical Society, and the Archaeological Institute of America. Many of these institutions had received charitable donations from the Vanderbilt family.

The service was shared by the Rev. Dr. David H. Greer, rector of St. Bartholomew's, and the Rev. Dr. Henry Morgan Stone of Trinity Parish, Newport, where the Vanderbilts worshipped during the summer months at their massive mansion (still standing) in that elite resort.

Everywhere curious crowds gathered to watch the grand procession of the carriages, one bearing the coffin, the others for close business associates, family mourners, and their servants. Police were needed to keep them back from the cortège.

The service in the church itself was as gripping and well choreographed as any Shakespearean play. Richard Herny Warren, the church's long-time organist played "the plaintive strains" of Chopin's funeral march. Wearing their formal white and black surplices, small round black hats, and bearing red-covered hymnals, the choir of sixty then entered slowly and silently to take their places in the chancel. Pallbearers with the coffin, still covered with the wreath of white orchids, followed by the mourners, met the clergymen and vestrymen from side aisles to proceed majestically down the main aisle. They placed the coffin directly in front of the chancel, and the huge wreath of white orchids from the cortège was transferred to it. The front of the church was "screened by large floral designs" tributes from relatives and intimate friends. Each side of the chancel was "a magnificent pillow of white roses, orchids, and lilies of the valley." A "superb wreath of white roses and orchids" covered the pulpit's front. Everywhere that there was space was filled in with "broken columns, crosses, more wreaths, and anchors of choice flowers.

Cornelius Vanderbilt had been a life member of St. Bartholomew's. Indeed, he and his wife, Alice Claypoole Gwynne, had met when they were both young teachers of Sunday school there. The musical selections had been favourite hymns of Vanderbilt's, including the musical version of Tennyson's "Crossing the Bar." All were "plaintive," which brought tears to the eyes of almost everyone in the large audience. One hymn, "Softly Now the Light of Day," had been Vanderbilt's favourite and Dr. George William Warren had composed music for it that he dedicated to him. This hymn was "tender and sweet," and the choir sang it with so much feeling that "many of the Vanderbilt servants gave way unrestrainedly to their emotions." All the contralto solos in this music were sung by Edith J. Miller.

After the service, crowds pressed in again and were restrained as the carriages drove to the ferry that would transport them to St. George on Staten Island, where more carriages and police awaited to see them six miles up the winding hill to the Vanderbilt burial grounds in the Moravian Cemetery as the bell tolled. There, the pallbearers carried the coffin into the Vanderbilt Mausoleum, a towering building that could house 300 bodies. From leaving the Vanderbilt home on Fifth Avenue and Fifty-Seventh Street to the return of the mourners took almost seven hours. The *New York Times* account was thirteen pages long.[10]

JEAN DELAYS HER RETURN FROM NEW YORK, 1899

It was widely understood that Jean Forsyth would return to Winnipeg the follow-ing September to resume her teaching and her Grace Church position when she left in March 1898. Her students were crestfallen to see her go at all. Even in 1895, Jean had been praised in the *Manitoba Free Press* as "a great acquisition to our musical world," especially in her role in the Grace Church choir. When Edith was in New York studying with George Sweet, Charles Wheeler wrote that Jean was "excelled by no vocalist in this city."[1] "Her thorough knowledge of teaching" had been a decided asset to the few pupils she had in her early years. The number of students grew rapidly and they were soon taking part themselves in musical events. As Charles Wheeler acknowledged in 1898, she was an outstanding teach-er, easily the best of the few in the city.[2]

From time to time while she was away, tempting snippets of her whereabouts were reported in the papers. *Town Topics* reported in mid-June that she would be back in September. "This will be good news to Miss Forsyth's pupils, who are warmly attached to her," ran the notice. It explained that Jean was studying teach-ing methods with George Sweet, "one of New York's leading teachers." He has "a fine baritone voice" and is full of "temperament—probably another name for keen musical perception, allied to enthusiasm and intelligence."[3]

"Temperament," especially in George Sweet, who—like Mme Marchesi—turned away all but the top singers, might well have had a different meaning. A columnist for *Town Topics* calling herself "Rosa Sub" (a reversal of the Latin phrase *sub rosa*, meaning "under the rose" or secretly) reported from a friend who had seen George Sweet teach his vocal classes several times. "Rosa Sub" was actu-ally Harriet "Hattie" Walker, a former New York child actress, who was a charter member of the Winnipeg branch of the Canadian Women's Press Club and had moved to the city with her theatre-director husband in 1897. Watching her friend's lessons, this woman had become quite critical of Sweet's methods. Sweet, she observed, had one "pet" exercise for all students, sung in "ah"; "they are meant for sustained tone only and are crescendos from '*pianissimos* returning to *dimin-uendos*'." She continued to say that this exercise (and the use of other vowels for it) was an improvement over the "scheme of 'placing'" (a technique that involved placing the voice in a spot that caused resonance). She also conceded that Sweet was a good coach for "style."

Yet Rosa Sub objected to Sweet's allowing visitors who were only partly hidden (Sweet claimed they were completely hidden) to observe his lessons, especially those of his best students. She found it a "harmful" practice, "especially to sensi-tive students." Her friend had told her that she felt "as though she were being used as a drawing card for further business." To Rosa Sub, far from being a cure for nervousness, as Sweet maintained, it was a "cruel embarrassment and a hindrance." As for "temperament," Sweet took every opportunity to illustrate his lessons by singing them himself; "he never spares himself in his desire to give the student the exact interpretation he wishes" in his "big, beautiful baritone voice." Further, she continues, describing George Sweet as a kind of popinjay: "On all occasions the students did next to nothing while he strutted up and down the room, talking incessantly in a pompous way, with frequent spoutings of Italian, and the invariable addition of—'as we say in Italy.' It all struck me as being an absurd show and worse than useless to the students." Rosa Sub insists that George Sweet "is an excellent man for the warm Italian style, and can make a good, well-placed voice effective in aria and song." Yet Sweet himself, though a fine actor who had "some vogue as a singer of much fire in Florence" and "some success in *Rigoletto*," has had a less-than-stellar career singing frivolous light opera, such as *The Queen's Lace Handkerchief* by Johann Strauss.

Rosa Sub's scathing remarks were directed to Charles Wheeler, who had objected to these same observations—more or less—in an earlier letter to the *Winnipeg Tribune*. He had used the experience of "a valued correspondent" to defend George Sweet. That "valued correspondent" was probably Edith Miller. She had kept Wheeler informed at each stage of her career, and he occasionally posted notices and at times paragraphs from her letters in his column. Certainly, she had studied with George Sweet; however, her eventual parting with Sweet in favour of Harry Luxtone might be explained by Rosa Sub's criticisms of Sweet.[4]

Edith Miller's name came up in Rosa Sub's response to Wheeler. He had maintained that some of Sweet's pupils—such as Mrs. Bloodgood, Shannah Cummings, Viola Pratt, Beatrice Prior, George Fleming, Harry Parker Robinson, and Edith J. Miller—held "commanding positions in the musical world." To this, Rosa Sub had replied indignantly, "None of the people mentioned quite deserve the word 'commanding,' for they are mostly singers who are not averse to accepting reasonably inviting engagements." She dismissed Mrs. Katherine Bloodgood, the best-known of the group, as having made her way in the musical world because her "beauty was a stepping stone to public favour." She singled out Edith Miller: "She as yet has little more than local reputation, but is rapidly gaining a prepossessing appearance and personal magnetism. I have no doubt she may soon lay claim to the term 'commanding.'" Truly "commanding" performers, such as Jean de Rezske, the most famous tenor before Enrico Caruso, who was one of the many performers on tour who performed in Winnipeg, charged $1,200 to $2,500 for each concert, plus a percentage of profits over $5,500. Sometimes other singers earned more than $2,000 a night.[5]

Another tantalizing notice in the *Manitoba Free Press* in early September promised that Jean would be returning "next week" to resume vocal teaching. "It is understood that this splendid vocalist will be open for a choir engagement on her return." Jean had spent August at Chatham and Detroit visiting relatives and friends.[6]

For whatever reason, Jean Forsyth stayed on in New York for another full year. It may simply have been that she was offered a position as accompanist for George

Sweet. It is hinted that she was also an accompanist for other vocal teachers in New York. And if indeed she, like Edith Miller, had found a lucrative position in one of the notable churches of New York, she might have been able to improve her financial position—which had fallen back from concert income to accompanist income—considerably.

Her students had begun to wonder if they would ever see their beloved teacher again, when two notices appeared towards the end of May. One said:

> Since she left the city over a year ago, Miss Forsyth has spent some time in New York, where she studied with the noted vocal teacher, George Sweet, and also act-ed as his accompanist. She, therefore, returns fully posted in up-to-date teaching methods, and when to this is added her old time intelligence and enthusiasm, her pupils may reasonably look for the best possible results. Miss Forsyth is re-suming her former position as leading soprano of Grace church, which, during her absence, has been filled acceptably by Miss Minnie Pace.[7]

Minnie Pace had been one of Jean's outstanding students the year before she left. Others of her students were finding positions too. Miss McKenzie and Miss Clara Bull, "an earnest student" whose "selection and renderings of her songs exhibits good taste," had also achieved success.[8] Jackson Hanby was headed for a strong musical career in Winnipeg. He had trained as a chorister in Leeds, England. When he was fifteen, his family moved to Winnipeg, where he kept up his vocal instruction with Jean Forsyth. He next went to Boston to study with J. H. Wheeler, the same man who had written the leaflet of advice to singers. He was tenor soloist in several large American churches, notably Calvary Presbyterian Church in San Francisco. He gave concerts in almost every state before returning to Winnipeg and quickly moved on to Edmonton in 1907 where he became the "efficient" and "enthusiastic" director of McDougall Church choir.[9]

There was no doubt that Holmes M. Cowper, who emerged in Jean's classes as a "most promising tenor," was by far the most successful pupil she taught, other than Edith Miller.[10] Once he began lessons with Jean, he was soon singing duets with her in concerts in 1895.[11] In the *Winnipeg Tribune*, Charles Wheeler was of the opinion that it was wise of Cowper to leave Jean Forsyth, whose training had taken him only "up to a certain point," and pursue further lessons "under a first rate London master."[12]

Before and after his London training, Cowper, a young bank clerk, was tenor soloist in Grace Church choir. At the church, a romance blossomed between him and the talented church and concert organist whose surname was his given name, the dimpled Katie Holmes, daughter of Lt.-Col. Holmes. They married in the late summer of 1895. A farewell concert before their departure for London was given by the friends and choir members in Grace Church. The program was entirely religious: a chorale from Stainer's "Crucifixion"; "Crossing the Bar," Tennyson's poem about death; Dr. Garrick's anthem "One Crying in the Wilderness"; and "But Who May Abide" from the *Messiah.*" Jean sang the woeful hymn "There Is a Green Hill Far Away" about the place of the crucifixion, Calvary.[13] It was hardly music to cheer on a newly wedded couple.

Three years later, after a brief return to Manitoba, the two of them left for Chicago, where he gave a concert tour of the northwestern states. A column in *Town Topics* expressed some trepidation about the challenge of forging a singing career "single-handed, without social or financial prestige" but simply by "artistic merit." Such a statement shows how important social connections and money were at that time in most undertakings. The column announced that he and Katie would return for engagements in Manitoba during October. "It would be popular if arrangements could be made for his talented wife—known so long and with such genuine esteem as Miss Katie Holmes—to accompany him and give one or more organ performances. Cannot one of our churches be induced to take up this scheme?"[14]

In October they did perform in Winnipeg in the very church where Katie had been organist and Holmes Cowper a choir member: Grace Church. "Very fitting," said *Town Topics*. During his years away Cowper "has been studying earnestly with the best teachers and is now winning laurels in the largest cities as a tenor soloist." His engagement in Winnipeg was creating "the very greatest interest." He and Katie "may count on receiving a very warm welcome from a host of admiring friends."[15]

In October 1898 word arrived from Jean in New York City. *Town Topics* made "an announcement which, they claimed, all her pupils will receive with pleasure." She will resume her vocal classes soon. Her students "were beginning to fear that the attractions and opportunities of New York would tempt her to remain." Winnipeg could "ill afford to lose Miss Forsyth."[16]

Yet Jean delayed her return to Winnipeg for several months more.

Finally, on May 27, 1899, Charles Wheeler reported that he has received a note from Jean "in hurried calligraphy" that he is scarcely able to read. She is ending her "long sojourn in New York, that metropolis of pedagogues," where she has accompanied "some of the most famed teachers—notably Mr. George Sweet." All he can make out is that she will resume her "vocal tuition studio." She had taken up residence again in the old Cauchon Block, now the Assiniboine Block. She will meet pupils in her rooms at number 39. She "knows how to teach," writes Wheeler, having "acquired the art of developing not only tone, but animation." She will have a large class of students, he predicts, "to polish up, and to inspire with the artistic zeal she always infuses into her own work upon the concert program."[17]

In early August, Jean Forsyth's advertisement for vocal classes at 39 Assiniboine Block appeared in the papers. By the middle of that month she was definitely back, for she sang a solo in St. Luke's Church on the 16th. Her pupils and friends were ecstatic. They "gave expression to their gratification" for the return of this "genial and popular lady" by giving her a party.[18]

WINNIPEG IN 1899 WHEN EDITH RETURNS

The Winnipeg Edith Miller returned to for late summer holidays from her job at Tompkins Avenue Congregational Church in New York in 1899 was far from the Winnipeg that had greeted Jean Forsyth in 1893. The population had almost doubled. The city had become even more prosperous. Its Anglo-Celtic elite was larger and more firmly entrenched. A future for Winnipeg had taken visionary shape as the central metropolis in the West, connected by railways east to central Canada and beyond, west to the coast, and south to Minneapolis–St. Paul and Chicago. No one could have imagined that journeys would soon be transformed by Henry Ford's invention of the car, or that radical politics and the cultural incursion of ethnic groups—especially Russian, Ukrainian, and Polish Jews—would take place in the near future.

Winnipeg was still a city divided between the British-based majority at the centre of the city and the pitiable immigrants in the North End working the railroads, peddling, or dealing in junk or ethnic fabric, food, and objects. Those working-class minorities still suffered rampant anti-Semitism and other powerful kinds of discrimination expressed in the most derogatory terms, such as "dumb hunkies," "Polacks," "bohunks," and "kikes." It was already a ferment of radical ideas and aspirations for a political say. So far, the only East European Jewish political figure was Joseph ("Fighting Joe") Martin, who would become MLA for Winnipeg and eventually, in 1900, premier of the province. Yet by the late 1890s astute Conservatives and Liberals alike had begun to realize that their candidates needed the Jewish vote if they were to win elections.[1]

Even so, a diverse and vibrant culture was gaining strength on and around Selkirk Avenue, the North End's commercial centre, where ethnic newspapers, literary associations, drama groups, sports clubs, alternative schools, and a plethora of music teachers had sprung up. For now, that culture remained hidden (or was suppressed or dismissed) by the Anglo-Celtic majority.

Worse was rampant degradation of Indians, whose land had been "bought" by early settlers and government agents at prices that were an insult. Phrases such as "The only good Indian is a dead one" peppered the newspapers. The exceptions were "honest, quiet, inoffensive" Indians. Mostly, they were "injuns," thieving "squaws" or "scalping" someone: objects of rough and denigrating humour such as "Chief Shoot-at-Him." A typical newspaper joke might be, "They seem to be making an unusual number of good Indians these days—several braves being run over by trains within a week."[2]

Even clothing had changed by the end of the 1890s. Overall, it had softened into less intimidating shapes and a greater degree of comfort. Only the corset remained a necessary discomfort for women. In fact, it had become more restrictive by lengthening the front over the abdomen ("Swan's Bill" corsets) to produce the newly fashionable S-shape with a flat abdomen, a wasp waist, an arched back and the hint of a bustle. Yet already there were discussions about how corsets harmed women's internal health—especially the health of pregnant women and their unborn children. The idea of more "rational" dress for women reflected a new interest in sports for women. The "bicycle craze" of the late 1890s that resulted from the refinement of bicycles into the "safety bicycle" suitable for women not only gave women a freedom and mobility unheard of before, it also led to the design and use of "skirtless" clothes, such as scandalous bloomer outfits. At this point, too, wool bathing costumes (some with sailor collars and other nautical motifs) for women, with short pants and an overtunic, appeared.[3]

These radical changes in fashion were reflected in the slightly more comfortable clothes that graced social occasions. Women's dresses had long been used to vie for attention to wealth and social status, especially in news reports of balls, teas, and concerts. Women had festooned themselves in lace and bows, frills and *passimenterie*, often using gauzy overdresses swept back into bustles that made them look like wedding cakes or tightly wrapped gifts. The "puffs" over the shoulders became bigger and bigger until they were cartooned as being "modeled on cricket bats, hot air balloons, or tennis rackets." By the late 1890s, these had become somewhat more natural "leg o' mutton" sleeves with just enough shoulder fabric to ease movement. Instead of the round, crinolined silhouette of the early 1890s, a more tailored, natural A-line shape like an upside-down tulip was created by narrower gored skirts. Afternoon dresses had high collars and draped bodices. The new, slightly masculine "shirtwaist"—a combination of blouse, skirt, and belt—became a popular informal outfit. Evening dresses were still quite frothy and had a squared décolletage, sometimes a slight train. Yet lengthy descriptions of women's dresses after social events had begun to disappear.

Hairstyles, too, changed. The curly bangs and ringlets and elaborately coiffed upsweeps—aided by hairpieces of various sizes—were being exchanged for an easier style without bangs that gathered the hair loosely into a bun perched on top of the head. It was this hairstyle (and the more mobile female shape) that was depicted by the illustrator Charles Dana Gibson as the "ideal American woman." No longer the fragile Victorian doll or the languid voluptuous woman of the 1880s, this was the vivacious "Gibson Girl."

Men's fashions were shifting too. Wing collars and stiff-fronted dress shirts with studs and ascot or four-in-hand ties (with white bow ties for evening wear) were considered "jolly good." The more comfortable blazer began to replace fitted jackets with matching waistcoats. The tweed Norfolk jacket, with easy pleats front and back, along with matching breeches, were popular for rugged outdoor pursuits and cycling. Beards, long sideburns, and other imposing facial hair were starting to disappear, leaving the neatly trimmed moustaches as the style of the day.

In Winnipeg, the musical scene had developed too. The most dramatic and tragic change was the burning down of the seven-storey Manitoba Hotel—the finest hotel in the city—in the early hours of February 8, 1899. The hotel stood at the southeast corner of Main Street and Water Street (now William Stephenson Way). Ironically, the fire that razed the building and its adjacent structure, the offices of the Northern Pacific Railway, began in the large, elegant dining room where so many concerts had been held since it opened in 1892.[4]

There were cries from all quarters for a new recital hall to be built, but that would take years. "It is a pity there is not in Winnipeg a hall of some sort where these recitals could be held," wrote Charles Wheeler in the *Winnipeg Tribune* after one of Jean Forsyth's student concerts at which her widowed sister Sarah Thompson, who had moved to Winnipeg, was accompanist. "Since the Manitoba Hotel was destroyed, the theatres are too large, and a church has a rather depressing effect on an audience."[5] Meanwhile, the ruins of "the finest Canadian hotel west of Montreal" stood as a sad reminder of loss, though all 400 residents in the hotel were rescued.

Earlier concerts at which sacred and secular music had often been mixed together in what seemed like random programs had now separated into definite categories where the type of music could be accurately anticipated.

Choral music would remain Winnipeg's main musical mode until the end of the Second World War. J. J. Moncrieff, co-founder of the main English paper, the *Winnipeg Tribune*, where Charles Wheeler would remain the music and drama critic for many years, was a moving force behind choral music. In 1899, Dr. James Tees, who directed the Methodist choir, was about to organize the first choral society in Winnipeg. By 1903, that choir would have 250 voices. He had already enhanced various choruses in the religious music he conducted by drawing from the choirs of other churches, especially for Christmas and Easter oratorios. Tees was credited with getting Winnipeg's choirs to "shut off the hissing sound of the 's' in *God Save the Queen*,"[6] that preceded most performances. Wheeler's forceful and British-centric views on what the city's music should be still held sway. It was very seldom that he was taken to task, as he had been by "Rosa Sub" over his praise of George Sweet.

There were still vaudeville-type events, some clandestine and risqué, others wholesome and filled with slapstick humour and pranks, such as the Firemen's Benevolent Association's entertainment at the Winnipeg Theatre. The stage was set as the interior of a fire hall, complete with horses and a hose wagon. One of the firemen suggests a concert. This "spontaneous" concert unfolds mainly with comic songs and recitations from the "firemen," with a few ballads and love songs, as well as banjo and guitar numbers. The climax is an "alarm" which spurs the firemen to harness the horses to the wagon and rush off stage. After an intermission, a double quartet of men in evening dress stand on a rear platform, while a row of three black-faced "Sambos" dressed as bones (skeletons) sit on each side and provide humorous mime throughout the quartet singing to the "hearty enjoyment" of the "very large and genial" audience. "Everything in sight was encored" with "outbursts of cheers," ran a review the next day. Jean Forsyth was the accompanist for this rowdy evening.[7]

Charity concerts, such as the Firemen's Benevolent Association, were common. Jean Forsyth organized several on behalf of the Winnipeg Humane Society. Such entertainments charged no admission, but passed the hat to raise money.

Concerts termed "popular," which had passed for classical music in the past, attracted an audience that enjoyed ballads from the "old country," sentimental

songs, such as lullabies, light classics with strong rhythms and melodies, and patriotic songs that glorified the British Empire.

Military bands consisting of the "gallant sons of Mars" were still on show, especially for occasions such as national holidays and military exercises. And small
"musicales"—such as those held by the Women's Musical Club of Winnipeg—
were still being held in private homes as entertainments for teas.

Classical concerts had finally reached the quality Charles Wheeler had hoped
to produce through his acerbic criticism and tireless attention. The "sugar and
honey school of a certain class of composer," as he called it, was fine for a certain
class of audience. For the discerning, however, more serious music than that of
Rossini and Donizetti (adored for their *bel canto* arias) was now heard at programs
set before a more "fastidious" audience.[8]

Into this changed Winnipeg arrived a changed Edith Miller. After her training
with Randegger in London, Mme Marchesi in Paris, and George Sweet and Harry
Luxtone in New York, she was no longer a prim Presbyterian girl from Portage la
Prairie. Not only had she spent a great deal of time in sophisticated world cities, she
had been enjoying an unaccustomed high income in New York. She might not have
been a "commanding" artist, as Charles Wheeler had claimed, but there was no
doubt the name Edith J. Miller was well-recognized abroad and in the United States.

Her first Winnipeg concert—which was the opening concert of the season
on September 14—would be an opportunity for her adoring home audience to
hear her voice again. Advance notice appeared twice in the same issue of *Town
Topics* twelve days before the concert. "Lovers of good music," one said, will
enjoy a "great treat." The other claimed, "the concert season cannot open more
auspiciously" than by "this young lady of whom all Manitoba is so justly proud."
Stanley Adams, who was proving himself a capable agent as well as a singer, had
organized the affair.[9]

The concert itself had an odd review. The audience in the Winnipeg Theatre
was very large, as expected, and "had got on its very best clothes and company
manners on." They were so polite, or perhaps were so intimidated by this now-fa-
mous singer they had not heard for two years, that they refrained from demanding
encores until the fifth piece. "This was a little trying for Miss Miller," the reviewer
observed, "who although by this time fairly well hardened, still would naturally
be rather nervous about making her appearance before a Winnipeg audience, all
anxious and critical to see what progress she had made."[10]

She undoubtedly *had* made progress. She had "improved immensely." That improvement was from the technical point of view of the professional vocal teacher:
"facility of expression, general confidence in herself and her powers were apparent
to everyone."

It is almost with shock the *Town Topics* reviewer writes, "We have evidently
heard the last of Miss Edith J. Miller, contralto." Two years of study and professional concerts and church solos had transformed Edith Miller into a mezzo-soprano. The reviewer concedes that, "there is no doubt about the improvement";
it is clearly an "obvious change from the amateur to the professional." Yet there
is a loss. "I think a good many of us, while feeling proud of the girl who has won

her way to such a high position in the East, still recalled with some regret the simple ballads that we used to hear some years ago from Miss Miller, of Portage la Prairie, who had a wonderfully rich contralto voice."[11] Had Edith Miller outgrown her home audience? Had training corrupted her natural voice by challenging her to reform it according to the fashion of the day? Was she nervous?

Nothing was going to stop Edith Miller's progress, however. The day after her Winnipeg concert she was off to New York for the Vanderbilt funeral.

Six months later, in mid-March 1900, the *Town Topics* reviewer declared: "A prophet has no honour in his own country. And this is doubtless the reason that it is hard to make a success of a concert in Winnipeg with nothing outside of local performers." He was not referring to Edith J. Miller, but to Jean Forsyth. "It is all the greater compliment, then, to Miss Jean Forsyth's popularity that such a good audience was present at her concert at the Winnipeg Theatre." The audience, he wrote, was "well repaid for its attendance." She was the principal soloist, among "a number of musicians among us of no mean order." "This lady," he continued, "has lately paid a visit to New York to gather the newest ideas on vocal production. Her singing showed what a thorough mastery she had of her subject and what a good claim she has to be considered one of our most successful vocal teachers. The two little French airs were sung as nobody else in Winnipeg could sing them but Miss Jean Forsyth."[12]

Jean was accompanied by the sister she joined on so many social occasions, Sarah, whose husband, John Hope Thompson, had left her a widow with their son Sydney. The program included Norman Douglas and Robert Campbell, two "promising" young tenors. Campbell was already well known in Winnipeg; he "continues to deserve all the high opinions" of his singing. Douglas has a "very delightful voice" and "an artistic and sympathetic temperament." His technical lapses on a few notes "will doubtless be remedied." There was also "a great ar-ray of pianists," six including Jean's sister. The reviewer praised the new soloist Miss McDowell. "Her playing is a delightful example of the latest and most correct Leipsic [German] technique," though he felt she showed a bit too much "restraint." Violinist Alex Scott "continues to improve," though his popular selection by De Bercat was "frightfully hackneyed."

All told, Jean Forsyth's concert was a delightful success.

THE EDITH J. MILLER COMPANY MAKES THE FIRST TOUR OF CANADA'S WESTERN CITIES, 1900

It would be the first time a thoroughly professional concert tour by Winnipeg artists through the major cities of Western Canada would take place. The Edith J. Miller Company, consisting of Edith, mezzo-soprano and contralto, Robert C. Campbell, tenor, and Stanley W. Adams, baritone, with Jean Forsyth as piano accompanist, set off on August 20, 1900. Professional photos had been taken of all four. These photos appeared in *Town Topics* three weeks before they left.[1] Edith had taken a three-quarters pose from the back in a sparkling black dress with short black lace

Jean Forsyth with her dogs,
already a Winnipeg "character,"
Town Topics, Oct. 13, 1900.

Edith J. Miller in her glamorous
New York gown, publicity shot for the
Edith J. Miller Company western tour,
Town Topics, Oct. 13, 1900.

Edith J. Miller in her glamorous New York gown, publicity shot for the Edith J. Miller Company western tour, *Town Topics*, July 28, 1900.

sleeves and a long front ruffle that was cut into a low square at the back. She had bought this glamorous dress in New York. Her coiffed dark hair is topped by a small black hat with a short black feather pointing obliquely upward. Her nearest arm, hand holding a partly opened fan, is gracefully draped around and below her waist. From this pose the full effect of the S-shaped "Swan's Bill" silhouette can be seen. Robert Campbell is casually dressed in a checked tweed suit with a slant-but-toned high dark waistcoat, topped with a high, round-collared white shirt. His san-dy hair is short and parted in the middle, his face clean-shaven. He is seated, his arms on the chair arms, leaning forward. His sweet open face looks like that of a schoolboy who takes his studies seriously. Stanley Adams wears a dark blazer over well-pressed grey flannels. His waistcoat is white and V-necked, exposing a high-necked white shirt with a small wing collar and a narrow dark tie. In his pocket is the jaunty inverted V of a handkerchief. He is leaning far into a table or desk, left hand in his pants pocket, right hand relaxed. His dark hair and small, trimmed moustache give him a roguish look. He is handsome, but the lift of his chin sug-gests an edge of condescension.

Jean Forsyth's photo is unlike the other three. She stands in her loosely gath-ered shirtwaist set off by a standup white collar and crossed black ribbon "tie" behind an ornate, high throne-like chair. She is wearing a plain brimmed hat such as Boy Scouts or Mounties wear. On the chair in front of her are her two white dogs in their collars: the larger one has folded ears and resembles a hound; the smaller one has black patches over each eye, a black nose, and black spots all over. It looks like a Jack Russell terrier. Jean appears serious, her mouth set as if she expected to be taken seriously. A photo of Edith Miller from the same photo shoot, from the side with her face turned to the camera, appeared in the *Winnipeg Free Press* the day she left. From it can be seen the deep round décolletage in her black spangled dress and the dark hair rolled back from her face with a hint of bangs at each side. That face is utterly beautiful.

Stanley Adams had organized the tour and did so with professional flair. He visited some of the cities to arrange lodgings and look at performance locations. He saw to it that enticing advance notices appeared in Winnipeg and in at least some of the cities the company would visit. These notices ran a full month before the tour began. Notices included locations in each city where tickets could be bought, and reserved seats selected ahead of performances. These locations were typically music stores and drug stores.

Off they went on the Imperial Limited train for Carberry and Brandon. It was the CPR's premier passenger daily train across Canada from Montreal to Vancouver, and had only been in service for a year. Its aim was to attract wealthy tourists to cross in comfort through the spectacular Rockies and stay at the elegant CPR chalets in Banff and Lake Louise. It advertised its luxurious sleeping and dining cars.

Carberry was not a major stop for the Edith J. Miller Company, but it was on the CPR line. Only 1,500 citizens lived in this prosperous agricultural supply

Robert Campbell, tenor, on
Edith J. Miller and Company's
western tour, *Town Topics*,
Oct. 13, 1900.

Stanley Adams, baritone and tour
organizer, on Edith J. Miller and
Company's western tour, *Town Topics*,
Oct. 13, 1900.

centre of seven grain elevators, a flour mill, a creamery, and a fair grounds. In 1900, the year the company performed there, the Union Bank built a red brick branch in the "free classic" style for $3,000. It was the most elegant and substantial structure in town.[2] Residents of Carberry were more interested in horse racing and the annual fair than in concerts, and the company left that same day in blistering heat to stay in the beautiful Langham Hotel in Brandon, so-named after the hotels in London, England, and Boston. There, they performed in a proper opera house. The *Brandon Daily Sun* enthusiastically reported that, "Miss Miller was given a hearty welcome. Her voice was heard to great advantage in the solo from *Lucrezia Borgia.*" This was a changed Edith Miller indeed. Lucrezia Borgia in Gaetano Donizetti's opera is portrayed as a notorious femme fatale renowned for her ruthless pursuit of power (even though she reveals a softer side when she encounters the son she has given up as a baby). Edith sang the closing aria of this opera (a mezzo role), which was one of the most demanding in all opera repertoire, with trills and coloratura passages that require extreme agility. Performing this role in her low-cut black spangles, she must have seemed a far cry from the quiet Presbyterian contralto who had performed in Brandon in the past. She was now the dark lady singing dark roles. She showed the amazing advances she had made, but the reviewer and audiences preferred the "exquisite melody" of her version of the oft-sung Tennyson's "Break, Break, Break."[3] Another review notes her "soulful voice." Campbell is merely mentioned (though in another review his "sweet tenor" voice is noted), and Stanley Adams is praised for being well received and given a "hearty encore." Accompanist Jean Forsyth was given "a great deal of credit for the artistic success of the evening." It was a "treat to all music lovers, and "a bumper house" was predicted for any return performances.[4]

After the concert the company was entertained by Dr. Stanley McInnis, MLA, and his wife at their residence on Sixth Street.[5]

The tour was off to a good start. It would only get better.

A week later, the company performed in Medicine Hat under the patronage of Lord and Lady Minto. This was a step up from the lieutenant governors who had formerly supported Edith Miller. Gilbert John Elliot-Murray-Kynynmound, Earl of Minto, was a flashy military man who was a friend of Queen Victoria (she was godmother to his first child). He had served in Canada as military secretary to Governor General Lord Lansdowne from 1883 to 1885, where he had been sent west to aid in the suppression of the Riel Rebellion. His new wife, Mary, daughter of Earl Grey (also a friend of the Queen), accompanied him cheerfully, for she was a sporting type like her husband.

In November 1898, Lord Minto was sworn in as Canada's governor general, replacing Lord Aberdeen. At a time when Prime Minister Wilfrid Laurier was encouraging British immigration and Canada was thriving economically, Lord Minto was considered the man for the job. At a farewell dinner, Lord Roseberry, a fellow Etonian, said that in Lord Minto, "Scotland and Eton are combined; you have something so irresistible that it hardly is within the powers of human eloquence to describe it."[6]

This larger-than-life hunting, fishing, riding sportsman who had served in several conflicts in the Far East took up Canadian sports such as cycling and skating with his wife.

To have Their Excellencies Lord and Lady Minto as patrons was but one remove from Queen Victoria herself.

Five days later, also under the Mintos' patronage, Edith Miller's company gave a "Grand Concert" at Hull's Opera House in Calgary. In an advance billing, Edith J. Miller was heralded as "Canada's Foremost Contralto and one of America's Leading Artists"; Jean Forsyth was "Soprano and Accompanist: Solo Soprano of Grace Church, Winnipeg"; Stanley Adams "The Well-Known Popular Baritone"; and Robert C. Campbell "One of Canada's Best Tenors." Reserved seats cost 75 cents and 50 cents; general admission was 25 cents.[7]

Hull's Opera House was a long, handsome building of sandstone and brick at 606 Centre Street (Albion Block). William Roper Hull, entrepreneur, rancher, and philanthropist (he willed his estate to build a home for "destitute and orphan children"), built the place that accommodated an audience of 1,000. It opened in 1893, the year Jean moved to Winnipeg. In this elegant venue with its dress circle and gallery the Edith J. Miller Company performed a two-part program that was typical of its time: romantic, dramatic, sentimental, with a few humorous pieces. The subtitle of an 1885 collection of Victorian songs sums it up: "Lyrics of the Affections and Nature."[8] Although these songs contain many religious words—such as "heaven," "soul," "pray," "angels," "spirit"—these are often used in secular, even erotic, ways to show the intensity of earthly love, especially love that is unfulfilled. Typically, Theo Marsials's "Go, Lovely Rose" (a duet with Edith Miller and Stanley Adams) is an elaborate address to the rose a lover is about to send to his sweetheart. Edith Miller sang the tender lullaby "Little Dustman (Sandman)" by Brahms. Robert Campbell offered a chivalric ode, "My Queen," by Jacques Blumenthal, who was Queen Victoria's pianist. Stanley Adams entertained—and provided what was probably welcome relief from the intense love songs and dramatic renditions—with three American humorous songs: "When Katie Tuned the Old Guitar (and sang my heart away)" by Arthur Bird; "Robin Goodfellow (the mischievous Puck)" by Scott; and "They Kissed (I saw them do it)" by C. B. Hawley. Even Edith Miller sang a humorous song, Paolo Tosti's "The Maidens of Cadix (Cadiz)," about Spanish girls who provoked male attention as they danced their boleros, but declined the advances of princes and peasants alike.

The centrepieces of the concert, however, were excerpts from the operas *Lucia di Lammermoor* and *Lucrezia Borgia*. Robert Campbell and Stanley Adams sang the famous and ominous Act III duet between Enrico and Edgardo from *Lucia*, "O, Haste Crimson Morn." Edith offered selections from *Lucrezia Borgia*. These operas by Gaetano Donizetti could hardly be more dramatic: Gothic settings, ruthless betrayals, bloodied scenes, passionate ill-fated loves, blind hatred and revenge, insanity, and abandoned women and children. Donizetti was the acknowledged master of the *bel canto* tradition, and the duets and arias he composed not only conveyed an almost inhuman intensity of passion, they were also designed to demonstrate this passion in wildly ornamental vocal gymnastics.

Even though it was a wet night in Calgary, a large audience turned out to Hull's Opera House. They were "very attentive and appreciative," said the review in the *Calgary Weekly Herald*, "liberally applauded all the numbers" and "demanded encores to not a few."[9] The reviewer praised Edith Miller, "a contralto of high order." The reviewer noted especially that she was "happily without the sensational methods which so attract the musically uneducated." People who expected to hear something "startling" were "very properly disappointed." It was not a concert for those who "desire to have their nerves harrowed or their vulgar sensations stirred." These comments imply that the concert scene in the West was still sometimes contaminated by vaudeville values, becoming the "circus" that Charles Wheeler deplored.[10] This was a real concert, a professional concert, with a contralto who sang "charmingly, powerfully, and artistically," an "old-time favourite" baritone whose voice had lost "none of its attractive ring," and a new tenor with a "round and pure" voice.

Then it was on to Regina and another successful concert. But, before that they were driven in the trap (small, open horse-drawn carriage) of the North-West Mounted Police to their military barracks for tea. Later, there was a formal entertainment at the grand Italianate Government House, the workplace and residence of Amédée Emmanuel Forget, lieutenant governor of the North-West Territories. *Town Topics* reported that everywhere Edith Miller's costumes were "much admired," especially her two "elegant New York costumes": her black spangled robe and "an evening frock of pink liberty silk, with a renaissance lace overdress, bodice, and sleeves with pearl trimming." With these two dresses, Edith Miller could play the seductive femme fatale or the fetching ingénue, as she wished.

Edith J. Miller had never visited the West Coast cities of Vancouver and Victoria, the locale of her next concerts. Once more, her company gave such a brilliant concert on September 6 that the reviewer said fervently that it would "bear repeating." The "large and fashionable" audience demanded many encores. Aside from these, their program was the same. Edith was "in excellent voice," the reviewer noted, "and it would be difficult to say which of her many contributions found most favour." "Break, Break, Break," Tennyson's sorrowful poem, was "exquisitely given"; "the Promise of Life" "charmingly sung." Again, Robert Campbell's "sweet and clear voice" stood out. But it was the "well-modulated baritone" of the "good looking young" Stanley Adams who "divided the honours with Miss Miller." Jean Forsyth, "a pianist of ability," did her part "admirably."[11] Much later, Charles Wheeler recalled in his musical reminiscences a letter he received from one of the singers in the Edith J. Miller Company. It said, "Miss Forsyth is well, but I fear she misses her dog. She pets all the dogs she meets in the hotels. 'Poor Billy, he missed a great trip, but I could not undertake to manage a dog even if he were musical,' she used to say."[12]

The concert was performed in Vancouver's Theatre Royal. This ornate building with almost 1,000 seats, designed to suggest Moorish exoticism, was named the Alhambra Theatre in 1899 when it opened. By the time the Edith J. Miller Company arrived in early September 1900, it was known as the Theatre Royal.

The *Victoria Daily Colonist* had advertised the forthcoming "Grand Concert" of the company in a long article a week before they appeared in that city. It quoted a review from the *New York Sun*, sent ahead by Stanley Adams: Edith J. Miller is "a truly beautiful woman, possessing a most lovely contralto voice. She not only has "an exceptional voice, which she uses with much art and intelligence, but she has the soulful temperament of a born artiste and a most attractive stage presence." "Undoubtedly," the reviewer continued, "she is one of the most promising singers in the United States today."[13]

This emphasis on the beauty and "attractive stage presence" of Edith Miller and the "good looking young" appearance of Stanley Adams in the *Vancouver Daily News* review was important. Robert Campbell and Jean Forsyth were also attractive people, their looks and personal auras far above average. Such performers were the stars and celebrities of their day, and their private lives, as well as their public appearances, were closely followed, often idolized. Occasionally, they inspired obsession. Divas of the day, especially, were discussed in terms of their personal attributes. Audiences attended concerts not just to hear singers' voices, but also to see them.

At Victoria's Institute Hall, formerly used by the congregation of St. Andrew's Roman Catholic Cathedral (and called St. Andrew's Pro-Cathedral), on View Street between Douglas and Blanshard, the Edith J. Miller Company performed on September 8, 1900. Again, Stanley Adams had ensured that advance publicity appeared. A long article in the *Victoria Daily Colonist* the day before the concert focused on Edith Miller's "first visit to the Coast Cities":

> A good stage presence is a wonderful help to an artist, but when a beautiful voice and a highly artistic temperament goes along with it, there is little left to wish for. Miss Edith J. Miller is one of the most attractive artists on the concert platform today and this makes her a great favourite wherever she goes.
>
> The programme will be sufficiently varied to suit all tastes. It is hoped that Victorians will give Canada's leading artiste a hearty reception.[14]

Tickets were sold at Lombard's Music Store: reserved seats $1.00 and 75 cents; admission 50 cents. Again, the concert was under the patronage of Their Excellencies the Governor General of Canada and the Countess of Minto. It was also under the auspices of Lieutenant-Colonel Gregory and officers of the 5th Regiment Canadian Artillery.

The review in the *Victoria Daily Colonist* offered one accolade after another. "Since the visit of Mme Trebelli, Miss Miller is by long odds the best contralto singer heard here for many years." Trebelli was the stage name of Zelia Gilbert, a French opera singer who had died eight years earlier. She was noted for her "trouser roles" (contralto parts for male characters) and—extremely unusual for her day—kept her hair cropped to play them. Edith Miller was praised as "an artiste of rare ability" with a voice "rich in quality, of great warmth and beauty of tone." Her expression is "earnest, but free from exaggeration." She was applauded with great enthusiasm and recalled often. Again, Stanley Adams's "fine rich tone" and "good contrast" are praised. Robert Campbell was a surprise; "his voice possesses that beautiful quality peculiarly adapted to sympathetic music." Jean Forsyth was praised more fulsomely than either of the men. "She is one of the best accompanists in Canada," the reviewer stated. "Being a vocalist herself, she is able to appreciate and interpret the aim of the composer and give the singer the proper support at the proper time."[15]

The four singers—no doubt tired from their long intense schedule—boarded the enormous (282 feet long), elegant CPR paddlewheel steamer *Yosemite* at the dock in Victoria. They took a much-needed, relaxed, four-and-a-half-hour trip, passing along the gorgeous North Arm at Richmond into Vancouver. There they lodged at the CPR Hotel Vancouver on Granville Street.[16]

The company gave a completely different concert in the First Presbyterian Church in Vancouver. This one was completely religious. Hymns and songs with titles like "The Rosary," "Oh, Divine Redeemer," "Awake, My Soul," "He was Despised," and "Night Hymn at Sea" were the main fare, although the program finished with the same trio as their tour program, "Queen of the Night."

Then it was on to Kamloops and homeward by rail through the Crow's Nest Railway, stopping at Rossland, Grand Forks, and Greenwood, with two nights in Nelson and Lethbridge. The remarkable performances the company had given on their outward-bound journey created a demand for another performance on the way back in most of the towns east of Medicine Hat. After one last appearance in Minnedosa at Pearson Hall (later the Lyric Theatre) run by George Farncombe, the four singers arrived back in Winnipeg on Sunday evening, October 7, 1900.

"Our tour was a great success," declared a jubilant Stanley Adams, "and I think we may safely say that we have broken all previous records. Thirty-six concerts in seven weeks is not a bad record for Manitoba's representatives, for when you take out the Sundays there are not many days left in which to rest."

His exuberance was impossible to contain.

> Everywhere our audiences were most enthusiastic and Miss Miller scored a pronounced hit wherever she sang. We had a most enjoyable time, too, and met hosts of friends at all points. Our programme has been very highly spoken of and while of course the higher class of music was more appreciated by the great majority, yet in the most remote places we always found those who were delighted to hear pieces which they had not heard since they left the mother land or their homes in the east. Our experiences were varied and interesting. Our last audience at Moosomin was a bumper.[17]

He took a breath, then ended with a wink of humour, "Miss Miller did not lose any of her diamonds nor was any member of the company waylaid, robbed or drowned."

Always the promoter, Adams added a reminder about the concert the company would perform at the Winnipeg Theatre on Monday, two days hence: "Miss Miller is resting in Portage la Prairie, but she has lots of new and taking songs."[18]

QUEEN VICTORIA'S DEATH DERAILS EDITH, 1901

The death of Queen Victoria on January 22, 1901 derailed Edith Miller's career. She had planned to go to Europe "not later than the last week of February."[1] A week after Victoria's death, as if oblivious to the fact that an era had crashed down, an item in the *Manitoba Free Press* announced that Edith J. Miller was off to England by the end of February. She had finished lessons for all but her most advanced pupils, and these she would finish within the few weeks before her departure.[2] Only three days later, "the gloom which hangs over the nation, and this city in particular"[3] had sunk in. "Owing to the death of the Queen and the consequent period of mourning and quietness in England," the *Manitoba Free Press* wrote, "Edith J. Miller has decided to postpone her proposed trip to London and will remain in Winnipeg for the next three months."[4]

She threw herself into five performances over the next three-and-a-half months, one of which was a grand concert featuring herself.[5] She was also the main performer of three (with Robert Campbell and Nellie Campbell) to sing at an elite reception given by Mrs. George Galt on Donald Street for Mme Albani, Canada's first internationally famous soprano, who was in Winnipeg on tour. Finally, Edith Miller would meet Mme Albani. By this time Mme Albani was as plump as a pouter pigeon, but her attire was duly described in *Town Topics*.[6] She was "handsomely gowned in black silk, the demi trained skirt made with a tucked flare. The bodice which was of tucked silk, had a vest and collar of Maltese lace and was finished with velvet straps and jeweled buckles. Her ornaments were a string of pearls and the Queen's jewel with a spray of pink carnations. A small toque shaped hat of black chiffon completed a very charming tollet [*sic*]."

By then past fifty, she had been spoofed in *Punch*[7] as a chicken with flounces everywhere. Her hat featured an open-beaked squawking chicken, and she wore a jewelled cross around her neck. Under the London stage she stands on, named COVENT GARDEN, an inscription reads "A Thing of Beauty is a GYE (Guard Your Eyes) Forever!" (This was doubly funny because Gye was also her married surname.) In Winnipeg, however, she was still a diva and nothing but the best by way of entertainment would do at her reception.

On April 27, Winnipeg music lovers were warned that the forthcoming choir concert in a month at St. Andrew's Church would "probably be the last chance" to hear Miss Miller, as she is "leaving shortly for England."

Indeed, it would be the last chance to hear Edith Miller in Winnipeg, apart from a few unimportant appearances.[8] But that was not because she left for England. That would not happen for another three years.

Edith J. Miller, known across Canada as the country's most famous contralto, had a breakdown.

Looking at the inhuman schedule she had managed to keep up, a breakdown was hardly surprising. Her western tour in the fall of 1900 was a physical feat—thirty-six concerts in seven weeks, followed by a triumphant concert two days after the four singers' return to Winnipeg, October 13.

Stanley Adams seemed to thrive on all the activity, but Edith was "resting" at Portage la Prairie. A week later, however, she was off again, with Jean Forsyth and Miss Ethel Burnham, a violinist who taught at her studio at 26 Assiniboine Avenue, on the Canadian Northern Railway for an extended tour through northern Manitoba.

Returning after a week of performances that began in Dauphin and ended in Selkirk, Edith had only three weeks to recover before giving another grand concert in Selkirk on December 6. Advance publicity was top pressure. Four notices starting a month before the concert urged people to attend. It would be "one of the most successful [concerts] ever given in Winnipeg";[9] Miss Miller would appear "three or four times" on the program along with a chorus of forty voices; "Miss Edith J. Miller in Popular Concert" ran the advertisement;[10] "hundreds of people did not hear this excellent artiste when she sang in the Winnipeg Theatre and doubtless all these will take this opportunity of hearing Manitoba's and even Canada's leading contralto"; she would sing "the lullaby 'Berceuse' from Jocelyn by Benjamin Godard, and Mr. Fred Alderson will play the accompanying violin obbligato, a beautiful composition well worth the price of admission by itself"; she would sing 'Abide With Me' by Liddle, one of the finest settings of these beautiful words ever written."[11] Stanley Adams would sing; his wife would play the piano. She and Jean Forsyth and Miss Maud Cross would take turns as accompanists. Tenor Bruce Eggo, a newcomer to the music scene, would sing. Admission was 35 cents, and children 25 cents.

The concert drew a huge audience, inspired encores and frantic applause, and Edith received so many flattering notices that "very little more can be said."[12]

Adding to her public appearances, her work with her advance pupils at the studio she opened at the Clarendon Hotel in Winnipeg, and her duties as choir leader at Knox Church in Portage la Prairie, she also advertised for "a limited number" of new pupils. It seemed she couldn't decline any invitation or forego any source of income. It was a marvel that she hadn't collapsed sooner.

She would need over eight months of "enforced rest" at home with her parents in Portage la Prairie before she could appear on the stage again in February 1902.

EDITH, SINGER; JEAN, TEACHER, ANIMAL ACTIVIST, SOCIALITE

Edith Miller and Jean Forsyth, the two singers who had ambitions for a stage ca-reer in the early 1890s—Jean having trained with William Shakespeare and Edith Miller having such success at the Toronto Conservatory of Music and in church solos and concert music in that city—had taken entirely different career paths as the nineteenth century became the twentieth. Apart from her few students in Portage la Prairie and later in Winnipeg, Edith had pursued single-mindedly her ambition to become a world-class contralto. She had established herself as "the best contralto in Canada" and was almost as famous in the United States. All that remained was to equal that fame in England and on the Continent.

Jean's career had become many-faceted. Her classes became larger and larger; she continued as soprano soloist in Grace Church; and gave Grand Concerts of her own, though not nearly as often or as successfully as Edith Miller did. She had encountered discouraging bits of criticism about her singing from Charles Wheeler, who very soon after taking up his position as music and drama critic at the *Winnipeg Tribune* had pegged Jean as an excellent accompanist and superb vocal teacher. Judging from several of Wheeler's comments, she was too "florid" or "artistic" a singer for his liking. Like Edith, Jean had gone to New York to study with George Sweet. But Edith paid George Sweet to develop and coach her voice, whereas Jean took instruction in how to *teach* voice.

By the time the Edith J. Miller Company made its major tour of the West late in 1900, Jean had, for the most part, become Edith's (and others') accompanist. Time and again she was praised for her versatility at the piano, her sensitive support of singers' voices, her intuition, derived from having been a singer herself, for the delicate task of sensing any vocalist's needs in terms of pace, volume, or rhythm. It was said, too, that she was able to understand the aims of composers as well. Jean seems not to have felt rivalry with Edith. They were friends, Edith staying with her at her Assiniboine rooms before they both left on the tour of northern Manitoba that followed shortly after their return from the western tour. Likewise, Jean stayed with Edith and her parents in Portage la Prairie for a concert they gave there in early January 1901.[1] It seems Jean Forsyth was as content in this role—perhaps more content—than Edith was in hers as the glamorous onstage star.

Jean still gave a few concerts and she still appeared with Edith on several occa-sions, though more often as an accompanist than a singer. The occasions where they both sang tended to be charity concerts, such as the one to raise money for the Free Night School in the North End, one of the first times the music world made a gesture of support for that immigrant area of the city.[2] Now there were occasions where Edith sang and Jean was simply a guest. Such was the case at yet another reception for Mme Albani at the Galts'.³ At other times Jean was not even a guest when Edith performed at special events. At a dinner for Mr. Shaunessy from out of town, attended by the lieutenant governor, Edith sang "some of her prettiest songs, Scotch, English, and Irish; the representatives of each country claiming that his song was the best."⁴

It might have been cutting to Jean that Mrs. Verner, whose sharp soprano voice Charles Wheeler had criticized in the past, was now featured—along with her picture—as "Western Canada's Leading Soprano."⁵ Jean had been favoured at first in Winnipeg over Mrs. Verner, but now Mrs. Verner was taking the soprano role, alongside Edith Miller's contralto, in the *Messiah*. Eventually Mrs. Verner would give concerts outside Winnipeg, such as the one in Fargo, North Dakota, on April 20, 1904, where she was soprano soloist in Mendelssohn's *Elijah* and received a standing ovation. In Winnipeg she opened a studio to teach vocal music, putting herself into direct competition with Jean Forsyth. From the photograph of Mrs. Verner run by *Town Topics* she looks demurely downwards, unsmiling. She is wearing a somewhat dowdy dark dress with two white striped ruffles around a moderate neckline. She has a locket that is almost a choker around her neck. Her brown hair is unfashionably twisted to the back of her neck. A prudish woman, shy perhaps. It does not surprise that she sings almost exclusively sombre religious music.

It might have been cutting, too, that Jean was not enlisted as one of the staff for the new Winnipeg College of Music that opened in September 1903. She had taken an active part—as had Edith Miller—in the vocal curriculum of the old, long-defunct Winnipeg Conservatory of Music. But a new, young cadre of teachers was employed for the new institution.

Jean's great delight certainly was no longer stage performance. As a woman of fifty she would probably have lost some of her vocal power and agility. She enjoyed accompanying, having the satisfaction of helping singers make the most of their performances, but even more than that, she enjoyed teaching. It had emerged as her *forte*.

Her annual recitals for her pupils had overflowing audiences. The number of her pupils grew and grew, as praise for her teaching followed each recital. She was now teaching the younger siblings of some of her former students. A few of her former pupils were making careers for themselves: some like Ina Hogg in Winnipeg; others like Holmes Cowper, her "most promising tenor,"⁶ who had emerged as a leading tenor in the United States and in other countries. One of her former students—Miss J. Perkins—had opened a studio to teach voice herself. Eva Clare later had a hall named after her at the University of Manitoba where she taught. Gabrielle Mollot set up a studio to teach voice in the city.

With each spring recital, Jean Forsyth showed more pupils. And with each recital the praise for her as a teacher increased. In mid-May 1901 after fulsome publicity in advance in *Town Topics* and the *Winnipeg Tribune* the review of her recital appeared. "Miss Forsyth's pupils were greeted with a house full to overflowing." Seven students were mentioned. Even the newer pupils gave "signs of promise."⁷

The following spring recital warranted a long column by Charles Wheeler. "When you find a singing teacher producing students who can really sing," he wrote,

There is no occasion for worrying about that teacher's "methods."

Come to think of it, did anyone ever hear of a really great artist or even a very good singer the product of the new-fangled "methods"?

Jean Forsyth is one of the teachers of Winnipeg who without any fads or frills or athletic exercises is actually turning out singers.

She proved it by a recital given last night in the YMCA auditorium and there was a large audience there to congratulate the teacher on the splendid results of her work.

Miss Forsyth's pupils did her credit and their selections evidenced rare good taste.[8]

To back up his view, Wheeler comments on ten of the student performances. Rita (Marguerite) Hogg, the younger sister of Ina Hogg, was one of them.

By way of contrast to the excellence of Jean Forsyth's recital it was noted in the *Manitoba Morning Free Press* that the recital of another Winnipeg music teacher, Miss Frida de Tersmeden (an assumed "European" name), did not draw the same crowds. "There was not the same uncomfortable overcrowding as at Miss Forsyth's recital the night before."[9] Although Edith also gave occasional recitals of her pupils, reviews were matter-of-fact and low-key.

By 1904 Jean Forsyth's pupil recitals were a cultural event in themselves. Advance publicity was a given. Despite bad weather, many "mustered up the courage to trudge through mud and moisture" to the YMCA auditorium. What they saw was "one of the most interesting of the season's students' recitals." "Each year at these annual demonstrations," Charles Wheeler wrote,

Miss Forsyth produces young singers who can actually sing. On the principle of the proof of the pudding, that is the best evidence of her methods.

Such teachers as Miss Forsyth, doing honest work along rational lines, deserve encouragement, for too often are they disheartened by the success of charlatans and humbugs permitted to ruin voices with baneful fads.

One of the most pretentious numbers was the always popular *Lucia* [*di Lammermoor*] sextette, the rendering of which indicated, that under Miss Forsyth's direction, the young people had been able to catch some of the inspiration of the work.[10]

It was "the most progressive and ambitious recital yet given by Miss Forsythe." The concert was repeated on May 19 so that those kept back by bad weather for the first performance could hear it.

Jean had chosen not to proceed to fame on the concert stage. That would have meant abandoning those she accompanied so well and, worse, abandoning her students. This praise for the unrivalled effectiveness of her career as a vocal teacher could only have been a warming source of pride and deep satisfaction, as did the consistent praise of her gifts as an accompanist.

That would have been so had she done little other than accompany singers. But her work with the Winnipeg Humane Society had not faltered through the years. She was now, after ten years, the first vice-president of the organization. She had seen it through lame horses rescued, sweltering horses given shade at the hay market, injured or tortured dogs saved, improved conditions at the city dog pound, education to help children develop fellow-feelings for animals, life-saving posts set up along the river, and awards given for heroic rescues of animals and people. The cases of child neglect and abuse were now matters for the Winnipeg Children's Aid Society that was an 1898 offshoot of the Winnipeg Humane Society.

The tenth annual meeting of the society on January 25, 1904, opened as usual with a prayer, was cause for celebration.[11] Jean Forsyth was often acknowledged as the originator of the organization in 1894: "The society owed its existence to Miss Forsyth," one of the directors once remarked. The president concurred. He praised her as "the founder of the society," and gave "emphatic testimony to the value of her work." In 1900 she had been elected third vice-president "with generous thanks of the society for the great work done in the early inception and organiza-tion of the society."[12] She had collected "funds that amounted to $70.00."[13] Even a much later article in *Maclean's Magazine* profiling four Canadian businesswomen, of which Jean was one, mentions her founding of the Winnipeg Humane Society and "her love of dumb animals."[14] Now, ten years later, the members assessed the tremendous progress they had made since. The organization had 100 members. There was now a junior chapter of young members. They held eight regular meet-ings a year. Jean continued to assist in raising funds not only by holding charity concerts, but also by convincing the directors to increase the fees for licensing female dogs from two dollars to five dollars in 1902.

Mayor Thomas Sharpe chaired the meeting. President Robert Barclay observed that "a great deal has been done towards ameliorating the suffering caused by negligence or direct cruelty among the lower animals, and should encourage every right thinking person to take an active part in such a noble enterprise."[15] He then listed the cases dealt with during the past year:

owners of lame animals warned, 131
horses relieved from hunger, 3
horses relieved from excessive whipping, 1
horses taken care of and stabled, 3
horses relieved from overloading, 5
horses ordered to be shot, 7
horses ordered to be inspected by the veterinary surgeon, 3
horses ordered to be killed, being totally unfit for work, 5
cows destroyed, 2
cats without homes destroyed, 5
boys warned for ill-treating dogs, 9
conviction of parties for ill-treating horses, 11

cases dismissed by the magistrate, 1
case of conviction of owner who absconded, 1

Barclay went on to say that in all these cases the Winnipeg Humane Society had had the cooperation of the city humane officer and the police. He praised the city for providing the drinking fountains for animals (and people) requested by the society. A new veterinary surgeon, Dr. Williamson, replaced Dr. Hinton. Jean Forsyth was thanked for founding the society and for the entertainments that "augmented the funds of the society." Those she had engaged to assist her financially were "the Hudson's Bay Co., Steele Co., Pengelly & Co., Mr. J. H. Ashdown, the Banfield company for stage equipment, and Mr. Chambers' orchestra."

Jean had played, and continued to play, a central role in the Humane Society, and her energy on behalf of animals had not flagged. She was still checking up on the treatment of dogs at the pound. Once she got into a dispute with a new pound keeper Jessen, who, she said in a formal complaint to the society, was "impertinent and insolent" to her over the telephone regarding a dog he had for sale. Jessen was no stranger to disputes and he was eventually prosecuted.[16]

Her steady initiatives at the Winnipeg Humane Society over its first ten years must have been a source of gratification and pride as she strode through the streets with a long walking stick in one gloved hand and her two leashed dogs in the other.

Far more than Edith Miller, Jean Forsyth was to be seen at every possible social event. Having a father who was a postmaster was not the same as having a wealthy businessman for a father. Jean had come from the social elite of the East, even if it had been pioneering Chatham. For this reason she was as much at home in Government House as she was at the euchre parties or celebrations of clubs such as the Snowshoe Club or the Cauchon Block's (now the Assiniboine Block's) bachelorette B & B parties. As a teacher of young people, she knew and was affectionately regarded by many, many families in the city. She was as comfortable and merry with young people as she was with visiting dignitaries and lieutenant governors. She had sung in most of the churches of Winnipeg; she had sung in too many charity concerts to count; she had been an accompanist to many, if not most of the singers in the city for over a decade. Though her own once-popular concerts were coming to an end, her audiences knew and admired her. It is not too much to say that her pupils—for whom she had teas and occasionally put out-of-towners up in her rooms—loved her.

In the spring of 1901, at age fifty, she decided to resign from the job that had brought her to Winnipeg in the first place, her position of soprano soloist in the Grace Church choir. At a special gathering of fellow members of the choir, she was given a beautiful gold-mounted umbrella. There was "much regret." "Aside from her experience and ability as a vocalist," ran an article in *Town Topics*, "her kindness and geniality have endeared her to her fellow singers in no ordinary degree." "With perfect truth and frankness, Winnipeg never has had a church singer more thoroughly capable and reliable." Jean Forsyth "intends confining her efforts to the large class of vocal pupils, which is growing very rapidly."[17]

Kindness, geniality, capability, and reliability: these are qualities that are exceptionally fine. And they were Jean Forsyth's.

Jean hardly missed a social event. She was among those who started the city's French Literary Club in 1902.[18] It was touted by its president, Madame de Bauvière, as "a mental gymnasium," a gathering that, as Canon Matheson ambitiously said, "might help "bring the French and English speaking people of Canada closer together." She attended the Women's Musical Club. She was there at Mrs. Macdonald's "delightful musical" at Dalnavert, her handsome residence on Carlton Street (now a heritage building). In subdued candlelight, with an orchestra in the background, guests mingled and chatted. Although descriptions of dresses at such occasions had been toned down or eliminated in the news, *Town Topics* couldn't refrain from describing the hostess and her daughter. Mrs. Macdonald wore white satin with an overdress of spangled mechlin (Dutch lace)" adorned with "exquisite crimson roses." Her daughter wore "a very pretty gown of Spanish lace over white silk." One of the many illustrious guests was Sir Charles Tupper, who had briefly been prime minister in 1986 and was now Conservative leader of the Opposition under Wilfrid Laurier. He had arrived with Lady Tupper in the city that morning and soon found himself surrounded by "a host of Winnipeg friends." Lieutenant Governor and Mrs. McMillan were there, as were scores of the city's wealthy couples and their eligible sons and daughters. So was Jean Forsythe [*sic*]."[19]

Jean was there, too, at an enormous afternoon reception in August 1901 given by the commissioner of the Hudson's Bay Company, Clarence Campbell Chipman and his wife. The occasion was the annual meeting of the Canadian Medical Association. Doctors from across Canada were present at this exciting affair that was held at the handsome stone barracks of Lower Fort Garry on the picturesque banks of the Red River. Guests were ferried by the 2:45 train, reaching Fort Garry to the sounds of the 90th Battalion band at 4:00. They were returned on the six o'clock train to the city in time for dinner.

This reception, that luckily drew fair weather, was mainly conducted outside, for there were hundreds of guests. So many guests, that the write-up of the event in *Town Topics*[20] listed the guests in sections headed by letters of the alphabet. Again, Sir Charles and Mrs. Tupper were present, as were the lieutenant governor and his wife. Senator Kirchoffer and his wife and daughter attended. There were judges, such as Chief Justice Killam and his wife and son, professors, military officers, and members of the clergy, including the archbishops of Rupert's Land and St. Boniface.

Jean was also at smaller gatherings, such as the garden party given by Mrs. J. Somerset Aitkens, on Assiniboine Avenue, at which "the persistent little mosquito did not add to the charm of the summer night, and many of the visitors who wore thin dresses found it more pleasant to remain in the pretty reception rooms."[21]

Jean was invariably present at such elite gatherings, large and small. Yet she was also present at special gatherings for the unmarried that were mainly intended to introduce young people to each other in hopes of marriage. The words "debut," "debutante," and "coming out" were never used, as they were on such occasions in the East. Yet these social events were more or less the same. Typically, one of these events was "a very pleasant gathering" for tea of young people hosted by Mrs. Kohl, Fort Rouge, to meet Mrs. McCullough and Miss Gilmour from Brockville, Ontario.[22] Other than the hostess and the married guest, Jean would have been the only middle-aged person present. She was invited to such gatherings because of her genial, witty personality. And she was not married.

On July 27, 1901, Jean was off to Seattle, Washington, for two months' holiday. She might have been visiting relatives, but Mme D'Auria was then living there, and she might have been Jean's hostess. Jean returned from her holiday "looking exceedingly well from her pleasant trip."[23]

JEAN VISITS DAWSON CITY, 1905

Jean Forsyth laughed, a merry tinkling laugh like silver clinking as a table was being set. She sat with her niece Dollie in the Camerons' small living room in Dawson City. Dollie smiled. "Yes," Jean said, setting the *Dawson Daily News* on the edge of the white wicker tea table that held a large pink-and-green *chinoiserie* punch bowl, "that was a delightful and most amusing concert last night. And it went so late. Too late, really. I confess I'm rather weary today."

Dollie wore a long, dark wool skirt and a white blouse with leg o'mutton sleeves and a wide high-necked collar. A long rope of pearls—no doubt real—hung below her waist. Her abundant, fair hair was loosely drawn up and back into a chignon. She looked the height of Edwardian fashion, even though it was Dawson City, a place only barely civilized. One must keep up appearances. The living room, too, was fashionably decorated with a corner bookcase full of books, net curtains, and gilt-framed paintings—landscapes and portraits—artistically arranged on the walls. It was a gentleman's living room, for Dollie's husband, Donald A. Cameron, was in charge of the Canadian Bank of Commerce, the first bank to open after the gold rush in the late 1890s.

Jean was Dollie's guest for most of a year in 1905. She had answered Dollie's almost desperate plea for company in the godforsaken place where she was raising her little four-year-old daughter Winnie.

Jean reached for the newspaper. She was not at all tired, though she had made what she humorously called "my Dawson debut" last night. Not quite true. She had already been soprano soloist in St. Andrew's Presbyterian Church choir.[1] She burst into laughter from time to time as she read the review of last night's many performances.

"It was mixed all right," she said. "Imagine putting those one-act comic sketches in with a children's chorus and the Highland fling—complete with..." She stopped to get her breath. "With...with...*bagpipes*!" Again, she fell into gales of laughter, bent over in her elegant Victorian chair.

"But my dear Pussy," said Dollie calling Jean by her family pet name and smiling in sympathy, "the old folks in Dawson are always taken with anything in child life that is a true impersonation of the affectations or peculiarities of adult life. Northerners seem to feel a strange sympathy for anything clever in the younger generation. Did you see Winnie? Her hair bow was all askew and she kept chatting with the girl next to her!"

"Yes," Jean replied, calmed at last. "That impersonation they did for an encore of the big sailor sweetheart and his lover was something rich! I haven't had such fun in years! In *years*! And their *encore*!" She began giggling again. "'Sweet Bunch of Daisies'! They captured the impassioned gesticulations of a lovelorn swain so well. One would think they had seen older moonstruck folk in person."

"They probably had," said Dollie. "This is such a small community. We all know each other, more or less. The children visit back and forth informally in a way that would never do in Toronto. Or," she added, "even in Chatham."

Jean shivered with laughter again. "And that fellow who played 'The Lost Chord' on his trombone! *Trombone!* That's supposed to be a soulful, philosophical piece. I've sung it myself. Arthur Sullivan's masterpiece. The house actually shook with applause afterwards. And then...then...then he couldn't do an encore—thank goodness—because the pianist forgot his music!" Jean held her stomach and shook with laughter. "Lost chord, indeed! It was a case of lost *music!*" Even Dollie laughed a little at this.

"And the vocal section! I scarcely know where to begin," Jean continued. But a glance at the paper reminded her. "The quartet I was part of was quite definitely off-key, nothing like the ones I've performed with in Winnipeg. Mrs. J. Harmon Caskey—now there's a name—sang 'Loch Lomond' quite well, but 'Fleeting Days' was a bit sentimental.

"Mr.—or should I say Monsieur—Laliberté cleverly sang both the French, then the English version of 'Tell Me With Your Eyes.' Surely that should be 'Speak to Me Only With Thine Eyes.'" She said this almost to herself, bringing the newspaper close to her eyes. She glanced over the top of the paper at her niece. "Did you know we have started a French Literary Club in Winnipeg?" she asked. Dollie shook her head 'no.'

"And that poor young thing who sang 'She's the Sweetest Girl I Know,' ending it with a dancing turn. Oh dear!" Jean consulted the paper again. "They say here that she had a 'tender voice.' Oh dear! No wonder they said I was 'in excellent form' and that I sang with the same 'vigor and skill' as I did when I was here before. That was when I visited a couple of years ago. Such fun we had! After all, 'Villanell'—they misspell it here—is a professional mezzo-soprano solo by the Belgian Eva Dell'Acqua. It's often sung these days. My silly encore about the merry robin was perfect for this audience.

"That last skit 'Stage Struck' was quite excellent. A great improvement over that 'Balm of Gilead.' 'Balm' certainly was *balmy!* One of those silly farces based on a secret wedding. Pretending to have a quarrel in front of the couple thought to be secretly engaged to 'teach' them about the perils of marriage? The perils of marriage are evident enough to me. And with complications leading to attempted murder? How easily your Dawson audience is amused. I believe they laughed throughout." She shook her head. "At least 'Stage Struck' required a smattering of education. Those two star-struck lovers who could not speak for themselves except in well-known lines from Shakespeare. Now *that* was entertaining."[2]

"You forget how rare such entertainments are here, Pussy," Dollie said a little sternly. "We have experienced a famine in things dramatic for months. Nearly all entertainments have been of the *olio* [slick, usually Italian, vaudeville] order. Few attempts have been made in carrying a story through the movements of drama."

"Have I told you that Stanley Adams, our naughty baritone, has turned to drama?" Jean interjected. "Two plays he's written, neither of them very good. He and his wife are off to England. Both, I believe, are to take lessons to improve their music. She, as I've told you, is a pianist of middling talent."

"How is your friend Edith Miller getting on?" asked Dollie, pouring tea that had been brought in on a tray by a silent local girl. "I do hope she recovered from her indisposition."

"Oh, yes, she has indeed. She returned to the Winnipeg stage after several months with a vengeance. She sang 'The Syrene's Song'—*Mon coeur s'ouevre a ta voix*—from

Samson and Delilah.³ You know, the grand opera by Camille Saint-Saëns? He's become popular recently. French, you understand. The Women's Musical Club had an all-French event last year. Edith was Delilah, of course, and that aria is the one in which she seduces Samson. It's a difficult one, legato singing over a very wide range. She's a mezzo-soprano now after all her training. Our Edith has certainly changed from the modest Portage la Prairie girl she was, though I believe she's still religious.

"She sang for Sir Alexander Mackenzie, you remember. Did I write you about that?"

Dollie set her tea cup down on the wicker table. "No, Pussy, I don't believe so," she said. "Perhaps...I'm not sure." She regarded her aunt, her face puzzled.

"Well, he did a cross-Canada tour gathering information on folk music. That's his great interest these days. It had a grand title. Something like the Cycle of Music Festivals of the Dominion of Canada. The idea was that choirs across Canada with their own conductors would prepare music—mostly British, of course. Then Sir Alexander McKenzie—principal of the Royal Academy in London, you know—would swoop in to each place and take over from the local conductors."

Dolly nodded. "I suppose Winnipeg was involved in all this?"

"Oh yes," Jean replied. "Our Welshman, Mr. Rhys Thomas, rehearsed the festival chorus until they could scarcely stand. He was so eager to have them in fine fettle for the great man's visit in May. Sir Alexander was to conduct them when he arrived.⁴ They did 'The Song of Hiawatha' by Samuel Coleridge-Taylor.⁵ I believe about 250 voices participated in Winnipeg alone. He had just received a medal from the Queen. Or did he get it while he was here? I cannot recall."⁶

"Surely you mean Samuel Taylor Coleridge, Pussy?"

"No, no," said Jean emphatically. "I don't mean the famous poet. Oh, I *do* enjoy *The Rime of the Ancient Mariner*. No, I mean the American composer. He has just composed this three-part cantata about Longfellow's epic legend of Hiawatha and Minnehaha. It uses North American materials, just as Dvořák used so-called 'negro tunes' in his *New World Symphony*. That's *still* causing a great to-do; the *Guardian* called it 'grotesque.'⁷ It's supposed to be completely free of European models, though I don't agree. In fact, I'm not sure 'Hiawatha' was a good choice at all. Surely there are pieces based on Canadian folk music that they might have used." Jean sighed.

"As I was saying," she went on, "Edith sang for him at a small supper party Sir Daniel McMillan gave for Sir Alexander and his entourage at Government House. That Verner woman was there. She has quite replaced me as the city's soprano."⁸ She sighed again.⁹

"But I mustn't complain. I have such a good life and I have reached a stage where singing becomes more trying. I can no longer reach the high notes I used to sing. Yet I take the greatest delight in accompanying others and teaching my dear pupils."

"And where is Edith now? Is she still in Portage?"

"Oh, no. She went to New York for the winter two years ago. Her health perhaps? We got word here and there through Charles's column. Apparently she sang at a most fashionable At Home for 250 guests along with our own sweet tenor Bobbie Campbell. And..." Jean leaned forward to pick up her cup and saucer and took a sip as if to increase the suspense. "She was offered her old position there at that prominent New York church at an increase of $300 over her former salary. And that was over $1,000! Imagine! I might have taken it. But she declined. The New York papers couldn't understand it.

'The young lady is attached to Portage la Prairie in a manner quite unaccountable in view of her superior vocal acquirements,' they said, or something like that."[10]

"Well!" said Dollie. "How could she decline such an offer? It really is incomprehensible. I can't tell you how much I look forward to the day when I return to Toronto. It's only about six months now. Civilization. How I long for it!"

"Edith came back to the West that spring," Jean continued, "to take up her position as organist, choir leader, and soloist at Knox Church. Quite a step down from a big New York church and an enormous salary. Perhaps her mother had something to do with it. Before you could turn around, she was resigning from Knox to go to England. She was persuaded to stay on until the end of August. No one is indispensable, but she was such a gem in Knox Church's crown they could only have been distraught that she was leaving so soon. She already had concert engagements arranged in the British Isles. Sir Alexander is behind this, I believe. Or, possibly, that scoundrel Colonel Mapleson. Perhaps both. She will be enjoying tea and crumpets there until sometime next year."

"My goodness! She has made a great name for herself, hasn't she? I wish her all success in her life there." Dolly smiled contentedly.

"Oh, well, tonight I suppose we shall have to endure Dawson City's talent again, along with William Douglas's encore. Surely his pianist won't forget his music *again*. The paper promised some improvements in handling, without the waits between the acts. I could show them how to do it efficiently and perhaps I will. I have a mind to organize and direct a production of *Patience* so that you don't have another long drought without drama and music.[12] But, never mind, I shall still be greatly amused tonight. I rather look forward to it."

EDMONTON

Jasper Ave., Edmonton, Alta.

Downtown Edmonton as
Jean saw it on arriving in 1907.

A CHANGE OF SCENE

"Well, my dear Blackberry, we'll just have to make do here until we find more suitable lodgings." Jean Forsyth is addressing the black collie dog she brought back with her from Dawson City. He is one of the pups fathered by her niece Dollie's husband's prize Scottish collie.

Jean has taken small rooms in a residential part of Edmonton that sits far from the downtown where she planned to live. It is 1907 and the city with about 15,000 citizens has just been named capital of the new province of Alberta. The place is drawing the same hordes of immigrants eager to make their fortunes as Winnipeg had a couple of decades before. Places to live are at a premium.

"At least we won't have to manage in a tent, Berry."[1]

Yet the optimistic Jean has no doubt that in good time she will find the kind of place in the centre of the city where she has access to concert halls and the students she intends to teach.

Berry wags his tail. "So, Berry, we shall just get along here for a little bit and it won't be long until I shall find us the kind of place I want. We'll make the best of it. The Riddells are looking for a place for us. And I've spoken with Gertrude Seton-Thompson. She tells me that the opportunities for everything are much greater here. She ought to know, for she is a writer and is very well connected and well informed about all that goes on in this exciting city. She hinted that she's looking for a roommate. Wouldn't that be grand! I can just feel the vibrations in the air. Can't you, dear Berry?"

After her visit to Dawson City, Jean spent a year in Vancouver and the Okanagan Valley with relatives and friends to see if she might teach and perform there. She remembers well the western tour she made with the Edith J. Miller Company in the fall of 1900. They were acclaimed everywhere. Surely by now there would be a desire for concert singers and reliable vocal teachers like herself? Yet there had not been enough response to her advertisements to sing and teach to ensure a decent living in that breathtaking part of the world. Everywhere one heard of the opportunities in the new western province of Alberta and particularly in its booming young capital city.

Berry wags his tail again. "I suppose you'd like to go out," Jean says, patting him energetically. She goes to fetch her coat and walking stick. "Come along then," she says, "Walkies? Let's venture out, even though the weather is far from perfect. You'll see. We'll soon have an excellent life here."

EDMONTON, 1907

When Jean Forsyth arrived in Edmonton, she found a city unlike Winnipeg, where she had lived for a decade. There, she had moved in a social elite intimately connected to eastern wealth and business and largely insulated from other groups in the city. The completely different community of North Winnipeg's ethnic poor had only begun to make a few impressions on the British society at the city's core. Yet Edmonton was far more egalitarian than Winnipeg had been or was. For one thing, zealous British sentiment had reached its zenith at Queen Victoria's Diamond Jubilee on May 24, 1897. From then on it had faded rapidly, partly because of colonial losses in the Boer War. That same British group settled in Edmonton at first, but their weaker political and civic hold was soon disrupted. It would remain merely one of several groups that vied strenuously for control of the new city. Before long, streets with names like Queen, Elizabeth, and Fraser were renamed with numbers as grid-like as New York City's. Only a few early names remained.

Still, Edmonton was a place of fast and dubious deals. Here, as in early Winnipeg, Indian land was appropriated for ludicrously low, or no, "compensation." There were a few feeble protests later on, such as the 1904 petition to Ottawa by a group of Edmonton bands demanding that the Indian Agent be removed for letting land sell for as much as 70 percent below market value. Most Indian bands only dimly sensed that they were being cheated. For the time being, their few protests did not seriously undermine the expansion of the settlement.[1]

More strident—and effective—were the protests of the trade unions that almost at once challenged the capitalists who were determined to build a community occupying virtually free land on the backs of ill-paid workers. Such had been the case in Winnipeg, where in 1907 there were at least nineteen millionaires.[2]

Even before Edmonton was incorporated as a city in 1904, a vast, unmanageable tidal wave of immigrants—far better informed than those who came to Winnipeg well after its establishment—followed hard upon the 1891 completion of the Calgary and Edmonton Railway into the settlement of Strathcona south of the North Saskatchewan River. The first immigration hall began at once welcoming vulnerable immigrants and helping them settle, especially into the fertile farmland that surrounded the city. There followed a long disagreement over the rail advantage Strathcona had over Edmonton until the Lower Level railway bridge was finally completed in 1902. In the meantime, a false burst of "settlement" followed news of the 1897 Gold Rush in the Klondike and Edmonton's advantages as a point of departure. Prospectors passed through and were armed, for a fee, with misleading information from "boosters" about what proved to be impassable routes to the Yukon.[3] By the time Edmonton was incorporated in 1904, the population was 8,350. (That same year Winnipeg's population was roughly ten times greater.)

By 1904 taxi service by horse and cart was available; students began to attend a fledgling Alberta College quickly built in Strathcona; the first car appeared in Edmonton; the city purchased the Edmonton and District Telephone Company; and the Edmonton Opera Company staged its first performance, *Les Cloches de Corneville* (The Chimes of Normandy) by Robert Planquette. A city market had been in place since 1900, while Edmonton's first union—Local 1325 of the United Brotherhood of Carpenters and Joiners—had been active for two years; the city's second union, of bricklayers and craftsmen, for one. The plumbers and pipe fitters union formed a local in 1904, which eventually become Canada's largest in the trade.

It was these trade unions—with many more to follow—that made Edmonton somewhat different from early Winnipeg. Here, workers would not be isolated in a separate district. They could—and did—make their presence and needs known vociferously.

These unions allied with ethnic groups and others who wanted progress and reform. Some businessmen sought efficient management while some reactionaries wanted a continuation of "the good old days." For this reason early politics in Edmonton seemed a strenuous tug-of-war between opposing objectives and visions.[4] The rivalry between North and South (Strathcona) Edmonton complicated matters until their final amalgamation in 1912.

Jean Forsyth would have heard of the lightning-speed, exciting developments in Edmonton. Both in Dawson City in 1905 (when Alberta became a province) and in the Vancouver and Okanagan areas during 1906 and 1907, news of the new capital of the new province would have been everywhere. She could not have entertained any thought of continuing a career in Dawson City; she had seen for herself the primitive state of music and entertainments there. Instead she attempted to establish a career on the West Coast. She had seen Vancouver and Victoria during her tour in 1900 with the Edith J. Miller Company. Both classical and sacred music must have progressed from what she knew was already a high professional level. Performance venues were excellent too. Perhaps she found too few families interested in vocal teaching for their children or themselves. Perhaps she found that the society there—cultured, but isolated, stagnant, and retrograde—was too stifling for her. She was no stranger to challenges. Indeed, she seemed uniquely fitted to face and deal with them. She had grown up in exciting pioneer Chatham, then experienced a life in early Winnipeg at a time when entertainments were just emerging from amateurism and there was no Humane Society. Her years in Chatham and especially Winnipeg had shaped her into what many held as a stereotype of the "Northwest Girl." She was independent, brave, and energetic. She was "as comfortable with a duchess as with a p'liceman's girl." She had "a freshness of soul, a wild freedom of spirit, a boundless and never-failing fund of hope, with a charming naiveté of manner."[5]

Whatever her reasons for moving there, Edmonton stirred her imagination. In 1907 she arrived in a city alive with the buzz of its creation. This was hardly surprising, since the pioneer entrepreneurs, such as John A. McDougall and *Edmonton Bulletin* founder Frank Oliver put forth extravagant visionary ideas of the city from a time when it had only 500 citizens.[6] Oliver's career as journalist and politician played a large role in Edmonton and Alberta generally. At the time Jean Forsyth arrived, he was already minister of the Interior and superintendent-general of Indian Affairs. She encountered a brand new city that was now a hub for railway travel, with the Alberta and Great Waterways Railway northeast to Fort McMurray and the Edmonton, Dunvegan and British Columbia Railway taking passengers northwest to the Peace River area. Almost a quarter of the residents already had running water; the first elevator was operating; the Alberta legislature had assembled the previous year in the Thistle Rink; and construction of a proper Alberta legislative building was underway. The University of Alberta had been founded (in Strathcona), though early classes in the Duggan Street School would not start for a year; mail carriers from what was the largest postal station between Winnipeg and Vancouver were delivering mail; the first rabbi, Hyman Goldstick, had just arrived; imported fine china had been available since 1903,[7] local unions—rail workers, blacksmiths, tailors, barbers, teamsters—were springing up everywhere and the first chapter of the Edmonton Trades and Unions Council had recently been established. Within the next year, 1908, the first motion picture would open at the Bijou Theatre, Diamond Park stadium for baseball would open, and the Edmonton Hockey Club (after 1910 the Edmonton Eskimos) would play in the Stanley Cup finals. It was all a dizzying, inspiring burst of activity.

Jean would probably not have heard that in the year she arrived, thousands of acres of the Michel Indian band's land had sold in a four-hour sale at the Empire Theatre, a sale from which the band received no profits.

Mayor William A. Griesbach had been elected for what would be, as usual in these early days, a short term of only one year. His mayoralty would have suited Jean, for he was one of those who wanted older days to return and ran the city with strict economy. He had been one of the members of the all-important Volunteer Fire Brigade as well as a hockey player in the Edmonton amateur league. But his delays in extending power and sanitary services and further delays setting up the dial telephone system and the street railway system ensured that he would be replaced (with 70 percent of the vote) in the next election by businessman John A. McDougall.

McDougall became "a legendary mayor."[8] He led those who favoured commerce and ran the city on business principles. He fired most of the city officials; he completed the dial telephone system (first in North America); and completed the street railway that cost passengers five cents.

Jean would have been especially interested in, and possibly already knew about, the state of entertainment in the city. Edmonton, she may have heard, strongly favoured the arts from the beginning. As early as 1879—when the population was less than 1,000—readings and recitations were given in various locations around town. Once the railway to South Edmonton (Strathcona) arrived in 1891, the Edmonton Amateur Society started giving performances. The town's first sheriff, Walter Scott Robinson, after seeing the first professional troupe perform in 1892, built a theatre on the south side of Jasper Avenue at the bottom of 97th Street (site of today's Edmonton Convention Centre). Robertson's Hall soon became the preferred place for social gatherings. In 1900 the Garrick Club was founded; in 1903 the Edmonton Operatic and Dramatic Society took shape.[9]

In 1904, Robertson's Hall burned down. At the same time, the Thistle Rink opened and presented plays in what must have been an unsatisfactory place until Alexander Cameron built the Edmonton Opera House two years later. In 1906, the first Empire Theatre (there were eventually three) opened to vaudeville shows, but closed for lack of interest in a couple of years. The year Jean arrived, Alexander Cameron opened his second theatre, the Kevin Theatre, but it—like Robertson's Hall—burned down, in this case only two months after it opened. Unlike Robertson, he began rebuilding at once and opened the renamed Dominion Theatre the next year. That same year, the first Ukrainian play, under the direction of Michael Gowda, was performed, establishing a tradition of ethnic theatre that combined entertainment with propaganda.[10]

Arriving in 1907, Jean was at the end of a surge of arrivals in the city. Construction of residences had not kept pace with the astonishing increase of population. Many—some 3,294 people—were making do in tents.[11] She had no option but to rent a large new store with double windows in a residential district far from the city centre where—as in Winnipeg—she planned to live.

Yet she had plans to brighten her surroundings. Before long she "converted it into a charming studio by covering the walls from the floor up with glazed chintz having huge roses on a dark green ground. Rugs, cushions and potted plants turned the embrasures of the curtained windows into cosy spots. The whole effect was most attractive."[12]

HAROLD SPEED CAPTURES EDITH ON CANVAS, 1906

Edith Miller stood still and upright in Harold Speed's studio at 8 Holland Park, London. She faced to the left, giving him her profile. She was dressed in one of her performance gowns. It was completely white. The long skirt was made of a rich material and fell in wide pleats from her waist, catching the light here and there. Her bodice was swan-like: three long layers of scalloped lace fell from her shoulder and circled around the front like waves. A softer layer, featherlike, fell to her elbow. Her arms were invisible, for she was wearing long white gloves—silk or perhaps fine kid leather—that concealed even her elbows. Her dark hair was gathered up into a simple bun on the back of her head.

It was 1906. Harold Speed was painting her portrait.

This was the second time she had visited his studio. The first time the horse-faced, balding red-haired man with an eloquent red moustache had welcomed her into his studio she had been wearing a simple navy day dress and a becoming hat with white feathers.

Harold Speed gestured to the "sitter's throne" and she moved across the cluttered studio and sat down.

"Well, Miss Miller," he said, moving about from right to left to appraise his subject. "I understand that you are a famous singer. I have been commissioned to paint your portrait and I can see that it will be a pleasure to do so."

Edith gave a slight smile. "Thank you, Mr. Speed. The pleasure is mine."

He could see that she was nervous. "You are from America, I understand. I know almost nothing of the place. I have travelled through Europe on a scholarship I received from the Royal Academy of Art School a dozen years ago. I won their gold medal."

He cocked his small long oval head, somewhat like a gnome puzzling over something in the woods.

"I suppose that is a coincidence," Edith ventured, looking more relaxed. "For I, too, won such a medal, at the Toronto Conservatory of Music in Toronto about the same time. And a scholarship that went with it—though not a travelling one."

He caught her accent, though she enunciated each word carefully. "Ah," he said, "so you are from Toronto. I've heard of it but haven't the least notion where it is. Is it on one of the coasts?"

She laughed quietly. "No, no. It is rather in the middle, but further east than west. I am from a much smaller place called Portage la Prairie. You won't have heard of it. It's in the province of Manitoba. That is closer to the middle of the country. Mainly people farm there. Grain," she added, seeing his bewilderment. "Mostly wheat, though I have learned that here you call it corn."

He shook his head, thinning red hair glinting in the sun. He wore a high-collared white shirt with a wide black silk artist's tie and an olive green jacket with wide lapels. This Edith noticed as she began to look around.

"Please, Miss Miller," he said. "Could you stand up now and simply walk about where your fancy takes you. You might like to examine some of my sketches and works propped here and there about the room." She stood at once as if ordered to do so and walked slowly towards the window. Stately, he thought.

She pointed to a red chalk sketch of a man's head and shoulders and, turning, asked, "Did you do this one?"

"No, my dear, that is by the great master Leonardo da Vinci. I keep it there for inspiration."

She nodded slowly. "And this one?" she asked of a pencil sketch that had all sorts of arms and legs in it.

"Yes, that is mine. I usually work on sketches before beginning a portrait. Trying out different methods. In those I was deciding whether or not to approach the portrait in terms of 'mass.' That is, blocks of light and dark areas for the composition. The rule of thumb is two-thirds light, one-third dark. Although, as you might guess, there can be exceptions."

And your portrait might be one, he thought. He had been observing her through-out, noting her upright posture, her reticence, the radiance that seemed to emanate from her. It is a certainty, he thought, that she has a commanding stage presence. She carries it with her in her proud neck. Yet, he mused, looking again at Edith, there is a vitality here, a spark of something almost flirtatious in the way her eyes lifted as she turned her head. But that is in the minor key. He chuckled aloud as he thought of how he had slipped into a musical comparison. She *is* music, he thought. That is her very essence.

She laughed too, a girlish echo. She was looking at his palette, splotched and scratched and looking for all the world, she thought, like a muddy accident of Red River clay.

*

Now, a week later, he held that same palette, resting it on his arm. He stood as he painted, peeking back and forth at Edith as he daubed oil paint on the large canvas. He had asked her to wear something white, something she had performed in. He had chosen to paint her in profile, as he had painted a few other subjects, such as Mrs. Laura C. H. Coxe, founder of the Watlington Library. Most of his sitters (or standers, as the case may be)—mainly peers, distinguished doctors, powerful civic officials, famous professors, military officers, high-ranking members of the clergy (though he had done a few of labourers)—had been three-quarter face or facing front. The year before he had done an official portrait of His Majesty, King Edward VII, in his royal robes.

He had placed a large pot of lilies overlapping the back of her skirt. She held a hym-nal. These symbols suggested religion: Easter, the season of sacrifice and redemption, and the religious music Edith had so often sung. Yet behind her on her right was a table draped in a gorgeous fabric that extended past her. Balancing on its front edge, "darkly visible," was a porcelain figurine—apparently of two mythological beings, lovers per-haps—that suggested only faintly that minor key Harold Speed had noticed at their first meeting. Such accoutrements, intended to suggest the personality of the subject, were typical in official portraits. Harold Speed called this "decorative pageantry."

"Lady in White" Harold Speed's oil portrait of Edith Miller,
1906, Royal Academy of Arts Library, London, England.

Occasionally he addressed Edith's right ear, which faced him. "Art, my dear, is the rhythmic expression of feeling." He swayed a little as he said this before raising an inquisitive eye to see what she did. Nothing. Good, he thought. She would be a steady, cooperative subject. He refrained from questions.

"You know," he remarked, "the portrait of Robert Burns by Rudolph Lehmann fails because he missed the essence. He painted Burns as people casually saw him—he looks like a prosperous businessman. But G. E. Watts's portrait of him, that's a different matter. There you see the man who wrote the poetry."

Speed had placed Edith standing tall in the middle of his painting, like a caryatid holding up the Erechtheion porch on the Acropolis. This was deliberate. Later he would write of the "hush and reverence" caused by positioning a figure this way, using as his example Raphael's *Ansidei Madonna*. Her uprightness implied morality, he thought. The vertical lines of her skirt pleats and her neck emphasized this. He placed the rear pleats in shadow and made the front bodice curve gently, rather than abruptly, to minimize the curved lines he believed indicated voluptuousness. The curled petals of the lilies hardly suggested voluptuousness, for they are white symbols of purity.

This was a white painting, one of those exceptions to the usual mix of dark and light. The dark background and Edith's dark hair blending into it emphasized the stark white figure, made more inaccessible because we cannot meet her eyes.

Speed believed that in a portrait the head was "a sort of chord of which the features will be but the component elements. It is expressive of the person." For him, "the habitual cast of thought in any individual affects the shape and mould of the form of the features." Edith's head was strongly upright, her gaze straightforward. Her eyes and brows were mild, her smile with closed lips was hardly perceivable. Her slightly retroussé nose hinted at a dash of mischief. Her upswept hair further softened the effect, for—again, as Speed wrote later—a chignon low on the neck sharpens the features, whereas a bun further up softens the profile.

As Harold Speed painted her, she was a kind of oxymoron: a strong, but gentle woman, a mainly moral, but slightly voluptuous lady, a restrained religious girl, but one with a few pagan tendencies and a hint of mischief.

He named his painting A Lady in White.[1]

While Jean Forsyth was keeping her niece, Dollie Cameron, company in Dawson City, Edith Miller emerged as a much-sought-after singer in Britain. Jean had produced the Gilbert and Sullivan operetta *Patience* in Dawson and she had sung in the choir of St. Andrew's Presbyterian Church where the Camerons worshipped, as well as performing in other entertainments. If she had been appraising the possibility of a career there, she must have come to the conclusion that it was not to be. She'd had a similar experience in Vancouver. She sang in the All Saints' church in Cedar Cove in 1906,[1] but in the end she left the West Coast for Edmonton.

During those same years in the stylish Edwardian era, Edith Miller had quickly risen. She had left Winnipeg for London and Paris in September 1904. Half a year later, the following announcement appeared in the *Manitoba Free Press* for those who were following her career abroad:

> The many friends of Miss Edith J. Miller in Manitoba will be pleased to learn that she is enjoying excellent health and making most favourable progress in her musical studies in Britain. Miss Miller has established a large circle of friends for herself in England and receives instruction and assistance from such able leaders in the musical world as Sir Alexander McKenzie [*sic*] and others. She will fill a number of important engagements during the coming season.[2]

Her first solo concert had been in Queen's Hall in London with the London Symphony Orchestra on the afternoon of Sunday May 13, 1906. Sir Alexander Mackenzie, who had been so taken with her when he visited Winnipeg on his cross-country tour in 1903, was the conductor. In a program that included works by Weber, Dvořák, Mendelssohn, the German composer Adolf Jensen, Cowen, and Rossini's overture to *William Tell*, Edith sang English, Italian, and German lyrics.[3] A major solo concert soon followed at the Aeolian Hall on May 25. The patrons of this concert were all royalty or nobility. The Earl and Countess of Minto had already sponsored Edith in Canada on her western tour in 1900. Donald Smith, Lord Strathcona, a Scottish-born Canadian who had been made a British peer and was about to be appointed high commissioner in London, and Lady Strathcona supported Edith as a Canadian singer. Other patrons were the Prince and Princess of Wales (later George V and Queen Mary), Princess Louise Augusta of Schleswig-Holstein, and the Earl and Countess of Aberdeen.

Edith was the only vocalist in Queen's Hall on May 6 with the London Symphony Orchestra conducted by Sir Alexander Mackenzie, which had recently won high honours in Paris. She sang the "Inflamatus" from Dvořák's *Stabat Mater* (an oratorio interpreted by several composers that presents the

Virgin Mary's brave anguish at the foot of the Crucifix). And, again, she sang Adolf Jensen's "Murmelndes Lüftchen, Blütenwind" (The Murmuring Wind). On May 25, she returned to the Aeolian Hall to give a solo concert. She had become one of the top singers in London's most prestigious locations. (She did not appear in Covent Garden, as that venue favoured opera, which Edith had not yet trained for.)

*

As usual, Charles Wheeler kept readers in Manitoba aware of Edith's successes in Britain. A long article in the *Winnipeg Tribune* in May 1906 quotes several reviews from various Irish cities where Edith had made a tour from April 23 to 28. She sang at Cork, Limerick, Dublin, Belfast, and Ulster. Her programs, designed to appeal to Irish audiences, included: "O, Mio Fernando" from *La Favorita*, "A Chain of Roses" by Lohr, Tennyson's famous "Break, Break" to an old setting, "The Organ Man," Children of London," a few Brahms's songs, "I Once Loved a Boy" (a traditional Irish ballad by Alice Needham) and "The Lament for Earl Patrick Stewart" (a ballad from the Orkney Isles), and other old Irish street ballads. At each concert she was applauded with hearty enthusiasm and encores were demanded.

"Miss Edith J. Miller is an accomplished and extremely pleasing contralto," went a review in Belfast, "Her voice is rich in quality, very sweet in tone, and free from vibrant defects in the various registers. She sang her encore 'Break, Break' with much tenderness and feeling."[4] Elsewhere she was admired for her "fervent and impassioned," "charming," and "well-phrased" interpretations. "Her voice is deliciously rich and mellow; she has a good range," said a Dublin review.[5] These concerts revealed Edith as unsurpassed.

London critics and reviewers, generally more fastidious than other British critics, also raved about Edith's performances. Her "artistic singing," "fine voice, under admirable control," "sentiment and feeling," were praised. "Everywhere the verdict of press and public has been that Miss Miller is a singer of unusual qualities who has a brilliant future to look forward to."[6]

During the previous fall, Edith had been touring the English provinces by a stroke of luck. She stood in for the contralto Muriel Foster when Foster married. Foster was hailed the greatest English singer to emerge early in the twentieth century. Though not an opera singer, she won fame as Sir Edward Elgar's favourite artist and key to success for his great oratorios *The Dream of Gerontius* (based on a poem by John Henry Newman that traced a pious man's soul from death through judgment to purgatory), *The Apostles*, *The Kingdom* and other works. She excelled as well in the music of Mendelssohn, Bach and a host of other masters.[7]

On May 25, 1906, Edith sang the new musical version of Sappho's poem "Hymn to Aphrodite" with a piano accompanist at the Aeolian Hall in London. Four months later, she sang it again with Henry Wood conducting the New Queen's Hall Orchestra.[8] It was the finale performance in the series of Promenade Concerts that year. This "Ode to Sappho" was the only one of Sappho's manuscripts to survive intact. Edith sang the role of Sappho pleading with Aphrodite to inspire love in a reluctant female lover. It is filled with the anguish of heart-break and the desperate hope that the goddess can change the situation. Partly because of her deep rich contralto voice, Edith was once again cast in the role of a temptress.

In the first few months of 1907, Edith's London schedule was full. These concerts included a Scottish performance to honour Robert Burns at Royal Albert Hall on January 26;[8] one for the Wimbledon Nine O'Clocks (a prestigious series of evening concerts) on January 28; Elgar's oratorio *The Dream of Gerontius* at Royal Albert Hall on February 13;[9] and one with the Amateur Orchestral Society in Queen's Hall on February 15.[10] For this latter concert, the Prince of Wales, who had heard her sing in Canada and had been a patron of her first two London concerts, had specifically requested that Edith Miller sing.

She was asked to perform for the opening of the Keats-Shelley Exhibition at Stratford House on March 20, where she would sing musical settings of the verses of these two Romantic poets. Again, this was an affair that involved many British aristocrats. Princess Louise, the Duchess of Argyll, was the patron of the event, which was given with the permission of the Duke and Duchess of Sutherland, who organized the display of relics of the two poets. The executive committee included more notable patrons: the Earl of Crewe (statesman and writer); Sidney Colvin (curator of the prints and drawings at the British Museum); Lord Curzon (famed former viceroy of India); H. Buxton Forman (antiquarian bookseller who compiled bibliographies of Shelley and Keats); George Leveson Gower (barrister and Liberal politician), Walter Leigh Hunt (descendant of the poet Leigh Hunt who was a friend of Keats and Shelley), and Hon. George Wyndham (Conservative politician, statesman, and man of letters), among others.[11] Edith had also been booked for performances in many private dining rooms in the months ahead.[12]

The "crowning honour" of Edith's career occurred on February 15, 1907, at a concert at Queen's Hall, the second of two held on February 14 and 15.

After the February 14 concert at Royal Albert Hall, Charles Wheeler reports from letters and clippings Edith has sent him, she was "warmly congratulated" in the artists' room by the conductor Sir Frederick Bridge. He told her that "she was so good a musician as not to give him an anxious moment during the entire performance" of *The Dream of Gerontius,* in which she sang the part of the angel. He also said that he was "very glad" that she was to sing in Elgar's new oratorio *The Kingdom* (1906), a narrative of the lives of Jesus's disciples and the early Pentecost church) in the same concert series. Edith would sing the same role Muriel Foster sang in its first production. Others famous in London's music world crowded around Edith too, overwhelming her with congratulations on her performance as the angel: Sir Hubert Parry, former director of the London Academy of Music, now music critic for the *Daily Telegraph*; Joseph Bennett, organist and the music critic preceding Sir Hubert Parry for the *Telegraph*; H. J. Wood, the Queen's Hall conductor; David Ffrangcon-Davies, a Welsh bass vocalist and author of the newly published *The Singing of the Future*; and many others.[13] The review concluded, "There can be no doubt some leading festival arrangements will follow as the result of Miss Miller's *Gerontius* success."

The next evening's performance with the Royal Amateur Orchestral Society in Queen's Hall on February 15 surpassed even this accolade. The occasion was a special "smoking concert" (for men to converse on politics, with smoking allowed), one of a series. Edith "the new Canadian mezzo soprano" was paired with Madame Suzanne Adams. She was an American soprano who had studied with Mme Marchesi and sung in the Paris Opera, returned to the U.S., and then sang opera in Covent Garden. She was the same age as Edith and also attractive. Signor Paolo Tosti was the conductor.

What was special about this concert? The king and several peers were in attendance. An armchair a few yards in front of the orchestra was set for Edward VII. Other chairs were placed in a semicircle around his. To the king's right sat the Prince of Wales and the animated Marquis de Soveral (a.k.a. the Blue Monkey because of his blue-black hair and swarthy skin), a Portuguese diplomat, who was a member of the "Marlborough Set," as close friends of the king were known. To the king's left were the Earl of Pembroke and the Austrian ambassador, Count Mensdorff, a second cousin of Edward VII. Others in the royal semi-circle were the Duke of Richmond, the Duke of Gordon, Earl Farquhar, Viscount Alverstone, Viscount Bridport, Baron Eversley, Admiral of the Fleet Sir John Fisher, the Lord Mayor of London, the Norwegian explorer Fridtjof Nansen, and "other notables in the musical and literary circles."[14]

Promptly at nine o'clock His Majesty arrived and proceeded without ceremony to his armchair to the singing of "God Save the King." When Edith sang the "Gavotte," "His Majesty's head was observed to be nodding to the rhythm of the music, and following his lead the courtly gathering gave our Canadian artist a double encore. Similar honors awaited her second appearance." The king ordered a lovely bouquet of flowers for Edith after her first song.

Singing for the king and his entourage would have been honour enough, especially since he stayed until the end of the concert, which was not always the case. Yet greater honour was yet to come. After the concert ended the king asked to have Miss Miller presented to him. He was kind and gracious "as to nearly overcome her self-possession."

"You sing most charmingly," he said at their private meeting, "You are a Canadian, I understand. From what part do you come?"

"Manitoba."

"Have you been in England long?" he asked.

"About two years, Your Majesty."

"You have a very beautiful voice and sing with great charm, and I am sure Canada must be pleased with a vocalist of your accomplishments."

The Prince of Wales also "warmly praised her singing."

To this account from Edith, Charles Wheeler added, "No doubt she was a proud girl that night. Manitoba is also proud of the success of her premier vocalist, proud of her social conquests, proud of the pluck, persistence and determination she has shown in overcoming all obstacles, reaching upwards and ever upwards until the goal of her ambition has been reached in listening to the praises of her king in person."[15]

THE EDWARDIAN EDMONTON THAT WELCOMED JEAN

Only two days after the *Edmonton Bulletin* announced that Jean Forsyth from Vancouver "will visit with relatives for a short time," the same newspaper declared, "Miss Forsyth of Vancouver, formerly of Winnipeg, where she is known as a talented soprano, intends in future to make her home in Edmonton."[1]

Both the Cautleys and the Pardees in Edmonton were related to Jean. Richard W. Cautley had moved to Edmonton after the Gold Rush in the Klondike, where he formed the land-surveying firm of Cautley and Côté, and his wife Mabel was involved in many women's organizations. Edwin C. Pardee was manager of the Edmonton Bank of Montreal and his mother was a Forsyth in Chatham, where he and his wife Marjorie (née Mowat) used to live. He was known as "one of Edmonton's ablest financiers."[2] These two couples must have made some arrangements for Jean while she was still in Vancouver. Less than a month after she arrived in Edmonton, an announcement in the *Saturday News* on May 4, 1907 said that Jean Forsyth, "the well-known vocal teacher who has lately come to Edmonton to reside will give a song recital in the Edmonton Opera House on Thursday, May 16. She will be assisted by some of the best local talent."

The same day the *Edmonton Bulletin* wrote, "Music-lovers in Edmonton are looking forward to the song recital. This will be the introduction to an Edmonton audience of a singer whose reputation as an artiste has preceded her from Detroit and Winnipeg, and will afford an opportunity of enjoying the performance of an operatic soprano who has profited by the musical tuition under masters on both sides of the Atlantic." Another announcement a few days later in the *Edmonton Bulletin* informed the public that Miss Jean Forsyth and Miss Seton-Thompson have taken apartments at 767 Fifth Street.[3] That same day, an advertisement appeared in the same paper:

MISS JEAN FORSYTH

VOCAL TEACHER

ITALIAN METHOD. PUPIL ROYAL ACADEMY, LONDON, ENG. FOR TERMS APPLY FIFTH STREET BETWEEN 5 AND 6 P.M. MONDAYS AND WEDNESDAYS. 767 5TH STREET.

Mrs. B. J. (Esther) Saunders, President of the Daughters of the Empire, held important executive positions such as president of the Hospital Aid and president of the Local Council of Women.

The "best local talent" who were to assist Jean at her concert were Miss Iva Wright, pianist; Howard Stutchbury, a baritone well known to Edmontonians; and William J. Hendra on the viola. Hendra had won medals in two of the largest musical competitions in England.

Gertrude Seton-Thompson was the daughter of Chevalier John Enoch Thompson of Toronto. Her uncle, Ernest Thompson Seton, was the naturalist writer who wrote the 1904 classic *Monarch, the Big Bear of Tallac* (the bear that appears on the California flag). Gertrude was also a writer. She was one of those Edmontonians— like the mayor, William Griesbach—who hoped to establish a facsimile of British society and customs in the new western city. Gertrude was almost the same age as Jean and would have been a lively, witty, and informative companion, not to mention a useful link to the newspaper.[4]

Naturally, Marjorie Pardee was among the "patronesses" for Jean's concert debut. Her husband, Edwin, had been the first manager of the Bank of Montreal, which opened in 1903 in an unpretentious frame building with a false front on Jasper Avenue. The bank paid $15,000 for the lot to build a permanent building— the highest price for city property to that date, which caused a rise in real estate value. When the permanent building "in imposing solidity" at the corner of Howard and Jasper with its massive Greek portico and high domed ceiling opened, the first and second floors—"handsomely furnished"—were allocated to the Pardees as a residence. Portraits of the financiers who had reputations on both sides of the Atlantic graced the walls—a kind of instant imported lineage. These included Lord Strathcona, Sir George Drummond, Sir William Macdonald, and others with British-Celtic surnames.[5]

There were eight additional patronesses for Jean's concert: Louisa Beck, Florence Riddell, Jessie Emery, Minnie Scott, Esther Saunders, Annie Nicholls, and Dr. Ella Scarlett-Synge. Dr. Scarlett-Synge was the grandniece of General Scarlett, who led the charge of the Heavy Brigade at the Battle of Balaclava in 1854 during the Crimean War. Her late father was Lord Abinger, General Scarlett's son. Her mother, née Helen Magruder, a beauty, was the first American girl to become a British peeress. Ella Scarlett-Synge became a medical doctor and practised in South Africa and Korea, where she was physician to the royal household

Mrs. J. H. (Florence) Riddell, wife of the president of Alberta College.

Mrs. Sydney B. (Ethel) Woods, wife of Deputy Attorney General, a patroness for Jean's first concert in Edmonton.

before coming to Edmonton. She was a small woman "with erect bearing, a rather absorbed expression, and an air of quiet determination,"[6] a familiar sight—often riding her horse Goldie—in and around the city.

Florence Riddell, a rather romantic-looking woman, was the wife of the new president of Alberta College, Rev. John H. Riddell, who—in keeping with its origins—was Methodist. The Rev. Riddell was a violinist who had been briefly on the staff of Wesley College in Winnipeg before moving to Edmonton in 1903 to help found Alberta College.[7] Jean already knew the Riddells. She and Florence had attended many of the same social events in Winnipeg before the Riddells left. The Riddells must have been an important contact for Jean, since she was hired by Alberta College to teach vocal music in the fall. It is possible that it was the promise of this employment that drew Jean to Edmonton in the first place.

Louisa Beck was the wife of the Hon. Nicholas D. Beck, Q.C., an Ontario-born and -educated lawyer who, soon after Jean arrived, joined the Supreme Court of Alberta. Her brother was the well-known Toronto priest Father John Read Teefy. She was already respected as an energetic philanthropist.

Jessie Emery, born and raised in Scotland, was married to Edward Emery, a lawyer in practice with Louisa Beck's husband until Beck was appointed to the Supreme Court.

Minnie Scott's husband was Justice David Lynch Scott, son of a Scottish farmer and raised in Brampton, Ontario. He had served in the military and had practised law in Regina before moving to Edmonton. Just as Jean arrived he was appointed to the Supreme Court of Alberta.

Esther Saunders, a stout matron of United Empire Loyalist (UEL) descent, was the wife of Major Bryce J. Saunders of the Alberta Mounted Rifles. She would hold several important executive positions in the city, notably as president of the Edmonton Public Hospital, president of the Local Council of Women, and president of the Daughters of the Empire (known in the East as the Imperial Daughters of the Empire).

Annie Nicholls was married to Dr. Alfred A. Nicholls, a graduate of the University of Manitoba, who worked at the Edmonton Public Hospital.

Ethel Woods, a handsome, formidable-looking woman, was the wife of the deputy attorney-general, Sydney Woods, K.C. These nine patronesses of Jean's were clearly married to a phalanx of upper class, rich, powerful men: two Supreme Court of Alberta judges, a military major, two doctors, a lawyer, a bank manager, a minister who headed the Alberta College, a deputy attorney general. The backgrounds and activities of these women included the usual British cues: the UEL, birth in Britain, the Imperial Order Daughters of the Empire (IODE), executive charity positions, membership in the Sons of London (that promoted fellowship and return trips to the old country for Londoners abroad), and Protestant affiliations. All were wealthy women whose names would appear frequently in the social pages of the burgeoning city. These were the types of immigrants Mayor Griesbach, who favoured the "old school," hoped in vain would dominate the city. For the moment they were a notable force, partly because their doings—no matter how trivial—dominated the news.

In Edmonton, Jean was welcomed by the same upper-class elites that had been her friends in Winnipeg. She could count on them to support the arts and patronize her concerts. If, in fact, Mrs. Riddell was a friend of her cousins Mabel Cautley and Marjorie Pardee, and had alerted her husband to the arrival of a qualified, extraordinary vocal teacher and performer for his college, Jean might have owed her employment at the college to her patronesses as well. Among the many announcements about Jean's recital was a short interview for the *Edmonton Bulletin*. The interviewer asked, "What differences do you note in musical conditions in Canada, east and west? Or have we any 'musical conditions' here at all?" To this Jean replied "with characteristic energy," "Surely, the West has talent, more latent than developed it is true; but in time it will be developed. I know that Sir Alexander Mackenzie on his Canadian tour remarked upon the exceptionally good quality of the choruses he met with in these Western towns."[8]

There were many announcements in the paper to alert readers to her upcoming concert. Even her program of songs was given beforehand: Benjamin Godard's "Chanson de Florian," Samuel Strelitzki's "Day-Dreams," "Villanelle," by Eva Dell'Acqua, and Coro Del Teatro Regio's "L'Amour," among others. Her patronesses saw to it that she whetted the appetites of friends by having her sing at teas, just as she had done before her first concert in Winnipeg.

JEAN FACES THE MUSIC AGAIN

Jean sipped her tea. It tasted bitter. "Oh no, not again!" she exclaimed to no one in particular. Gertrude had gone off somewhere. The two collies stirred at her feet. She had taken in the black-and-tan Zip from the street, an exact match for Blackberry, apart from Berry's white flash of bib.

She was reading a review of her recital in the *Edmonton Bulletin*. "Why was I nervous?" she wondered, her lips uncharacteristically tight. "When I have *so* much experience, sung *so* many concerts, stood on *so* many stages, faced *so* many audiences filled with top-ranking officials and the cream of society!"

"My 'first group of songs,'" she read. "'She was not at her best.' If only it weren't true," she sighed, "I haven't slowed down *that* much!"

Nor, she thought, did they appreciate my East Indian love lyrics. "'Quaint!'" they said, "'Uncommon'! 'More suited to a drawing room than a recital'! Nonsense! Of course they were uncommon. That's why I thought an audience would find them engaging, refreshing, challenging. Instead they admired what has been accepted as concert fare for decades. My French songs, especially their 'wealth of feeling,' and Del Teatro Riego's 'L'Amour' were sung with 'dramatic force.' *That* 'delighted' them. The only one that got an encore was 'Chanson de Florian.' As if an encore was the exception and not the rule at my performances! Then they found my last group of songs 'airy, musical, bright' giving me 'a suitable medium.' 'Airy'? 'Suitable'? 'Bright'? So much less than I hoped for, though I confess I was nervous at the start and knew it, which only served to make me *more* nervous."

She sighed deeply as she added another cube of sugar to her tea with the silver sugar tongs. She read further. How annoying, she thought as she stirred her tea, noting that the other two performers were praised. Of course, they are known so well here. And William Hendra just played in the first Alberta Music Festival. I'm sure I saw my student Jackson Hanby in the male chorus.

She tapped the teaspoon on her saucer and took a sip of tea. Her thoughts drifted to Jackson Hanby. He's moved his Schaeffer piano business here, and he's become choirmaster at McDougall's United Church. He's well on his way.

Of course, she reflected, I am the newcomer here, else I should have been in that festival too. Jean sighed again.

She cast her mind back to the recital, which she knew had drawn the *crème de la crème*. There was a party from Government House, including Mrs. Bulyea herself, with Miss Middlemiss, her guest from Brantford, and Mr. Babbit. Surely he's Annie Babbit's brother. Of course Justice and Mrs. Scott were there, and my dear cousin and her husband Marjorie Pardee. My other supporters were there too: Florence Riddell, Esther Saunders, Jessie Emery, Ethel Woods, Annie Nicholls, Louisa Beck. Gertrude, of course.

And so many others! Oh, dear! I noticed Mrs. McDougall, Lovisa, I believe her name is. Her husband John A. was one of the original pioneers from Ontario who profited from the Winnipeg real estate boom before moving here. He and his partner Secord were fur and outfitting merchants—and more real estate, I think. Now they have just begun a financial business, I believe. Rich as Croesus. And their daughter Alice. I fear I have disappointed them all.

Jean folded the paper briskly, as if to make it disappear. She patted Berry's head, then Zip's. She poured herself more tea thoughtfully. "Oh well," she reassured herself. "I mustn't let this lower my spirits. I've overcome the same thing before, and I shall do so again." She lifted her chin defiantly.[2]

JEAN TAKES UP HER EVER-INCREASING INTERESTS

"The perfection of a really enjoyable tea is that at which one may enjoy music, flowers, a cosy chat, and the comforting brew that women the world over like best of all at the mystic hour of five." So wrote "Peggy"—Gertrude Balmer Watt—in her society column "The Mirror" for the *Saturday News* on May 11, 1907.

The tea in question had been held a few days earlier at the home of Ethel Woods, one of Jean's patronesses. It was "a veritable poem in roses." "Splendid roses were massed, great bunches of them," everywhere. Dark red roses on the piano and on small tables. In the tea room "they rose from the table in bewildering pink splendour." Centred on the polished walnut table a silver fern pot rose "from a sea of pale green tulle." Four smaller fern pots stood at the four corners bracketing high cut-glass vases of pink roses at each end. Above the table hung a pagoda-shaped *electrolier* [chandelier] swathed in pink *crêpe* paper and hung with a "riot of long trailing marsh grasses, deep purple flags [irises] and other quaint blooms." The light was subdued into a rosy "fairy gleam."

Even the hostess was gowned in "pale pink chiffon, with a lovely lace overdress of the handsomest Battenberg (an American tape lace in which areas of elaborate patterns are linked by bands of net). She was, as always, according to "Peggy," "the sweet and gracious *chatelaine*."

Jean had not left behind the "teas galore" which brightened her social world in Winnipeg. And, as before, she sang at this one. Now the ladies' costumes, hats, and hairstyles were fully Edwardian. Most, like the senator's wife, blonde beauty Helen Roy, and Cecile Côté, the land surveyor's wife, wore tailored suits with soft A-line (or "Princess") long skirts. Helen was the granddaughter of pioneer Rev. George McDougall, twice mayor of Edmonton. Her suit was brown, her hat deep shades of *bordeaux*. Turban hats were the latest style and some guests wore these. The most lavishly dressed was Constance Hamilton. She wore "a handsome black costume with ermine furs and a jaunty pale blue turban with plumes." Mrs. Metcalfe, a widow from Port Hope, appeared in "the smartest of black and white tailor mades, a striking black hat and ostrich boa." Her daughter, Mrs. Swaisland, "always one of the prettiest women at a tea," was married to a city bank manager. The doctor's wife, petite Mrs. Biggar, wore a "very chic jaunty tailored suit of soft grey, with chapeau to correspond." Mrs. Buchanan, married to the recently appointed provincial librarian, wore "a pretty *bluet* [cornflower or blueberry] tailored costume with a hat in the loveliest tones of brown." These, and other ladies at the tea, were as attractive as youth and wealth could make them. For most, their husbands' important jobs had brought them to Edmonton within the last few years. As "Peggy" noted in the *Saturday News*, "What a tremendously large number of smart people are making Edmonton their home. It was remarked on all sides the number of new faces present, such pretty women too, that one almost despairs of making the rounds to meet them all."[1]

Only two weeks before Jean arrived in Edmonton, the first meeting to organize a Humane Society had been held at city hall. Mayor William Griesbach presided. It had been the agitation of the two chapters of the Daughters of the Empire that had made the issue an urgent matter. As in Winnipeg, the humane treatment of animals concerned the wealthy elite. In Edmonton, however, the more powerful members of society, including politicians, lawyers, and business owners, were involved from the outset, not brought on board gradually as the organization evolved. Griesbach would continue as president. The first vice-president was ex-mayor William Short and the second vice-president was Victoria Bouchier (her husband William J.O. Bouchier advised on rural town sites), Jennie Braithwaite, Dr. Braithwaite's wife, was treasurer and Edmund F. Slocock was secretary.

Life memberships were set at $25; annual memberships were $1 for adults and 25 cents for associates and children.

Several examples of cruelty were raised at this meeting, in particular the use of restrictive reins on horses to prevent lowering of their heads.

It would be no time at all before Jean was involved in this new Edmonton Humane Society. Within a year she was secretary of the organization.[2]

After her first concert in March, Jean and her Winnipeg friend Edna Sutherland, a well-known drama reciter, performed at the opera house in Fort Saskatchewan.[3] Jean stayed with Mrs. Baltz, whose husband was the secretary of the Liberal Association, while Edna stayed at the Manse. The idea was that they would both perform in the opera house. Jean would sing; Edna would give one of her splendid dramatic recitations. It was, according to the *Edmonton Bulletin*, "a diversified programme that gave unqualified enjoyment."[4] Edna Sutherland—almost twenty years younger than Jean—was the daughter of Scottish immigrants to Cobourg, educated at the Emerson College of Oratory in Boston, then a teacher of voice culture and expression at the University of Manitoba. (Later she would be the first Dean of Women at the University of Manitoba.) Edna had a passion for correct pronunciation of English and would leave most of her estate to the University of Manitoba to create a scholarship for students to travel to England and learn to speak proper English.[5]

Not long after Jean and Edna returned from Saskatchewan, the *Edmonton Bulletin* announced Jean's appointment as a vocal teacher on the staff of Alberta College. Jean might have known of this appointment long before through the Riddells, via her cousin Mrs. Pardee. The announcement itself was fulsome. It outlined her education: Royal Academy, London, England, and George Sweet, New York, "who has coached most of the prominent singers in that city." (By then, just as Jean moved to Edmonton, George Sweet huffed off to Florence with all his New York students to open a studio there.)

The announcement then listed her previous posts: in Detroit, she was in "one of the best quartette choirs" and "soloist at the Reformed Jewish synagogue," and "soloist in the Detroit Musical and Harmonic Societies"; in Winnipeg, her work as an accompanist; her soprano solo status in Grace Church under the direction of the late James Tees; her solos in Holy Trinity in Winnipeg.

Finally reference was made to her virtues as a teacher, "proved by the success of her pupils, many of whom occupy leading positions in Winnipeg choirs, while her pupils' recitals were always looked upon as an interesting event in Winnipeg's musical circles."[6]

Jean, and others of her contemporaries in Winnipeg, might have been overlooked in the re-institution of the Winnipeg Conservatory of Music in 1903, but here in Edmonton she had found a niche as a vocal teacher in Alberta College.

The college was relatively new, had expanded dramatically, and was in dire need of qualified instructors. No doubt Jean would have emphasized the fact that Grace Church—her first and main post—was a Methodist institution. Alberta College itself was established mainly in connection with the early Methodist church, a log building known as the McDougall Methodist Church after its first minister George McDougall. It was the Rev. Dr. Riddell—along with other Methodists—who first thought of establishing the college. Riddell was the college's first administrator. The first building was put up on the grounds of the church. It opened in October 1904 to seventy-three students. In bounds and leaps the college grew—a reflection of Edmonton's quickly rising population as well as the college's appeal to students outside the city. In its second year, there were 183 students and a new building to accommodate them. Again, the necessity of larger quarters became a vital question. The summer of 1905 saw further building double the capacity. In 1906 the old McDougall Church was refitted as a dormitory for one teacher and fourteen students.

Now, in 1907, 430 students enrolled—some boarding off campus—and a new residence building was underway.

The college was co-educational and had three streams: academic (based on the equivalent to the first two years of McGill University in Montreal), commercial, and musical. There were practice rooms with soundproof doors for music staff and students. The third floor housed boys with a few male teachers; the second floor housed girls and teachers; the main floor had classrooms, a dining hall, an assembly room, and a library "with most of the classics of English literature and translations."

Overall, Alberta College aimed to provide a social environment similar to home environments where boys and girls mixed freely and common rooms encouraged groups. They expected that this co-ed arrangement would "exert a refining influence upon the boys" and give the girls "a more sensible view of life generally." Alberta College, then, was based on quite different principles than those of the elite private schools, such as the Ladies' Presbyterian College Edith Miller attended, which were favoured by wealthy families in the East and throughout Canada. Independent life—especially for women—was encouraged. Jean Forsyth who, at age fifty-six, had been living such a life with great pleasure and success, would have been an ideal teacher.[7]

By the end of 1907, Jean was not only well employed, she was also ensconced in the high society life of teas as a singer and often seen in concerts in Edmonton. Through her ads she had assembled a sizeable group of her own vocal students.[8]

She had joined the Edmonton Ladies' Musical Club just as the fledgling group organized its first public concert.[9] All this, as well as her involvement—partly through her tea party friends—in the city's Humane Society. In Gertrude Seton-Thompson she had found a roommate who was more than suitable, connected through her column as "Penelope" to social and musical events. The two ladies had found convenient central apartments downtown.

Jean had produced a "Vaudeville" concert in early December.[10] And soon she not only acquired her stray dog Zip as a companion for Blackberry, but also a black cat called Mischa and a bird.

A LETTER FROM EDITH IN LONDON
TO CHARLES WHEELER IN WINNIPEG, 1908

Mr. Charles Wheeler
Music and Drama Critic
Winnipeg Tribune

June 10, 1908
Dear Charles,
  As you know, I am now in my third year of residence in London. You will be glad to hear that I have made more money this year up to date than for the two past years put together, and am now getting more private concert work than I can manage. I never sing even one song for less than twenty guineas, so I am trying to take as many bookings as I can attend.

Yours sincerely,
Edith J. Miller

Wheeler summarized what was a long list from Miss Miller of important engagements in his June 10, 1908 column. She had appeared in numerous public concerts. The most important of these were concerts at Bechstein Hall (now Wigmore Hall), where she sang first at a fashionable and expensive function with Arthur Shattuck "the sympathetic soulful pianist"[1] in piano recital. (Shattuck, the son of a founder of the American paper company Kimberly-Clark, was a European-trained piano virtuoso and humanitarian.) Then, at Strafford House, under royal patronage again (the Duke and Duchess of Sutherland), she performed for high admission prices. The other artists at that concert—all international stars—were the daughter of her former teacher, Madame Blanche Marchesi, along with Marie Brema, who was an unusual English dramatic mezzo-soprano who came to singing late, after marrying; Landon Ronald, a pianist, soon to be conductor of the New Symphony Orchestra in London; the Welsh singer Ben Davies, who was currently the top tenor in England, specializing in opera and oratorio; Efrem Zimbalist, Sr., the Russian violinist; the popular British actor and comedian George Grossmith, known for his work in and alongside Edwardian comedies; and Mademoiselle Natalia Janotha, a Polish pianist who had been a student of Schumann and pianist at the imperial court of Berlin.[2]

  Edith J. Miller was also contralto principal at the Handel Society concert in Queen's Hall on May 27 under the direction of the composer, Samuel Coleridge-Taylor. The four-part program included Dvořák's *Stabat Mater*.[3]

  On the side she promoted a Winnipeg girl's compositions by including them in some of her performances. Laura Gertrude Lemon's "My Ain Folk," "Canada for

Ever," and "The Rose Garden" now found audiences far from the Canadian city already enjoying them.

It could certainly be said that Edith J. Miller now had a "commanding" position as a singer, even if "Rosa Sub" had challenged her status only a few years before. As Charles Wheeler wrote, "One Canadian, at least, seems to be doing well in London."[4]

At the March 18, 1908 meeting of the Edmonton Humane Society where Jean Forsyth first appeared as secretary, there was a new board member—Emily Murphy. Wife of an Anglican priest, she was to become an indisputably important figure in Edmonton and across Canada. There is no doubt that if she had not moved and stayed in Alberta, the development of the new province would not have been the same, especially for women and their children. She had moved with her husband and their two daughters to Edmonton from Swan River near the western border of Manitoba, the same year that Jean arrived in the city as part of the extraordinary growth of the new capital of the new province.[1]

Emily Murphy was a person of sympathy for the have-nots—whether they were animals or people—and she quickly noticed and deplored the poverty in the city, especially its effect on women and children. She was also a person of action. On turning forty, as her four daughters began to need her less, she organized women's groups where discussions of ideas and plans to remedy social ills could take place. Struck by the pathetic case of a farm woman whose husband had abandoned her and their children, taking with him the entire proceeds of the farm they had built together, Emily began a campaign to entitle women to a fair share of property rights.

Although Emily was not opposed to social teas, her own tea in Edmonton on Friday, September 18, just as schools and the social "season" got underway, showed that she took a different attitude to them. The *Edmonton Bulletin* reported that the event was "delightful," but it was out of step with the lavish teas given by the wealthy elite ladies. There were no gushings about flowers and ferns, nothing said about atmospheric lighting, no comments about what the hostess or the guests were wearing. The tea was held in Emily's "cosy" (i.e., small) library and two of her daughters, Kathleen and Evelyn, helped her receive the guests. No mention was made of extravagant "dainties" or a "heavily laden board." Two friends—Mrs. Ferris and Mrs. Wallbridge—served the tea, but it was passed to guests by her daughters and her friends, Miss Belcher, Miss Forin, Mrs. Jackson, and Miss Brown. Twenty other guests were mentioned, including Jean Forsyth, her cousins Marjorie Pardee and Mabel Cautley, and two of Jean's original patronesses, Louisa Beck and Ethel Woods.[2] Nothing was said about anyone singing. This was a tea at which the main point was not food, dresses, and hats, or decorations, atmospheric effects, entertainment, or large numbers of guests. In the library, surrounded by books, significant conversation was meant to enhance the tea. And Emily wanted her daughters to hear and take part in it.

Although British social customs would continue for women in Edmonton, the *zeitgeist* was changing. Unionized workers were demanding attention. Non-British immigrants were pouring into the city. The car was accelerating the pace of life. Women's fashions were easing to accommodate bicycles and greater physical activity while hairstyles became more casual, in imitation of Queen Alexandra's upsweeps—all of this a shift in the notion of womanhood from ornamental "doll" to active, thinking personhood. Edmonton in the early 1900s was already more progressive and more accepting of ideas of equality—whether between the genders or among classes of workers and employers—than Winnipeg had been in the last decade before the turn of the century. That *zeitgeist* turned the page of history—social, cultural, and political.

Jean Forsyth had already adopted independence as her *modus operandi*. She had managed to negotiate a delicate balance between all the elements of her life in Winnipeg: the social elite, the world of performance (on one hand religious, on the other hand secular), the profession of teaching, the charity work on behalf of animals at the Winnipeg Humane Society that she had founded, the work as an accompanist to singers she had shared the stage with. Juggling all these interests had called upon her remarkable flexibility. Now in Edmonton, that flexibility would result in a different emphasis and unexpected initiatives.

Jean's Edmonton cousin, Mabel Cautley (née Helliwell), doubtless steered Jean in the direction of various rights issues beyond the Humane Society. Mabel came from Toronto United Empire Loyalist families and was educated at the Presbyterian Ladies' College (that Edith Miller had attended), then at the University of Toronto. She had married Richard W. Cautley, who had come from Ipswich, England, to apprentice with his brother, Reginald, in Dawson City before joining him in their Edmonton practice as land surveyors.

In Toronto Mabel had begun a career as a writer. Her first story was published when she was twelve; she won the *Boston Globe* competition for short stories by children under eighteen when she was fifteen. She contributed short stories to various Canadian and American magazines, then took the position of editor for the women's department of a Canadian magazine. This intelligent, experienced woman of independent politics had quickly "identified herself with progressive movements of various kinds" when she arrived in Edmonton. She became president of the local branch of the National Council of Women of Canada, would soon initiate and preside over the crèche to help destitute mothers with their children so they could work, and serve on the board of the Children's Aid Society. She also played a major part in such organizations as the Ontario Historical Society, the Imperial Order Daughters of the Empire, the Edmonton YMCA, the Arts and Handicrafts Guild, the Victorian Order of Nurses Association, the Canadian Women's Press Club, and various local church societies. Everywhere she was praised for her "executive ability."[3]

It could be said that while Jean's cousin Marjorie Pardee fostered her social and musical life in Edmonton, it was her cousin Mabel Cautley[4] who encouraged her natural independence and sympathy for the have-nots of society.

Suddenly Jean found herself in the company of such independent-minded women as Dr. Ella Scarlett-Synge (who was already giving first aid seminars for women)[5] and Emily Murphy.

Within a week, Jean gave a Sunday evening concert at the Dominion Theatre on July 16, 1908, assisted by the Edmonton Citizens' Band[6] and was one of eight guests at a luncheon on August 4 for Miss Agnes Laut, hosted by the Edmonton branch of the Canadian Women's Press Club at Cronn's Club Café. Agnes was a well-travelled writer from Ontario, the daughter of a Glasgow merchant who had moved his family to Winnipeg in 1873 when she was two. A schoolteacher in Winnipeg for several years, she returned to school herself at the University of Manitoba for her teaching certificate. She was an editorial writer for the *Manitoba Free Press* from 1895 to 1897, the period when Jean knew her.

After 1897 she travelled Canada, paying her way with articles contributed to magazines. In 1900, she settled in Wassaic, New York, where, for the next two years, she researched and wrote historical novels in the hope of informing more people of their history. Her early work included the history of Montana and the story of settlers on the Santa Fe Trail, but her later work, which encompassed two dozen titles, were Canadian in subject matter. At the time of the Edmonton luncheon she was working on *The Canadian Commonwealth*, which was published in 1909. Her books sold extraordinarily well.

The members of the press club's Edmonton branch, which had formed in 1908, were enthusiastic, Katherine Hughes, who wrote for the *Edmonton Bulletin*, had been one of the club's founding members. So was Gertrude Balmer Watt, wife of another Ontario journalist, Arthur Balmer Watt, with whom she had set up a new newspaper, the *Saturday News*. Gertrude used the pseudonym "Peggy" to write a social column called "The Mirror" for their paper.[7] The other two Edmonton members were Anne Merrill and Georgie Shibley. Mabel Cautley and Emily Murphy also attended the press club luncheon along with Jean. The press was still using phrases more suitable for large dressy teas, though that would change in time. This luncheon for eight was described as a "pleasant little affair." Agnes Laut was described as a "sweet, unaffected girl" as well as a "brilliant young Canadian authoress and magazine writer."[8]

At this gathering "good fellowship and a guest of honor who could talk well and entertainingly were the important factors in the feast." Agnes Laut spoke "in a most interesting manner of her work and the object of her trip to the West."[9] The next day Agnes left on a trip down the Saskatchewan River to Winnipeg to prepare for her next book: *Hudson's Bay Company.*[10]

The mercury hovered between forty and fifty degrees below zero on January 7, 1909. That did not deter fifty or so women from making their way through the snow and piercing winds to Edmonton's YMCA Hall. Their "genuine interest" in the first annual session of the Edmonton branch of the National Council of Women—the first of Canada's local councils—was palpable as they gathered to elect officers for the current year.

The warm round face of Grace Ferris, a graduate of the University of Toronto, beamed over the crowd as she led the meeting. Known for her "good judgment and common sense,"[1] she was regent of the Daughters of the Empire. After completing bits of business, she spoke about the "excellent work" accomplished so quickly and effectively over the past year. The Crèche Committee had been appointed less than three months earlier at the council's quarterly meeting and had already leased and furnished a "comfortable house" at 840 McDougall Avenue and hired a "capable matron," thanks to the managing skills of Mabel Cautley, Grace Ferris herself, Ethel Hyndman (a "pretty, vivacious, and clever amateur actress" who was elected treasurer), and Jennie Braithwaite (who founded the Edmonton branch of the Humane Society on which Jean and Mabel both served).

An "active and benevolent circle of girls in their teens" known as the "Busy Bees" raised $100 towards furnishings, which was supplemented by other donations. In all, $475.45 had been donated to the crèche fund, and more had been promised. Despite expenses a balance of $289.85 remained. "The house stands as an eloquent testimonial of the generosity of Edmonton's citizens," said Grace Ferris, "and a tribute to the enthusiastic work of the committee."

Since the crèche opened on December 7, it had been put to good use for both day and overnight care. Three children stayed while their mothers worked. One child was cared for while its mother was sick. An application was made and accepted for a permanent home for another. A destitute mother and her two children were housed there after travelling forty miles to see her husband in hospital. The children stayed on. The Salvation Army, informed of the situation, was looking for work for their mother.

Dr. Ella Scarlett-Synge read a report from her Committee on Public Health, currently trying to prevent spitting on the street and in other public places. Treasurer Ethel Hyndman reported receipts of thirty-two dollars from the seventeen affiliated societies that had donated to the crèche and expenses of six dollars.

Emily Murphy reported on her Committee for Laws to Secure Protection for Women and Children, which was appointed in October 1908. Already she had written to Alexander Rutherford, the Ottawa lawyer and Liberal who had become

Dr. Ella Scarlett-Synge on the horse she rode around Edmonton.

Miss Gertrude Balmer Watt, Vice-President of the Canadian Women's Press Club and writer for the *Saturday News.*

Alberta's first premier, to enact a law for the better protection of women and children. Rutherford, who resembled a kindly walrus, had replied that such a law was already in the works. She and her committee then turned their attention to the question of dower rights for women. The case of the abandoned farm wife left destitute with the children by her husband still irked Emily Murphy. A vote was taken that decided the matter would be forwarded to the government during the coming session.

The election of officers for the upcoming year took place. Mabel Cautley was elected the new president. Dr. Ella Scarlett-Synge and Emily Murphy were reappointed heads of their committees. A new committee was formed to set up a free employment agency at the crèche for women looking for work by the day.

A robust singing of "God Save the King" with Jean Forsyth accompanying on the piano ended what was an inspiring and fruitful meeting.

Gertrude Seton-Thompson published an extensive article that year with twenty-nine photos titled "The Women of Edmonton" in *Canada West.*[2] In it, most of the women who attended the first annual session of the Edmonton branch of the National Council of Women in Canada and their various accomplishments are praised.

The photo of Jean Forsyth with her two dogs Berry and Zip—both collies, one tan-and-black, the other black—is the only one that is featured on its own page. In it she wears a long light shirtwaist dress belted at the waist and a large hat festooned with flowers. She has dark leather elbow-length gloves and holds the chains of the two dogs in one hand and a narrow walking stick in the other. Her chin-up attitude is assertive. She is described as a "sterling musician and singer of charm and cultivation." Her love of dogs is a "dominant note in her character." Another is "her intensely humorous turn of mind." "Her bright wit and individualistic sayings make her much sought for."[3]

Emily Murphy is pictured in her usual dark clothes and hat, looking magisterial, though she was not yet a magistrate. Known for her "quick wit and readiness of speech," she is "to the fore" as a writer (her Janey Canuck books had just begun to appear) and in philanthropic projects of a "progressive and upward trend." A natural leader.

Jean Forsyth, a striking Edmonton figure with her two dogs Zip and Berry, *circa* 1908.

Ella Scarlett-Synge appears in a photo on horseback. She is described as a women with an "air of quiet determination."

The popular humorist Gertrude Balmer Watt is seen sitting at her desk in a well-stocked library. Her columns are "racy, lively, and vigorous"; her company is "amusing and stimulating." Her 1907 collection of "Peggy's" best "Mirror" columns between 1905 and 1907 in the *Saturday News* had been published as a book: *Woman in the West*. This lively illustrated book is a personal humorous description of scenes and occasions that reveal much about early Edmonton from a woman's point of view.

Mrs. W. D. (Grace) Ferris, a University of Toronto graduate, who led the Jan. 7, 1909 meeting of the Edmonton branch of the National Council of Women.

Mrs. A. C. (Mattie) Rutherford, wife of the Premier of Alberta, active in church work and charitable enterprises.

Mrs. Richard (Maggie) Hardisty, Jr., a "statuesque beauty" from Kentucky who excelled in tennis.

Mrs. J. D. (Ethel) Hyndman, an amateur actress, treasurer of the Edmonton branch of the National Council of Women.

Mrs. R. Percy Barnes, who organized the church embroidery group.

Mrs. Richard (Eliza) Hardisty, wife of the late Chief Factor and a leading society hostess at the "Big House."

Women's roles were in transition in the city. Yet not all women had achieved the professionalism of Dr. Ella Scarlett-Synge, Emily Murphy, or Jean Forsyth.

Some were still entrenched in the old role of "angel of the house." Maternal devotion, expert hosting of events like teas and bridge, even mere beauty, anchored these women to the past. This was especially true for the wives of powerful men. Mattie Rutherford, for instance, "a woman of much sweetness of nature, devoted to her children," was dutifully married to A. C. Rutherford, the first premier of the province.

If a woman like this ventured past the threshold it was to do charitable church work. If she were sporty she might play tennis and garden like Edith Macdonald. Or, like the "statuesque beauty" Maggie Hardisty, she might sing at teas, but never in concert.

Maggie was from Kentucky, part of the yeasty cosmopolitan mix that was Edmonton. The city's base drew largely from UEL backgrounds. Yet at any gathering there might be people from Britain or the British colonies, such as Australia, New Zealand, or India. Several came from the U.S.—New York, in particular, and California. Still others had arrived from China, Japan, Russia, or European countries such as France and Italy. This mix disrupted the UEL base, providing the city with a more open context in which women could move away from domesticity into more professional roles.

Gertrude Balmer Watt was far more accurate than Gertrude Seton-Thompson in her depiction of the population of Edmonton, perhaps because of careful firsthand observation. She, too, notes the city's "cosmopolitan" composition:

> You pass the smartly groomed man and encounter a step behind his brother in sheepskins. Down the middle of [Jasper Avenue] pounds an Indian mounted on a broken-down pony, and behind him comes an officer of the Mounted Police, in the smartest get-up on the continent. Pretty Galician girls with shawls on their heads jostle milady in the latest spring headgear. French, German, "United States" and dear knows what jargons are wafted in on your ear, but you are unheedful of anything but the faces of the crowd. We are a truly cosmopolitan people, and every type from the slick Yankee to the stolid Redman has joined the procession to see the "toot."

> In the distance came the strains of some long-dead favourite played by an "Uncle Tom's Cabin" band.[6]

"The Women of Edmonton" shows ideas of the Western Canadian elite woman in flux. As it had for some time before, lineage matters, a husband's rank matters, wealth (unstated) matters, grand homes matter, beauty matters, hospitality and manners matter, popularity matters. Churches are mentioned: for example, the rather plain unfashionable Mrs. Robert Percy Barnes had organized the Church Embroidery Guild. Yet churches were becoming less important as centres for women's activities than they had been during Jean Forsyth's years in Winnipeg.

Many of these women are young. Several are recently married. Though there are "old-timers" with more than one generation in the area, most are recently arrived. Fashions vary. Some wear elaborate hats lavish with flowers, other hats take large bold shapes. Others appear without hats, their hair swept much more casually up behind the head or at the nape. Fringes and bangs have disappeared. Some dresses recall Victorian fussiness; others are simpler, more tailored in the Edwardian fashion. Some women take the coy angled stances of ornate dolls. Others, especially Emily Murphy, Gertrude Balmer Watt, and Jean Forsyth, position themselves as upright, forthright, and self-possessed.

It is true, as Gertrude Seton-Thompson writes, that about half the women in her article "are mothers and homemakers first and society women afterwards." Yet there are several for whom the demands of society—whether these be service in the interests of women, children, or animals—or the challenges of the arts, such as music and writing, clearly take precedence over domestic ideals. In the froth of transition, gatherings of women for tea and bridge were drawing closer and closer to gatherings of women for purposes so serious and significant that they were to change society altogether.

EDITH J. MILLER RETURNS FROM ABROAD, 1909

She stood centre stage in the spotlight. The intense light caught the opalescent sequins on her overdress and bodice. Underneath was a gown made of what the *Town Topics* writer will later describe as shell-pink *"enchantreuse."*[1] This is an error, for there is no "r" in the name of the rich patterned or striped fabric. The error is telling. *Enchantreuse* means "enchantress" and that, surely, was what Edith Miller was. She breathed deeply, her dark hair gleaming, her bodice alive with light as she sang "Rose in the Bud," a romantic ballad by contemporary American pianist Dorothy Forster. The audience had endured the suspense of waiting to see and hear her. Three performers had preceded her before she finally walked onstage, to thunderous applause.

It was April 5, 1909, in Halifax. Edith J. Miller had returned after almost five long years abroad to give a cross-Canada tour. She had brought with her "some of the best rising talent of England." This tour, after being hailed abroad, would be unlike her western tour in 1900 with Stanley Adams, Robert Campbell, and Jean Forsyth. Now, a diva at thirty-four, she was "desirous of being supported by a first-class party." The young tenor successor to the famous Welsh performer Ben Davies, with whom Edith had sung in London, was Alfred Heather, a small, natty, long-faced man with a twirled moustache. The pleasant round-faced Thorpe Bates was the baritone of the company, young and rising. Maud Bell, Edith's cellist, had "created a furor in London on her first appearance a few months ago."[2] With her heavy-lidded eyes and flowing wavy dark hair she resembled a Pre-Raphaelite painting.

Edith had expected to return to Canada from the "old land" two years after she left her post at Knox Presbyterian Church in Portage la Prairie in 1904. At that time, she had planned to study further and to sing in a number of concert engagements abroad.[3]

Yet four years later she was still in England. So great was her success there that she delayed her return plans. "It was Miss Miller's intention to return in the autumn of 1908," the *Edmonton Bulletin* announced after a rundown of Edith's training and accomplishments and lavish praise for her "beauty," "power of voice," and delightful vocalization,"[4] adding that her career in the British Isles had been "one of continuous triumph." It was her "numerous engagements in England" that had caused the delay of another year.

Now, however, she and the company of three English artists arranged by her agent, Mr. Tillitt, of London's noted Ibbs and Tillitt artists' management agency, trained under impresario Nathaniel Vert, and joined by their accompanist Mr. Caxton, would go on from Halifax to perform in Montreal, Toronto, Winnipeg, Brandon, and Edmonton.

Charles Wheeler was beyond excited at this prospect. It was he who had singled her out for international success from the first time he heard her in Winnipeg. Before she even arrived, he ran long columns in anticipation of what he considered a major cultural event. Large headlines in the *Winnipeg Tribune* on February 22 announced

TOUR FOR MISS MILLER—Noted Canadian Singer is Coming to Canada in April—Will Be Heard in Winnipeg.

Wheeler spoke of the "very great headway" she has made in England, her recitals "attended by royalty and the cream of London society." He referred to her concert for the king and his request to see her afterward. He mentioned her recent successes in London: Elgar's *Dream of Gerontius* and the *Kingdom*, as well as a concert performance of *Carmen*, with the Royal Choral Society. He had already learned of the other artists from England performing with her, Alfred Heather and Thorpe Bates, "who will no doubt take the Canadian musical public by storm." The "young and charming cellist" Maud Bell, he wrote, "apart from her musical ability has a big following in society."[5]

Two weeks later another announcement appeared by "CLEF" the music reviewer in the *Ottawa Journal* recalling Edith Miller's performance in *The Messiah* with the Ottawa Orchestral Society a few years ago and noting her upcoming tour. She "enjoys a reputation few can excel" and is a great favourite with Royalty," went the write-up, and "was presented to His Majesty King Edward at the latter's special command" after a performance with the Royal Amateur Orchestral Society.[6]

Charles Wheeler reported on the opening performance in Halifax. He wrote of the praise for Maud Bell's "splendid selections" and found Alfred Heather "a tenor of no ordinary ability," even though he was too "diminutive" to be convincing as Sampson in Saint-Saëns's *Samson and Delilah*. Thorpe Bates as Elijah the High Priest was "simply grand." The Halifax review focused on Edith.

> Miss Miller was a perfect Delilah, even her physique and sequin costume with its clinging effect was redolent with the luring wile of this ancient Circe. Her acting of the part was perfect.

> In her second part selections showed her range of accomplishments. Whether her excellent rendition of Donizetti's *O Mio Fernando*, the semi-sacred "Song of the Cruise," her coquettish version of "I Once Loved a Boy," [and] "The Little Dustman." [Which of her two] encore selections—favourites from [her] earlier days "The Spring" and "Break, Break"—was her best, is hard to decide.[7]

Charles Wheeler went on to say, "If last night's reception from strangers is a criterion, it will be hard to imagine how the music lovers of the Canadian west, where Miss Miller is already well-known, will express their appreciation of their returned songstress and her accompanying artists."

Edith J. Miller as a
sultry Delilah, *Winnipeg
Tribune*, May 1, 1909.

He needn't have wondered about Edith's reception in the West. She sang in Montreal and in Ottawa, again to ecstatic crowds. In Montreal on April 22 the Governor-General, Lady Grey and their entourage attended the concert in Her Majesty's Theatre. Her "splendid" program before a "crowded house" included a scene from that originally scandalous opera *Carmen*.[8] At least one bouquet was thrown onstage after each number.[9]

As Edith's Winnipeg performance drew near, Charles Wheeler grew more eloquent. On May 1—a week before her concert—he offered "her hundreds of friends and admirers throughout the entire North West, to Vancouver and Victoria" summaries of some of Edith's reviews filled with "unstinting praise" in England and Ireland. The *Morning Post* of London, for example, had written somewhat condescendingly, "In music as in other subjects the Colonies are beginning to take a by no means unimportant part. Canada has sent us a charming recruit in Miss Edith Miller."[10] The quotation continued:

> The young singer has an excellent voice of contralto quality. Its range is extensive and its character most pleasing. The tone is singularly full and sweet, and its natural beauty is augmented by the artistic manner in which it is used. There is plenty of colour in her voice, her diction is clear, and her vocalization is of the best.
>
> Miss Miller's method of using the mezzo [soprano] voice is excellent.

This last comment wss important because Edith had learned to extend her range upwards into the mezzo-soprano register. Even Joseph Bennett, the veteran music critic of the London's *Daily Telegraph*, was "puzzled in what category to place her voice." Other competent music critics had the same problem. "Hers is not the 'veiled voice' of the ordinary contralto, her tones are not 'muffled,' but on the contrary, are bright and exultant."[11] Edith's voice was not only compelling, it was unusual and unique.

Wheeler emphasized the fact that "our Manitoba Nightingale," as he called her, had not merely been lucky. Her "successes have been gained by her own individual accomplishments as a highly trained vocalist, enhanced by an elegant platform appearance as to costume [performers were responsible for their own costumes],[12] and presenting the finished manners of a gentlewoman, at ease in any society however distinguished."

"Surely," he continued, "these English triumphs will stir Manitobans to give the warmest of welcomes to their own cantatrice whose indomitable pluck and perseverance in the face of almost insuperable difficulties has made her famous in the world of music," writes Wheeler.

After several half-page ads in the newspaper, Edith finally appeared in Winnipeg. She arrived the afternoon of May 7, the day before her performances in the Walker Theatre. En route she had performed in Fort William to the usual wild applause. On her arrival in Winnipeg the Women's Musical Club and the Women's Canadian Club hosted a joint reception for her. She gave two concerts on May 8: one in the afternoon, one in the evening. Charles Wheeler took one of his daughters to the afternoon performance. The lieutenant governor and his wife, Sir Daniel and Lady McMillan, and most of Winnipeg's elite were in the full-to-bursting audience. So were Edith's "very proud" parents. Edith wore "a gown of palest mauve satin with a tunic overskirt of pale blue chiffon bordered with pipings of the satin; the sleeves were of Limerick Lace, the bodice trimmed with the same lovely lace and gold embroidery." This light, shimmery costume set off her dark upsweep.[13]

Charles Wheeler was rapturous in his review two days later. It was headlined VERITABLE TRIUMPH FOR MISS EDITH MILLER. "She has arrived at the apogee of her art," he wrote.

> She has mastered that exuberant temperament observable five years ago, which now serves gladly artistic commands. With such a lovely voice, especially in *sotto* and *mezzo voce* effects, no wonder His Majesty King Edward the Seventh became fascinated and commanded an introduction to the fair singer. Miss Miller's tones are now so limpid, her natural vivacity so amiable in certain of her songs, her personality so full of charm, that her chief difficulty lay in avoiding encores, but without avail, for her thirty-five hundred friends proved so insistent that she had to respond in every instance.[14]

Her aria "O Mio Fernando" was "exultant." This exuberance was "enhanced with luscious beauty of expression" in Saint Saëns's *Samson and Delilah.* Some of her top notes of ringing soprano were "marvelous in power and quality of tone." Her duet as Delilah with tenor Alfred Heather, "without a false note in its intense, dramatic, impassioned vocalism...will not soon be forgotten." Wheeler found "the vocal and physical allurements of 'Delilah' well nigh irresistible, savouring "those delicate, yet Satanic touches with which she enticed the strongest man in history from his high duties." He went on to praise her "thrilling" use of "tone colours" in "Softly Awakes My Heart."

Though Wheeler was besotted by Edith Miller's performance, he also had high praise for Alfred Heather—"small in stature, but a giant in song"—and for baritone Thorpe Bates, whose interpretations outdid all others. "My word! How the audience reveled in his delivery of songs, serious and jovial." Wheeler noted that the cello "is rapidly gaining ground among the fair sex owing to its power of expressing womanly feelings" and praised the "virtuoso skill" and the "rich," "warm," and "pure" tone of "this young English girl," Maud Bell.

Almost as an afterthought, Wheeler noted "society was out in gala attire," many being Edith's "warm personal friends." The "beautiful" singer's "radiant smiles and graceful bows revealed the pleasure she felt at the warmth of the greeting bestowed upon her." Her Portage la Prairie friends, now living in Winnipeg, sent a huge basket of American beauty roses to the stage. So many loose flowers and bouquets were flung onto the stage as she took her final bows before a standing ovation that the stage—and even the piano—was covered. This was, according to Wheeler, entirely appropriate for "the Queen Rose herself."

AN UNEXPECTED CLASH FOR JEAN AND EDITH

After the overwhelming response to her concerts in Winnipeg and in Brandon—attended by even more Portage la Prairie admirers who "showed right royally that they had not forgotten their own little Edith"[1]—Edith Miller and her agent faced an unexpected problem in Edmonton. Jean Forsyth had already booked the Edmonton Opera House very close to one of the days Edith was to perform there. Edith was scheduled for Thursday the 20th and Friday the 21st of May. The opera Jean was producing was to play the following Tuesday, Wednesday, and Thursday. There were only three days between the two performances. Each one promised to be exceptional.

Jean had been working for some time on a production of Gilbert and Sullivan's *Patience*. It was the same opera that she had produced in Dawson City in 1905. Now, with a much greater array of musical talent in Edmonton, she was determined to stage the first performance ever seen in the new province. As usual, Jean's charitable streak induced her to share the proceeds with the public hospitals' Ladies' Hospital Aid Committee. She promised that it would be "the very best opera ever produced in Edmonton."[2] There would be a "splendid" chorus of forty voices and a ten-piece professional orchestra. Jean would have full control of the casting and musical direction. She would conduct the orchestra herself, unheard of for a woman at that time, and unusual even today.

Patience was a satire. It made fun of the arts movement in the 1880s and 1890s that emphasized aesthetic values—such as style and rhythms—over moral social values. More broadly it satirized human foibles, such as hypocrisy, vanity, and pretentiousness. The simple milkmaid Patience was the heroine, swearing to marry only for "unselfish" reasons. Her two suitors were poets: Bunthorne, whose poems were emphatic, alliterative, and obscure, and Grosvenor, whose poems were simple and pastoral. Both poets were given to reciting their poems aloud in an affected manner to a bevy of enraptured maidens (like today's groupies). Long-haired Bunthorne in his velvet jacket caricatured Swinburne and also made fun of Oscar Wilde's knee breeches worn to show off his legs. Grosvenor mocks poet Coventry Patmore, who was a humourless idealist and Arts and Crafts artist William Morris, who glorified rural simplicity.

The two-act plot—like all Gilbert and Sullivan operas—was tangled, silly, and ended happily. The opera was the second-longest running musical performance when it appeared in London in 1881.

Jean's choice of this opera reflected her great sense of fun, her knowledge of English poetry and the fact that the opera had been, and still was, exceptionally popular. It was a major undertaking. The *Edmonton Bulletin* promoted it with all the superlatives it could muster. "*Patience* stands in the front rank of comic operas," ran one column. "Its music is delightfully tuneful. The solos, duets, trios, quintettes, sextettes and chorus have never yet been surpassed in comic opera. The comedy is equally as clever and is of the real, genuine, wholesome character." The next day, the same newspaper declared, "'Let the Merry Cymbals Sound' is one of the many delightful choruses in *Patience*, to be performed for the first time in this city. The music throughout is bright and sparkling. This opera, which is creating such interest in the city, is being produced in the Edmonton Opera House. The principals are happily cast: Miss Pinckston, the popular soprano, and Mr. H. G. Turner, the well-known tenor, are Patience and Grosvenor, while Mr. A. E. Nash, who has been prominent in amateur theatricals for some time, will play Bunthorne. The other principals include Mrs. Mahan, the Misses Buck, Gerdung, and Heatherington, and Messrs. Cope, Griffiths, and McIsaac. The plan of seats are on sale at the Edmonton Opera House."[3]

The majority of the eleven cast members were students of Jean Forsyth's. The three major roles—dairymaid Patience (Alice Pinckston) and poets Bunthorne (Albert E. Nash), and Grosvenor (Herbert G. Turner)—were all played by her students. So were three of the women with solos: Lady Angela (Constance Buck), Lady Sophia (Mary Gerdung), and Lady Jane (Anne Heatherington). One of the Dragoons, mocked for their military mishaps, was her student too: Colonel Calverey (an irreverent pun mixing "cavalry" with "Calvary"), played by Alfred McIsaac. In fact, only four of the eleven major roles were played by singers who were *not* Jean's students.

At the same time as these inducements to attend *Patience* appeared, advance publicity for Edith Miller's forthcoming concert was given in the same paper. "Miss Edith Miller, whose beauty and power of voice and delightful vocalization had firmly established her in the hearts of her English audiences, claims Portage la Prairie, Manitoba, as her home."[4] After summarizing her education and early career, the column continued, "She made her debut in London in 1905, under the patronage of Royalty, and since then her career has been one continuous triumph." She has "engaged the service of some of the best rising talent of England" to sing with her, and the dates of her performances are given.

Much was made of Edith's impressive farewell concert in London at the new St. James Hall. Mr. Henry Wood had directed the Queen's Hall Orchestra and Maud Bell—who was now one of the artists accompanying her on her Canadian tour—supported her with the cello at her last concert in England. The concert's patrons were Their Royal Highnesses the Prince and Princess of Wales, the Duke and Duchess of Argyll, and many other worthies. It was noted that she had studied with Paolo Tosti ("a favourite pupil" of his), composer of light or Italian songs, and had had "the benefit of his suggestions in the interpretations of his songs." At the end of the concert, she was recalled eleven times, which she acknowledged by giving two extra numbers. The "floral tributes" were so many that they had to be taken off in a separate carriage. After the concert crowds of her "enthusiastic admirers" clustered outside the hall to wish her *Bon Voyage*.[5]

After that, on May 19 and 20, Jean Forsyth's production of *Patience* and Edith J. Miller's concert shared equally an ad in the *Bulletin*. Edith's ad was above Jean's. It emphasized "Canada's Great Contralto" with Edith's name in bold capitals. It mentioned the patronage of the lieutenant governor. Jean's ad emphasized the opera itself, with *Patience* in bold capitals. Jean's name, as musical director, is in small print at the bottom of the ad. The prices for the two entertainments differed; for Edith's concert, tickets were $2, $1.50, or $1, depending on the seats, for *Patience* exactly half those amounts.

Someone at the *Bulletin* made an error in Edith's favour. Her ad stated that 5 percent of her gross sales would go to the Ladies' Hospital Aid for the new Public Hospital. Actually, half the proceeds from Jean's production would go to sponsor this charity, but no such statement was made in the ad for *Patience*. Once Edith's concert was over, the oversight was corrected in an ad for *Patience* in the *Saturday News*.

As the final curtain fell on the first performance of *Patience*, it was clear that the large audience was thrilled. "In the midst of a most capable orchestra stood Miss Forsyth as she [had] directed the opera through all its stages. Great praise was showered on her as success after success was scored by the choruses and the soloists." There was mild criticism: that the military chorus was better than the love-sick maidens' chorus, and that the dancing was "not the acme of elegance." Yet "over the entire production was the glamour of well directed and whole-hearted endeavor."[6] The second night was even better. "The well filled house that a second time greeted the second production of the opera *Patience* in the Edmonton Opera House last night was decidedly the most appreciative that has graced this theatre for many months. No company in recent times has received the spontaneous and hearty encores accorded the performers last night. A most unusual occurrence in even professional productions was the triple curtain on the finale to the first act. The picture was beautifully set and the music magnificently sung, and reflects the greatest credit on Miss Jean Forsyth, the musical directress."[7]

Although Edith Miller's concert preceded *Patience* the reviews of it came later. It was as if the local production was more important. Edith might herself have treated it as a lesser occasion than her overwhelming welcome in Winnipeg and Brandon. She did not attend the welcoming reception tea held by the Edmonton Women's Musical Club and the Edmonton Women's Canadian Club. She sent a message saying that she was "fatigued by her travels."[8]

Gertrude Balmer Watt's write-up in *Saturday News* on May 29, more than a week after her concerts (in which there were two different programs), focused on the tardiness of the audience. "People in Edmonton have one weakness," they "usually prefer to be late instead of being in time."[9] The Edith Miller concert was advertised for 8:30, and the performers were "strictly on time." After fifteen minutes, when Lieutenant Governor George Bulyea and his party had been seated some time, the concert commenced. As soon as it was "nicely started" people began to arrive.

"The performers had to wait for these people to get seated. Then another start would be made, then another stop had to be made for more people to arrive and be seated." The "artiste smiling serenely" waited for all folks to be seated. After another piece of music, more people came in. "Not till about one third of the programme was through did we really settle down. It doesn't worry those who come late, it's nice to be able to show off clothes and be stared at or make a sensation. But fine musicians find it hard to do their best with their nerves on edge with motion and movement or rattling, rustling or banging." "We who knew that everything in Edmonton starts from half an hour to three-quarters of an hour, or perhaps an hour after advertised time were not surprised." It was hardly a review of the performance. Nor was it the kind of tribute Edith Miller was used to on both sides of the Atlantic.

Another item towards the end of the social pages of the same newspaper—in among news of "coming-out teas, tennis teas, the comings and goings of those wealthy enough to take holidays away from the city, a ball given by the IODE, and birth announcements—was so brief as to be an insult to the Edith J. Miller Company. It treated the "very delightful vocal recitals given by Miss Edith Miller and her clever company" as a mere social event: "quite everyone I knew [was] present on either the first or second night. On Thursday I noticed His Honor and Mrs. Bulyea with Major Thibideau and Miss Babbit in their party." There followed a description of Mrs. Bulyea, "beautifully frocked in palest green satin á la Directoire, with a corsage knot of gold and green satin flowers and was looking bright and well."[10]

Not a word was mentioned about the program of music, Edith's voice or the skills of her company, and nothing about what she was wearing.

It is impossible to ignore the comparison between the reception given to the performances so close together of the diva Edith Miller and the woman who had once been her teacher, Jean Forsyth. It indicates several things: that Edmonton was already a cohesive community proud to the hilt of its own amateur singers, musical director, and stage manager; that no diva—no matter how impressive and skillful, no matter what royalty patronized her in England, with her better-than-thou supporting singers and musicians from abroad—was going to upstage their much-loved local talent; that generous charity outshone token charity; that the kind of touring performers that had drawn such crowds and attention in Winnipeg a decade earlier—especially if they hailed from England—would now fall into the category of interesting social events and not be seen as high points of culture to which local artists should aspire.

It must have been a relief for Edith to return to Winnipeg for two more concerts. After these were done, in triumph as before, a brief note appeared in the June 3 Winnipeg Tribune. "Miss Edith Miller and Miss Maud Bell are spending a short time with Miss Miller's parents at Portage la Prairie." A week later another notice appeared in the same paper. "Miss Edith Miller and Miss Maud Bell, who have been visiting in Portage la Prairie, left last Monday for Montreal, and are sailing next week on the Allan liner Virginian for England."

A month later Jean Forsyth was directing Patience at the Drill Hall in Lloydminster, a town 250 kilometres east of Edmonton along the Canadian Northern Railway. She must have revelled in this performance, which followed the annual interprovincial sports events of the Alberta Amateur Athletic Association on July 5. The weather was remarkably fine, and 3,000 people arriving by train from east and west attended the event, which included band competitions and horse races (featuring bareback riding and "Indian races") as well as athletic trials. At the end of the day, after medals and cash prizes were handed out, *Patience* was performed in the hall "packed to the doors."[11] It proved to be "one of the most successful items in the long programme of events."[12]

> Every seat was occupied, and 'standing room only' was announced shortly after the commencement of the performance. From start to finish, the opera went with a swing, smoothness and finish that did immense credit to the performers, the stage manager, the directress (Miss Jean Forsyth), and all concerned.
>
> That painstaking care must have been expended in rehearsals was evident.
>
> Miss Alice Pinckston, as 'Patience,' won the audience by her acting, singing, and admirable stage presence. Her enunciation was clear, and her voice true and fresh. Miss Pilot, as 'Lady Jane,' was clever and amusing in her part. The parts of 'Bunthorne' and 'Grosvenor' were well sustained by Mr. Nash and Mr. Turner respectively, and it is difficult to say with which of these clever actors the honors lie,—both were equally good. Mr. McIsaacs as 'Col. Calverley,' with his fine baritone voice, and 'looking every inch a soldier,' earned well-merited applause. Possibly the sextette, 'I hear the soft note of the echoing voice,' was the best piece of the evening. Voices and orchestra were shaded to an almost perfect balance.

It is not difficult to imagine Jean Forsyth's state of mind as she returned by train to Edmonton with some of her students and other performers.

"Celeste" is a French name for boys or girls. It means "heavenly" or "celestial." A "celeste" is like a small piano that produces a "heavenly" sound, somewhat akin to the bell-like *glockenspiel*, but with a softer, subtler timbre. The famous "Dance of the Sugar Plum Fairy" in Tchaikovsky's *The Nutcracker* is played on a celeste.

"Celeste" was the name Jean Forsyth chose as a pen name for her weekly column with the *Edmonton Journal*. It was a name tied in with the Blue Moon Tea Room that she would soon open and the Starland Theatre where she had often sung. Since 1903 the *Journal* had been a Conservative alternative to the Liberal *Edmonton Bulletin*. Jean's full-page columns began in 1910 under the following heading:

THE JOURNAL'S PAGE FOR WOMEN: FROM A WOMAN'S POINT OF VIEW

Items of Interest in the World of Fashion and Fancy—

Social and Personal Affairs of the Capital City of Alberta

The page was modeled on her friend Gertrude Balmer Watt's society columns for the *Edmonton Bulletin*. But Jean's columns ranged far wider and deeper than Gertrude's. The page was divided into five sections: PERSONALS, SOCIAL, ITEMS OF INTEREST, RECIPES, and THE FASHIONS. Jean filled any extra space with jokes, poems, or odd events.[1]

The following are typical excerpts from Celeste's "Page for Women."

Miss Stewart of the post office inspector's staff, who has been visiting the east for the last six months, returned Monday. Miss Stewart has had a most enjoyable summer holidaying in Toronto, Muskoka and Hamilton.

The visit of Archbishop Syptikyi to Edmonton on Wednesday was a very picturesque affair. From three to four hundred Ruthenians met the train on which his excellency arrived, the women dressed in gala attire, the men wearing shades of purple and orange, the Ruthenian colors. When the prince stepped onto the platform the strains of the Ruthenian song of welcome greeted him and as he passed through the crowd his countrymen kneeled before him for his blessing.

If you have a telephone in your house, the mouthpiece of the telephone should be cleaned every day, just as we clean the dishes we use, and the table, and it should be thoroughly disinfected at least twice a week. Germs of pneumonia, bronchitis, tuberculosis, and other things may be caught from a telephone. A good formula for disinfectant is a few drops of formaldehyde in a two ounce bottle of water, adding enough extract of lavender or some other pleasant-smelling extract so that after the mouthpiece is cleaned well it will be agreeable. Any druggist could mix such a disinfectant for you very easily and inexpensively.

Miss Marshall Saunders, a well-known authoress who has been in Vancouver, says: "I spend a lot of time in the United States, and my books [especially Beautiful Joe] have a large sale there, but I am a Canadian woman and I am proud of it. I am intensely loyal to my own country." Miss Saunders is a brilliant conversationalist, possesses a most engaging personality, and is deeply interested in every cause having for its object the advancement of woman. She secured material for future stories during her visit to the out-of-the-way points in the prairie provinces, and at the CPR mountain hotels. Miss Saunders spent last winter in California. She recently sold her farm for one of the show places in the famous Annapolis Valley of Nova Scotia, and now resides in Halifax, frequently making trips abroad. In her Annapolis Valley home near the historic village of Grand Pré, she maintained a regular menagerie of birds, dogs and goats. She has written much about animal life. She is an authority on birds, and the care of her aviary and its inmates, although entailing much work, has been a source of much pleasure to her. Her education was largely the result of her father's tutelage [a Baptist minister]. At eight she began the study of Latin, and at fifteen she was sent to Edinburgh, Scotland. Then she was sent to France.

Long velvet coats are to be used this winter. They are just as effective as the long fur cloaks of last year and less expensive. Very supple velvet is used, giving soft, rich folds and varying from one-toned effects and iridescent patterns to cashmere designs. Skunk fur is favoured for edging the skirt, sleeves and collar, this latter by the way not so long and rolling as last year. Large muffs to match these full-length coats are trimmed with ribbon velvet and are frequently combinations of silk velvet and fur.

Curate (at Sunday School) "Now children, we'll close with Hymn 389, 'Little drops of water.' Now do put a little more spirit into it!"

Nothing is more wonderful in these days than the great change which is coming over the women of the East. It is perhaps to be doubted whether the influence exerted by many of these women has not been underrated in the West where conditions are so different. Those veiled women cannot, it would seem, have all been subservient to their husbands. Nor their lives as far apart from their interests and ambitions as we have been taught to believe. At any rate some of them are now taking a part in public affairs as prominent as any of their western sisters would venture upon. In the Turkish revolution ladies of high rank hid documents and brought them to the revolutionists. Unsuspected they carried messages from one plotter to another. What was even more important, they kept up the spirits of their husbands and brothers and urged them to activity in their struggle to overthrow the power of Abdul Hamid [Abdul Hamid II, sultan of the declining Ottoman Empire, the last to have absolute power, known as The Great Assassin for his persecution of Armenians.]. More remarkable still has been the attitude of the Persian women. During the struggle for a constitution many of them sold the ornaments so greatly valued by Eastern women and put the price of them in the treasury. Some of the older women disguised as men actually fought in the ranks. More recently they have been active in the movement to prevent the country from accepting a foreign loan, fearing that if this was done their country would lose its independence. In Egypt the women are working against British occupation. In India education has made great progress among the Mohammedan women. There are colleges in many of the provinces three of which have been founded by an Indian princess. In Lahore a Mohammedan woman edits a magazine in which she urges her fellow women to demand a better social position. A native writer says: "Whereas the Moslem woman of yesterday never left her private apartments on any pretext, today her daughter goes driving for pleasure. After dark, of course, swathed from head to foot in the folds of the burgla [burka or burqa] which custom ordains that she must wear, viewing the world from the little net-screened holes cut in front of her eyes. And the grand-daughter is chafing at the veil longing to cast it aside, yearning to come out from the shadow of the purdah. Even desiring to travel abroad and there secure an education that will enable her to help along the evolution of her less favoured sisters."

THE KNEE BAND SKIRT

[known as the Hobble Skirt, fashionable 1900–1910]

Lovely lady as you wobble,
In your new, knee-banded skirt,
E'en as if you wore a wobble.
Does it hurt?

Does it never make you worry,
Never cramp or hamper you,
What, when you are in a hurry
Do you do?

Gentle lady when you wear it
Where you have to jump or slide,
Do you never long to tear it
Up the side?

Often have I wondered whether
If it were the latest fad
To bind women's feet together
You'd be glad?

If Dame Fashion someday stated
That two legs were not good style,
Would you have one amputated
For a while?

Pretty lady, you're a blessing
To mankind, upon my word,
But you have a way of dreaming
That's absurd.

"THE TATLER"

Queen Alexandra, who is at present in Denmark, is retaining possession of selected carriages and some of the best horses from the Royal Mews placed at her disposal by King George. Seventy thousand pounds a year is ordinarily a large sum, but when the establishments which the Queen will keep up are considered and when her private benefactions so numerous and so generous are remembered, there's very little to spare. This is the opinion of those about the widowed Queen. A court official speaking on the subject exclaimed: "£70,000 a year; why she will give away as much as that." Of course, this is an exaggeration, but it is well-known that Queen Alexandra's kind heart prompts her generosity far in excess of what her income justifies.

Honey Cakes.—Bring one and one-half cupfuls of honey to a boiling point, skim if necessary. Add one-fourth cupful of butter and cook. Add two cupfuls of pastry flour, stirring it in carefully. Let the mixture stand overnight, when ready to bake stir in the grated yellow rind of one lemon, two tablespoonfuls of lemon juice, one half cupful of chopped blanched almonds. Add in a little lukewarm water, and bake in a small round tin. Ice when cool.

Maud Marian Adelaide Ward is an English woman who is touring this country in the interest of ballots for women and the proper feeding of school children. She is a remarkable woman and has had a remarkable career. She is well-educated and a keenly logical student. Her forbears included clergymen and scholars. When her parents died she refused to accept the support of her brother, rebelling against the "parasitic life." She went to London and there studied cookery, working eighty or ninety hours a week. After she learned the art, she gave lessons and often prepared dinners for sick and titled persons. Soon the subject of half-starved school children of London interested her. When the Fabian Society [British socialist society for reform] started the experiment of feeding the poor in certain schools she offered her services in preparing the food. With Dr. Harde Davenport she got under way an experiment that promises to be copied soon in every city in the world where there are ill-fed children.

Jean predictably used her "Page for Women" to publicize her Blue Moon Tea Room from time to time.

The new "Blue Moon Tea Room" opened with a rush on Saturday afternoon, many people being unable even to get to the inside. The rooms, though small, are prettily decorated and on Saturday were filled with flowers, gifts of the many friends who wish success to the venture. It may not be widely known as yet that a hot luncheon is served each day from 12 to 3 o'clock, tea during the afternoon and tea, coffee, chocolate and other light refreshments until 9 o'clock p.m. Arrangements may be made for engaging the rooms for afternoon teas, suppers or small bridge parties. Everything will be done by the management to give satisfaction to the patrons of "The Blue Moon."

—CELESTE

BRITISH SUFFRAGETTE PROTESTS SPUR
WOMEN'S ORGANIZATIONS IN EDMONTON

A startling announcement appeared in *Saturday News* on August 7, 1909. Sylvia Pankhurst and 108 women and 14 men in the Women's Social and Political Union had been arrested on June 29. They had approached the British House of Commons straightforwardly at first, then—after Prime Minister Asquith refused to meet them—violently. The event was one in a long and increasingly intense and violent campaign by suffragettes campaigning for the vote for women since 1906. Sylvia Pankhurst herself struck a policeman in the face five times during the rush. Later, thirteen of her followers broke windows with stones tied in brown paper and attached to strings.

This event was far removed from Edmonton. Yet it had an impact there. Among the suffragettes in the "onslaught" on the House of Commons that night was Mrs. Haverfield (née Scarlett). Evelina was married to a Royal Artillery major, then, after he died, to another Royal Artillery major. She accompanied this second major to South Africa as an assistant for two years during the Boer War, took part in rifle practice, and established a retirement home for horses. Back in England she rode a bicycle called "Pegasus."

Evelina was Dr. Ella Scarlett-Synge's sister. The news report of her arrest vividly piqued the attention of those—like Emily Murphy—who were already deeply involved in the movement. It soon became known that Dr. Scarlett-Synge's sister had been involved in the Women's Social and Political Union for a few years. She had taken part in the Bill of Rights March of 60,000 that turned violent, on March 1908. She was among those at the Albert Hall meeting on October 13, 1908 at which close to 10,000 suffragettes raised nearly £7,000. It was then that she joined the Women's Social and Political Union.

Evelina and Ella Scarlett were women to be reckoned with. The suffragette movement was one that would take hold in Edmonton more strongly than elsewhere in Canada.

The women's organizations in the city that were already well established now grew in importance. For the first time in newspaper reports of women's gatherings—especially political and professional ones—women were sometimes referred to by their first names instead of as "Mrs. so-and-so" or "the wife of so-and-so." They were on the way to becoming "persons" in their own right. For Jean Forsyth, who remained determinedly single, this was already a given.

The most active women's club at the time was the Edmonton Women's Press Club. A visit to Edmonton by Dr. Helen MacMurchy, editor of *Canadian Nurse* and the first woman to intern at the Toronto General Hospital, and her sister Miss

Mrs. Arthur (Emily) Murphy, first female magistrate in the British Empire, and famous women's rights activist.

Marjorie MacMurchy, president of the Canadian Women's Press Association and literary editor of the *Toronto News*, prompted a gathering of professional women in the city. They stayed with Mrs. Emily Wilson on Sixth Street, who gave them a tea on August 3.[1] Partly because Dr. MacMurchy was a member of the Toronto Local Council of Women, it was members of Edmonton's Local Council of Women who entertained them. These included Mrs. Jean Blewitt, Mrs. Mabel Cautley, Mrs. Edith Watt, Mrs. Emily Murphy, and Miss Jean Forsyth. They drove their guests through the city, pointing out locations of interest. Afterwards, they had luncheon at the Yale Hotel. The conversation would have touched on information about Edmonton, women's and children's difficulties being dealt with in the city, comparisons of Toronto and Edmonton women's organizations, and ideas about how to improve life for women, children, and animals. No longer were the set topics of conversations at women's gatherings restricted to who was wearing what, the difficulties of getting and keeping good servants, and gossip about social events and personal relationships.

A meeting of the Alberta and Eastern British Columbia Press Association in September[2] would appear to have shifted the emphasis back to male journalists, some of whom brought their wives for the two-day conference. Yet with Gertrude Balmer Watt, Gertrude Seton-Thompson, and Jean Forsyth organizing events for the ladies, and Dr. Ella Scarlett-Synge presiding over a tea for them, the conversation must have veered towards concerns for women journalists.

Early in the New Year, the Edmonton Women's Press Club met for tea at Mabel Cautley's Belton Lodge to elect officers for the coming year. Gertrude Balmer Watt became president; Mabel Cautley, vice-president; Gertrude Seton-Thompson, secretary, and Jean Forsythe [*sic*], treasurer.[3] In May, the *Edmonton Bulletin* reported on a meeting of the Canadian Women's Press Club in Toronto. Three speakers from the Canadian Women's Press Club gave addresses. One was Marjorie MacMurchy, the same Marjorie who had visited Edmonton with her sister Dr. Helen MacMurchy five months before. Along with Jean Graham and Jean Fraser, she spoke about "How to Make a Paper of Interest to Women."[4] According to the *Toronto News* (where Marjorie MacMurchy was an editor) "the whole three speeches were models in phrasing, in clearness of statement and in brevity." Miss MacMurchy's talk had "delicate touches of humour, and excellent literary finish and was spoken with much grace and effect." Miss Graham, editor of the *Home Journal*, was "entertaining and practical and altogether gracious and womanly." Miss Fraser spoke more briefly, "but not less acceptably."

Sadly, Gertrude Seton-Thompson had decided to return "home" to Ontario. The Edmonton Women's Press Club gave her a farewell tea. Emily Murphy—who had been invited to write a series of columns for *Collier's* magazine[5]—was "unavoidably absent." Otherwise it was the literary women of the city—Mabel Cautley, Jean Forsyth and Katherine Hughes who gathered at five o'clock for "tea and toast and cakes and much gossip" at the Cosie Corner, a local café. It was, wrote Katherine Hughes in her *Saturday News* write-up[6], "the pleasantest kind of a feast. I think we were trying to make Miss Thompson regret her going and succeeded so well that her parting words were that 'she supposed she would do as everyone else did—end up by coming back.'"

Hughes continued her assessment of the situation of women journalists in Canada, quoting "Kit" Coleman, first president of the Canadian Women's Press Club (known by its detractors as the "Cats with Pointed Claws"):

> You would be surprised at the number of women journalists who compose that club, and at the camaraderie and good feeling of each member for the other. As our wittiest comrade, Miss Jean Graham, editor of the *Home Journal*, says, "There is not a cat in the club."
>
> We respect each other and accord to each without jealousy or that lower passion, envy, the place she has won by her work. We have many brilliant members, whose work will be known later, young girls stepping courageously on the first rung of the journalistic ladder, and women who have "arrived."
>
> Our motto is, "Every stroke upward," and it is a great motto to live for. Women are working in all journalistic paths. There are some who write editorials, some who act as special correspondents, others who are free lances, others again who do what is really difficult work, advertising and social paragraphing! It is not as easy to write up every day a stack of weddings and say something pleasant and different of each one, not to speak of not mixing [up] the gowns.
>
> Miss Cora Hind, who is commercial editor of the Thunderer of the West, the *Winnipeg Free Press*, a mighty newspaper, with four editions daily, was at our late meeting. And all these women meet in harmony, generously giving, the one to the other, her mead of praise, or of encouragement.
>
> The Canadian Women's Press Club is an organization to which any member may be proud to belong, and it is growing in size and strength every day.[7]

Women who actively worked for change—whether they were suffragettes like Emily Murphy or suffragists like Katherine Hughes or were busy with any of the women's organizations in the city—seemed to recognize the importance of having a voice in the press. Not just in a women's section devoted to teas, weddings and bridge parties, but more importantly as editors and columnists writing about serious political issues for women. They were quickly acquiring this voice and putting it to good use. The term "suffragette" was coined in London's *Daily Mail* to refer to women who were protesting actively for the vote. ("Suffragists" were those who used constitutional methods.)

And, for the first time, professional gatherings of women began to include husbands, just as men at conferences were attended by some wives. Mabel Cautley welcomed the Imperial Order Daughters of the Empire delegates from Toronto and their husbands, who visited Edmonton at the end of October 1909. She entertained them on Friday evening at Belton Lodge, along with the executives of the three Edmonton chapters of the Imperial Order Daughters of the Empire and their husbands. The next day Mrs. Bulyea held a reception in their honour at Government House.[8]

This is not to say that women shifted all at once from elegant social teas and balls and receptions to professional gatherings. The longstanding social entertainments, often with musical entertainment, continued side-by-side with meetings of women's organizations bent on changing the world.

Jean Forsyth was as involved in these "old-fashioned" entertainments as she was in the charities and serious women's organizations. She was still secretary of the Edmonton Humane Society and had added the job of treasurer of the Edmonton Women's Press Club, which reflected the prestige she had gained from her new "Celeste" column.

Less than two months after her production of *Patience* at Lloydminster, the effervescent Jean hosted "a merry bridge party of three tables in her "delightful[ly] appointed studio." "The large, and to almost anyone else, impossible room to decorate, under Miss Forsythe's [sic] clever fingers has a fine smack of art and Bohemia, and on Tuesday great vases of Golden Glow [coneflower] and other flowers lent their quota of charm and colour." Jean greeted her guests in "a light summery costume of champagne linen, with heavy embroidery on the bodice. She had a "bright word and a smile for everyone."[9] Later on, the men stopped in to enjoy Jean's singing.

It was a busy Christmas for Jean. She disproved the myth that single women might languish alone on this family holiday. On Christmas Eve, she attended a "jolly dinner" given by Mr. and Mrs. Ambrose Dickins.[10] The hosts had set a miniature Christmas tree in the centre of the table, with a present for each guest as decoration. "Each gift was a funny one and provoked much laughter and gaiety, being accompanied by a suitable inscription." That, however, was not the end of the party. They all went over to Mr. and Mrs. Clarke Bowker's where a dinner party was also in progress. The combined parties played "jolly" Christmas games.

On Christmas Day itself, Jean was off to another dinner party.

If it is possible, Jean—quickly approaching sixty—was busier in Edmonton than she had been in Winnipeg when she was younger. She attended teas (even the Ladies' Curling Club tea, where Emily Murphy was vice-president)[11] and musicales[12]—"really-truly music, not the music-hall makeshift";[13] attended the concert

Miss Katherine Hughes, a Christian suffragist and journalist.

Mrs. George Hedley Vicars Bulyea, wife of the Premier of Alberta.

given by Russian pianist Mark Hambourg on his first Canadian tour (the same year he began cutting records);[14] and she was one of the "musical enthusiasts" on the executive committee that organized the third Alberta Music Festival[15] with 200 voices and 50 orchestra members.[16] She even performed in a comedy at the Empire. She played Mrs. Pilkington, wife of the hero, in *Innocent as a Lamb.*

"The part is one that produces great fun," ran an advance notice, "and Miss Forsyth's vein of comedy will find good scope in the role."[17] She also attended a late roast chicken dinner at Lewis's Café after a performance of *Twelfth Night* by the local Amateur Dramatic Club. The players arrived in costume to the vivacious scene that had "the real smack of Bohemianism" as its "chief attraction."[18]

Jean was one of the guests at a huge ball at Government House on February 10, 1910, in honour of the Alberta MLAs. The *Saturday News* went to extraordinary lengths to describe this entertainment for more than 300 guests, at least a third of them MLAs and their wives.

> The rooms and halls on the entire three flats represented a surging wave of fashionably frocked humanity. But, whereas the ordinary billows are only snowy-capped, this particular wave was rainbow-hued, a mingling of red coats, and black and white, of queer bobbing heads abreast the billow, marcelled and plain, bald and turban-topped. You looked from a face to a gown, and the identity was lost before you could arrive at a conclusion. The general effect was magnificent. Often back of the figures, was a frame-work of lovely blooming things, next moment the "moving row" had obliterated the flower faces. You got the impression of a moving picture performance.[19]

Of course, the "Queen of the Salon" was Mrs. Bulyea "in a magnificent creation of white Duchesse satin with a garniture, or over-dress of chrystal [sic] and raised embroideries, silver threads and beads just suggested here and there, and a strikingly

Mrs. Joe (Margaret) Morris, wife of the Liberal politician "Fighting Joe."

modish note appearing in a knot of pale pink roses caught at the hem of the train. The new turban arrangement of her coiffure was the finishing touch to a very stunning *toute ensemble*, which was admired by all present." Even the lieutenant governor's clothes were observed. "His Honor still wore his Windsor uniform of the afternoon and looked very smart and stately." The "artistic" table of refreshments, "a host of nodding yellow daffodils on a long mirror base, was enhanced with a dash of yellow satin streamers, with red shaded-candles in handsome brass candlesticks on the four corners." Turner's Orchestra "played delightfully in the upper hall-way."

Jean also attended "one of the most brilliant functions ever given in Edmonton," a dance hosted by Mr. and Mrs. Joe Morris (an early grocer, alderman, and member of the Board of Trade who owned the first car in the city—a 1903 Model A Ford bought in 1904)[20]—in the dining hall of the King Edward Hotel. Turner's Orchestra "furnished irresistible dance music."

As in the old days, the women's dress was described in detail. The hostess, Mrs. Margaret Morris, was "a graceful figure in an elegant toilette of white spangled with silver sequins, her lovely white hair dressed with the new turban effect." Mrs. Scobie appeared in a "filmy white lace robe with a wreath of tiny rosebuds in her pretty wavy hair." Mrs. Bannantyne, "a pretty piquante woman, [wore] mauve satin, with deep fringe and gold sequin ornamentation." And on and on.[21] Jean Forsythe [*sic*] was "a striking figure in handsome black lace." The ball was romantically staged with softly gleaming lights, softly tinted walls, a staff of "irreproachable men waiters," and a "perfect floor." The scene, according to the *Saturday News*, "was more like an incident one would expect to take place in the Savoy Hotel in London or the Waldorf Astoria in New York, than a private dance at an outpost city of an empire. Who could believe that this was faraway Edmonton, and the ball a western, and not a metropolitan affair?"

JEAN PERFORMS AT SILENT FILMS

Theatres in Edmonton at the end of the first decade of the twentieth century hovered in a limbo between serious drama, vaudeville, and silent movies. Serious drama continued on a separate path, appealing to more sophisticated audiences, as it does today. Vaudeville appealed to the less sophisticated, typically offering a mixture of unrelated separate acts including rollicking comedy, popular music such as ballads, magicians, animal tricks, one-act plays (usually farces), and sly jokes. Meanwhile, silent movies were growing in popularity. (And after the introduction of "talkies" in the early 1930s, movies would eventually supplant vaudeville.)

Jean Forsyth had mainly associated herself with the church and the concert hall. She had given endless musical entertainments for teas, charity events, and other gatherings of high society in both Winnipeg and Edmonton, but now she found herself drawn in the direction of vaudeville, performing with the Edmonton Amateur Drama Club in "screaming farce" comedies such as *His Excellency the Governor*, which made saucy fun of the very upper-class social events she was attending.[1] Such plays had acquired at least a touch of dignity by being performed at the Empire Theatre.

She was no longer taking part in the Ladies' Edmonton Musical Club.[2] Almost as if sensing the increasing shift of popular entertainment to "store theatres" that in time would become movie theatres, she began singing at the Starland in what amounted to a slightly more sophisticated type of vaudeville, for the Starland billed itself as "The Popular Family Theatre."

A notice in the *Edmonton Bulletin* on October 4, 1909 showed yet again how adaptable and entrepreneurial Jean Forsyth was:

> The management of the Starland Theatre announces that they have secured the services of Miss Forsyth, the well known and popular soprano of this city, to sing the illustrated songs. Miss Forsyth's beautiful and well-trained voice needs no recommendation than to hear her sing. Her renderings of classical vocal music and interpretations of difficult selections from the masters' works are above criticism, and music lovers in general in Edmonton have before recognized in her a lady of unquestionably high musical attainments and artistic ability.

> Miss Forsyth will make her first appearance at Starland today at the usual matinee.[3]

"Illustrated songs" suggests that images appropriate to the songs Jean was to sing would be projected on a screen of some sort—usually a hanging cloth, such as muslin, or a large board painted white. Jean performed five times on different weekdays that October, her songs marking the conclusion of each matinee and evening program.

A typical program, such as the one reported on October 12, included two highly dramatic illustrated stories: the "thrilling" "Last Day of Pompeii" and "Napoleon and Josephine." The latter film highlighted Josephine's Creole background, her reign as empress, and her divorce. A newsreel-type presentation followed of the "principal views" of Edmonton when the governor general, Earl Grey, laid the cornerstone of the legislative buildings less than two weeks earlier on October 1. An impressive procession along Jasper Avenue through huge crowds gathered beneath the flags and bunting, preceded the event. (The magnificent legislative building would not be completed until 1912.) After these "superbly illustrated" presentations were done, "Miss Forsyth ended an entertainment of the highest merit."[4]

On October 14 the presentations seem to have been either short plays or illustrated recitations with the titles "The Janitor's Bottle," "Landlady's Portrait," "He Couldn't Dance," "The Empty Sleeve," "Making Tambourine," and "Host of New Year's Dinner," finishing up with a song by "Edmonton's celebrated soprano," Jean Forsyth. On October 23 "a triumph of photographic art (A Romance of Old Madrid)," and Jean's closing song made up the whole program. Admission for these performances was ten cents.[5]

Before long these visual presentations would include very short, unsophisticated films cranked on projectors. (Such films were already being shown in "store theatres and black tents" in major cities across North America.) Not until 1918—a decade later—would the first feature-length silent film be shown in Edmonton. Yet the productions at the Starland Theatre were a step in that direction—including the music. Jean's songs, though she could not have known it, were precursors of the piano honky-tonk and waltzes that accompanied silent films.[6]

JEAN OPENS HER BLUE MOON TEA ROOM, 1910

Jean Forsyth looked at her watch. It was 4:30 and soon her guests would arrive, climbing up the stairs from the Starland Theatre. This was her boldest venture yet—her own tea room, up among the telegraph wires, looking out over the city roofs with their jagged pattern of false fronts. Jean glanced at the advertising painted on the side of the building opposite, then down to the canopies below shading windows displaying all kinds of merchandise. It was Saturday, October 29, a fine day. Thank goodness, she thought as she nervously arranged the Delft blue curtains over the window. Windy rains would have kept some away.

"I couldn't have asked for better advance notices for opening my Blue Moon Tea Room," she said, turning to Evelyn Mackie, one of her students who had arrived to give her a hand with the tea and muffins.

Dear Gertrude, she thought. She couldn't have been kinder in her "Peggy" column a week ago. Of course, she's my friend, but she did go a little bit overboard describing me as "The High Priestess of the cult of tea." She laughed her high tinkling laugh. And I the "Lady—rather than the Man—in the Moon"? She *does* let herself get carried away! I wonder what she meant by anticipating something different because she knows me. Was she suggesting that I am "different" in some way?

"Gertrude did ferret out the meaning of blue moon," she said to Evelyn, who was disappearing into the kitchen to start the kettle. "I haven't seen her in a blue moon. That's it. That's what we all say when we meet for tea—or anything else," she added. "And it's sailing away over 'Starland'!"

There were already tea rooms and cafés in the city. She had attended them all.

Cronn's Café had opened the year before she arrived in Edmonton. Back then it was Cronn's Club, to entice men who didn't belong to a *real* club to go there. Then Robert Cronn sold the hotel. Lately it was felicitously placed next to the Grand Theatre over on Jasper Avenue East. It was really the Alberta Café, but no one ever called it that. Cronn had made a success of the place, all right, but it mainly attracted men. No wonder, since its ads usually pictured men dining on things like quails on toast or frogs' legs.

Advertising *frogs' legs*, Jean thought. *Imagine!* No wonder his waiters have their noses in the air! And ads in *French*! In 1906 "*L'Homme satisfait*" indeed! *Pshaw!* He called Edmonton "a man's town," with pictures of stout chaps in their waistcoats and bow ties smoking cigars and drinking wine!

"Well," she said to Evelyn, who had reappeared, "we'll just show him that this is also a *woman's* town!" Evelyn looked perplexed, but said nothing. "One thing I certainly know," she continued, "this place will not be as tiny as that little Tip Top Tea Rooms on a *balcony*, for heaven's sake. Roof Garden? Ice cream? Or that other one further down McDougall Hill. Ye Cosie Corner Café? That's no more Old English than I'm a monkey's uncle...aunt, I mean. Only six women can fit in there. *Six!* And I should know, my dear, because I was one of six regulars who used to go there."

Jean smoothed her white-grey hair, bound in a loose Grecian style with a blue ribbon, and her blue gored ankle-length skirt. She patted her cream lace blouse with its high collar and delicate layered sleeves. She smiled at Evelyn. "Here they come, dear! And plenty of them!"

Gertrude Balmer Watt was the first through the door. She was wearing her navy wool tailored walking suit with matching slanted hat. She walked to Jean at once, extending her hand straight out. "My dear Jean," she said warmly, "Congratulations! I'd like to introduce Mrs. Sifton. Mary is the wife of our new premier. Her daughter, Nellie Dennis, will be along later."

As the other women chatted, Gertrude glanced around at the room, "Ah, this is everything I anticipated—and more!" she said, turning back to Jean. "You have outdone even yourself, Jean. Such a talent for everything artistic!"

Others crowded up to Jean, shaking her hand, offering their congratulations, and swivelling their heads so as to take in everything and everyone.

"Mathilda! Welcome!" said Jean, smiling broadly at Mrs. Harwood. "And how was Paris? I want to know all about your trip, perhaps not now, but later." Jean stood back to take in Mathilda's ensemble. "I see you have dressed for the occasion—in that lovely blue linen frock, so finely tailored. Did you have it made in the great city of fashion?"

Mathilda nodded and said, "Yes, it is from Paul Poiret's in Paris. And so is the hat." She turned her head back and forth so Jean could see the hat swathed like a turban and plumed with black feathers from both sides. "I brought back several things for the season."

Evelyn handed Mathilda a cup of tea in a Blue Willow cup and saucer and guided her to the table where the cream and sugar, muffins and jam were pleasingly displayed.

Jean went over to the table occupied by the Women's Press Club, which had been joined by Florence Lowes, wife of Freddie Lowes, the millionaire realtor from Calgary, and Mrs. George W. Swaisland, a pretty, vivacious lover of gatherings and dances.

"I can't tell you how happy I am to see you here," Jean said, looking round the table after introductions.

"My goodness, Jean, this is a wonderful spot," Mrs. Swaisland declared. "It is truly a study in blue. I love blue! The Blue Willow is delightful, especially against the cream and brown walls. And your hammered brass trays have such...such *élan*!"

"Yes, yes," joined in various members of the press club.

"And we shall greatly enjoy having our meetings here," Kathleen Hughes added, the rest nodding.

"Yes, this is not simply a place for ladies to meet when shopping," said Gertrude. "This is a place to encourage the discussion of ideas, a place that gives women a chance to meet for conversation other than gossip, though we wouldn't want to miss out on that either, would we."

They all laughed heartily.

Just then the French-speaking friends known as the "French Literary Club" hurried up to Jean. "*Bonjour, bonjour!*" They all carried exquisitely wrapped small boxes. "*Ouvre les, ouvre les!*" they chimed together.

Jean sat at one of her tables to do so, even though more guests were coming through the door. Each package held a pretty blue cup and saucer.

"*Merci, merci beaucoup. Ces tasses et soucoupes sont très jolies, très, très jolies!*" Jean exclaimed.

"*Souvenons-nous par ces petites tasses,*" said Mme Delavault, who was from Paris and whose husband was E. E. Delavault, a consular agent to France. "*Bien sûr,*" Jean said. "*Sans doute! Comment pourrai-je oublier? Les tasses bleues pour La Lune Bleu!* Oh, *c'est dommage,* but I must go."

Now a crowd pressed through the door. More waited behind them on the stairs.

As she hurried to the door, Jean's cousin Jessie Dawson with her daughter Jean leaned after her to call out, "These muffins and jam are simply delicious, Jean, dear. If they are typical of the Blue Moon's menu, I shall be here often. It will be such a delicious sensation, after a hot afternoon at the theatre downstairs, to come up here to enjoy a soothing cup of tea, a few healthful delicacies, and a quiet chat with a friend or two."

They were joined by Nellie Dennis, who added, "Yes, it is a delightfully cozy tea room, altogether 'homey.' Such a *coup,* Jean. Is there anything you *can't* do?"

They all laughed.

Just then a jolly little *côterie* of men burst as best they could into the crowded room and made for the tea table, where the younger set was chatting with Evelyn Mackie and Jean Dawson. They helped themselves to muffins. Jean looked over at them and said to Nellie, "Oh, I'm delighted! I had so hoped that men would feel comfortable here as well as women."

Both the *Saturday News* and the *Edmonton Bulletin* reported with great delight on the opening of the Blue Moon Tea Room. "It was christened," wrote "Peggy," "with such tremendous good-will and *éclat.*" The Lady in the Blue Moon "suffered so overwhelming a reception, I wonder she is still alive to tell the tale. It has sailed off under flying colours, to what one hopes and predicts will prove a long and successful voyage."[1]

A HUSBAND'S LETTER OF COMPLAINT

Not all men were interested in going to tea rooms. Some were dead against tea rooms. One was so annoyed about tea rooms that he complained to "Peggy" at the *Saturday News*. She turned his objections into a column:

> I had an interview with a young husband a day or so before I left for the East. The burden of his refrain was that he "wished we would go home."
>
> I told him please not to be so Mad-Hatterish and tell us what he meant, when he explained "that when he went home, he wanted his dinner."
>
> "Why don't you take it then?" I said when he told me that "we" wouldn't let him.
>
> I wanted to know who "we" were, and this is what he said: "Well if you really want to know, it is you tea-partying women who come presumably to drink an afternoon dish of tea, and stay—until the husbands imagine you must be waiting for a bid to dinner."
>
> "Now my wife tells me that her 'tea' cards read 'From 4 to 6 o'clock.' Very well, I stay hanging around town until 6:30, my usual dinner hour. I would like a chance to fix up a bit for the evening meal, but I can forgive that. What I can't stand philosophically is waiting around until 7:30 or later, until the last of 'you' have flitted, and the maid and my poor tired little wife can rustle the dinner, a half-cold one—between them. Now I work hard all day. At night I am ready for a good, hot dinner, served promptly, so that I can settle down for an evening's rest or recreation.
>
> I am glad, if it gives my wife pleasure, to have you all come and drink tea under our roof.
>
> I should like to be home and have a cup with you—but, by Jove, I wish some of you had a better idea of time.
>
> It's just as bad when my own Frau goes out. It's nearly seven, or a quarter to, before she gets home, and the dinner standing, and the girl cross over her spoiled meal.
>
> I don't know what you women with children do, I'm sure—I mean what the children do. They must be awfully tired and fractious by the time you blow in.
>
> And then my wife has no appetite for dinner—little wonder, with her tea just over—and I wish you'd write it all up, and ask every person to please go home

at six anyway. "I suppose," said I, "you'd like your name published? The women will be so interested."

"Not on your life, Peg," said he. Some of the women have had my views already, and I'm ambitious, don't you know. And some day you women may have the vote."

"You're a Cowardy Custard," I told him. But there really is something to what he says, isn't there?

You know some of us are famous.[1]

EDITH PERFORMS AT THE "FESTIVAL OF EMPIRE"
FOR THE CORONATION OF GEORGE V, 1910

King Edward VII died on May 6, 1910 from the last in a series of heart attacks, complicated by bronchitis. He did not die in Paris in the special chair he had had made to enhance his pleasure at his favourite brothel, as he might have. The stubborn, profligate king who smoked twenty cigarettes and twelve cigars daily died at Buckingham Palace, to all appearances a devoted family man. His last words were "I am very glad." They were in reference to his horse, Witch of the Air, winning the race at Kensington Park that afternoon. Thus passed the Edwardian Age, a scant nine years since it began after his mother Queen Victoria died in 1901. Pulitzer-prize–winning American historian Barbara Tuchman described his state funeral on May 20, 1910 as "the greatest assemblage of royalty and rank ever gathered in one place and, of its kind, the last."[1]

There followed an official year of mourning before his second son (his first predeceased him at age twenty-eight), the forty-four-year-old George, who had married Princess Mary of Teck sixteen years earlier, was crowned.

As a part of the series of celebratory events that led up to the Coronation on June 23, 1911, a Festival of Empire was held at the Crystal Palace in South London. It was sixty years since the original temporary palace in Hyde Park had been built to house the Great Exhibition of 1851, the first world's fair, which displayed cultural and industrial progress from around the world.

By 1911, however, the Crystal Palace was in financial difficulty. It was thought the Festival of Empire would save it from liquidators[2] as well as pump up British patriotism throughout the Empire by making a link to Queen Victoria, whose reign established the Empire "on which the sun never sets."[3]

The Festival of Empire was "pure Imperialist propaganda."[4] The souvenir brochure referred to "a Social Gathering of the British Family" to encourage the "firmer welding of those invisible bonds which hold together the greatest empire the world has ever known." A massive historical four-part pageant over three days by 15,000 volunteers that ran for four months chronicled "the gradual growth and development of the British nation, as seen in the history of this, the Empire City." Each of the major colonies held demonstrations related to their culture and histories—once they became British, of course—displaying products and exhibits from their countries in pavilions that were three-quarter-size replicas of their houses of parliament.

The opening concert on May 12, 1911 was dazzling. The vast central nave of the Crystal Palace was filled to capacity. The choir, drawn from the major choirs of Greater London, was 4,500 voices strong. There were 400 in the orchestra from the Queen's Hall Orchestra and the London Symphony Orchestra, plus the Festival of Empire Military Band. Four conductors shared choral and orchestral direction: Sir Henry J. Wood and Sir Alexander Mackenzie, who had both often directed Edith Miller at her London concerts; Dr. Charles Harriss, a Canadian composer and organist who passionately wished for closer ties between Britain and Canada; and Sir Hubert Parry, a religious English composer favouring chorales who had recently been the Heather Professor of Music at Oxford.

Donald Smith, Lord Strathcona, the CPR magnate from Canada, had ordered special silver medals struck for all the choir members—the Imperial Choir Strathcona Medal.[5] Lord Strathcona, a precise man with a jutting pointed white beard, had maintained a house in London since his appointment as Canadian high commissioner in 1899.

An enormous and boisterous crowd cheered all along the route taken by the Royal Parade from Buckingham Palace to the Crystal Palace.

When King George V in his frock coat, dark vest, and white winged collar, his cane in hand, and Queen Mary on the arm of their son, the Prince of Wales, and their party of family and aristocrats appeared, "a rousing fanfare" and Elgar's arrangement of "God Save the King" greeted them. Someone in the choir shouted out, "Three cheers for the King!" and the response from the huge crowd and musicians alike was one of "the greatest zest." The Queen's attire was much praised in the papers. It was "a beautiful dress of orchid mauve *charmeuse,* her small, neat-fitting hat being trimmed with *pleureuse* plumes [ostrich feathers extended and thickened by more ostrich feathers] exactly the same colour." Her bouquet—small "in accordance with Her Majesty's special desire—of Catyler [actually Cattleya, or large] orchids and white flowers also "matched her dress."[6] Photos show a somewhat sombre Queen, her hat stacked high with plumes, the bodice of her dress covered in lace with only a neck-high collar instead of the chin-high collars favoured by her mother-in-law, Queen Alexandra.

The concert itself featured patriotic music, mainly British music about Britain by British composers: Sir Alexander Mackenzie's "Britannia Overture," Harriss's "Empire of the Sea," Fletcher's new anthem "For Empire and for Sea," and Dyke's "rousing recessional" "God of Our Fathers" sung by choir and audience. The Elgar favourite "Land of Hope and Glory" drew wild cheers. The single soloist, Madame Clara Butt, sang "The Enchantress," a song about the enormous power of love by John Liptrot Hatton, a Liverpudlian composer and pianist. Though her deep contralto voice could not be heard far from the stage despite its power, because she was statuesque at six feet, two inches, she could be seen: a "living Union Jack" with "her dress of brilliant blue silk gauze being draped across with a crimson ribbon, the upper part of the corsage being chiefly white."

Music remained a prominent part of the Festival of Empire and the Coronation on June 23 at Westminster Abbey. On Tuesday afternoons from May 30 to July 18 "a series of grand Empire concerts" were given in the Crystal Palace. "The most eminent artists will appear."[7]

The first in this series at 3:00 p.m. on May 30 was the "Grand Canadian Concert." The "eminent" artists chosen to represent Canada were soprano Mme

First Canadian soprano star
Emma Albani, *circa* 1872.

Emma Albani and Miss Edith J. Miller. Edmund Burke (on loan from Covent Garden), a Toronto-born international opera star with a bass/baritone voice, was also a part of the concert, as was the Smallwood-Metcalfe choir, which sang "O Canada" and other Canadian choruses. The program also interspersed orchestral numbers: "Canadian Rhapsody" by Alexander Mackenzie; Elgar's "Cockaigne Overture"; and "Aire de Ballet" by Percy Pitts.

Yet Mme Albani and Edith J. Miller were the centrepieces of the concert, and their performances were at the core of the program. Edith sang first, then Mme Albani twice, then Edith again, which gave Mme Albani pride of place at the centre of their program. Albani sang "A Coronation Song" ("The Bells of Peace" written for the occasion by English composer Robert Coningsby Clarke), "Dove Sono" (aria from Mozart's *Marriage of Figaro*), "Souvenirs de Jeune Age" (aria from Ferdinand Hérold's opera *Le Pré aux Clercs*), and "A la Claire Fontaine" (a traditional French-Canadian children's song).

Edith Miller sang "Le Nil," a song by Xavier Leroux, "Pastorale" a song by Henry Carey, eighteenth-century English composer, and "Vive la Canadienne," the well-known traditional French-Canadian song.[8]

Edith Miller was by now in her prime at age thirty-six. She must have out-performed the now excessively stout Mme Albani, who was long past her prime at age sixty-four. Only six months later Mme Albani would make her last appearance on the English stage.

The concert ended with the rousing "Rule Britannia."

Edith Miller also gave a solo concert at the Aeolian Hall on June 8 as part of the lead-up to the Coronation. Others performing in the series of concerts around London were Spanish Catalan cellist Pablo Casals; Czech violinist, Jan Kubelík; French flautist Yvette Guibert; Irish tenor John McCormack; and—as might be expected—Nellie Melba.

Now aged fifty, Nellie Melba had become a scandalous divorcée. Her "rogue" of an Australian husband, Charles Armstrong, finally heard (through gossip columns in Paris)[9] about the reckless affair she was conducting with Prince Phillippe, Duke of Orléans, nine years her junior. Melba had become a London snob, using her fame in the Covent Garden Opera and her friend (and Oscar Wilde's friend) Gladys de Grey, whose husband Lord de Grey was chairman of the Royal Opera's directorate, to gain entrance into London high society. She settled at the new luxurious London hotel, the Savoy, and bought a mansion in Regent's Park. She was "palatial in her tastes" and—despite the scandal—"achieved quasi-royal status" and did as she pleased, including taking many other lovers and turning down performances she disliked. It seems there was "no more liberated class of woman in Europe" than rich successful stage performers. Recently she was beginning to be upstaged at Covent Garden by Luisa Tetrazzini, a much younger coloratura soprano, though, thanks to directing her "pathological criticism" of other lyric sopranos at Luisa, she largely held her own.

Her performance in the series of Coronation Concerts in Royal Albert Hall on May 27 "under the immediate patronage of Their Majesties the King and Queen" included Wagner's "Elsa's Dream" from *Lohengrin*, Ophelia's "Mad Scene" from Thomas's *Hamlet*, the "Jewel Song" from Gounod's *Faust*, and the "Prayer" from Puccini's *Tosca*. These songs were derived from highly wrought scenes: Elsa, accused of murder, dreams of a knight on a boat to whom she pledges her virtue; Ophelia, driven insane by Hamlet's neglect, goes mad and drowns herself; Marguerite, the rural maiden in *Faust*, tries on the jewels she finds and admires her own beauty; and Tosca's prayer asking God why he is punishing a righteous woman, after which she is stabbed. It was an exhausting emotional roller coaster.

In contrast Edith sang a set of songs by modern English composers. Her solo concert was billed as "The Only Recital This Season."

JEAN SUCCEEDS AS A BUSINESSWOMAN

Jean Forsyth's decision to go into business by opening her Blue Moon Tea Room in October 1910 had been an astute move. Her decision a year later, in December 1911, to shift to larger quarters in the Bellamy Block at 108 Rice Street at the Corner of Howard Street was brilliant. Her new Blue Moon Tea Room was much more spacious. It consisted of two rooms that could be rented out for any number of activities: meetings, recitals, teas, dances, receptions, displays and sales—activities for which anything from a cup of tea to a lavish banquet might be needed. The rooms could be expanded to full capacity or turned into intimate nooks with clever arrangements of furniture and various sizes of screens. Jean took a room (#10, then #3) next door to the Blue Moon in the Bellamy Block.

Her new business was also hard-headed. She dealt only in cash. She said that this was to avoid the headache of keeping books.[1] Whatever her reasons, her business earned her a place in a later *Maclean's Magazine* article about Canadian women in business. (The other women in the article were Cecile Holmes's [a.k.a. Miss Cecile] Ottawa dress shop; Mrs. H. M. Simpson, Montreal prime real estate agent; Mrs. Jane Hample, Winnipeg caterer; and Ottawa's Miss Flora Ann Campbell, that city's first policewoman.)[2]

By this time—at age sixty-two—Jean's experience had shown her exactly what sort of setting was needed for the social and professional needs of the city, especially women's needs. With the shift towards women's activist and intellectual organizations, a simple ladies' tea room was not sufficient. She saw that she could attract a much larger clientele if she ran a place that was congenial to serious endeavours and intellectual, political, and religious discussions. If she welcomed male clients and created a décor that was not too ruffled and fussy, the place could attract men as well as women. The Blue Moon Tea Room replaced the churches and parish halls and rinks that had been community centres in the past, especially during her time in Winnipeg. It was not only a place that could be rented out for many events, it was equally a place to finish an evening after events around the city. Living next door she could easily oversee the staff she needed for any number of activities, even those that might be held simultaneously.

In 1911 the local economy surged. Edmonton's population (including Strathcona's) was now slightly more than 31,000, a startling near-doubling since Jean's arrival in 1907, when it was about 18,000. Of that population about 70 percent had Anglo-Saxon roots. By far the next largest group—over 15 percent—was from Slavic stock, some Poles, but mainly Ukrainians (then called Ruthenians). Though a good number of these were illiterate and hoped to keep alive their language and customs, they had high ambitions for the education of their children.

The Blue Moon Tea Room, interior,
Maclean's Magazine, Jan. 1915.

It was not long before a parallel Ruthenian/English Reader was produced. By 1912 Ukrainians were printing their own newspaper *The New Society*, edited by Tom Tomashewsky. The same year the new Boian Society began a reliable series of Ukrainian plays.[3] Germans (8 percent) and Scandinavians (3 percent) were groups with similar interests. A smattering of Belgians, Chinese, Dutch, Greeks, Hungarians, Italians, and a few blacks from the United States made up the rest of this cosmopolitan city.[4]

Real estate speculation floated sky high. The new meatpacking plants, such as Swift and Burns, staffed mainly by eastern European immigrants, introduced mass production techniques. Some practices spurred grumblings that unions were imminent, though that was not to be until the 1940s. Yet the garment works—mainly women—established Local 120 of the United Garment Workers of America that same year. This helped set a standard for wages and working conditions in non-union places in the garment industry.[5]

In September 1912, the Industrial Workers of the World (IWW) organized the first strike of sewer construction workers in the city. After five days, the strike failed, but the IWW (known as Wobblies) would continue to organize unskilled unemployed workers in a series of other protests.

These strident, highly visible protests from labour and service people, though often unsuccessful, were the harbingers of more to come. They were also an enduring force from the Left bearing in on city and provincial politics. The year 1912 fostered prosperity and civic projects partly because George. S. Armstrong was smoothly elected mayor. For once, the seesawing of city governance achieved a balance. Armstrong "had the support of several 'professional aldermen'; one or two 'business' aldermen won [seats], and the 'populists' made a breakthrough, electing four aldermen out of ten."[6]

In this harmonious context, 1912 flourished. Strathcona and Edmonton finally amalgamated. The first graduating class from the University of Alberta celebrated. The building of the High Level Bridge, designed to serve rail, streetcars, cars, and pedestrians, ushering the Canadian Pacific Railway into downtown Edmonton the next year, was underway. The local branch of the Women's Canadian Club was organized. Emily Murphy built her arts-and-crafts-style house at 11011 88 Avenue in the Garneau district (now a historic site) where she would later settle until her death. The first ski tournament was held on Connor's Hill. Annie Jackson joined the Edmonton Police Service, the first female police officer in Canada. The Cree athlete, Alex Decoteau, competed in the Stockholm Olympics, the only Albertan competitor. Finally, after years of blocking downtown development, the Hudson's Bay Company sold off its enormous land holdings that had forced suburbs to spring up along its northern and western edges. The lineup of potential buyers ran for blocks.

It is almost symbolic of the year that the severely handsome, authoritative legislative building, which had begun construction in 1907 when Jean arrived, was finally completed.

Luck is sometimes said to be a matter of being in the right place at the right time. This was true in Jean's case, but it was not the whole truth. She could not have known that Edmonton in 1910 and 1911 was on the verge of unforeseen expansion and prosperity.

Yet her many connections also gave her a decided advantage over some diligent matrons who meant to serve afternoon tea in boudoir-like surroundings to ladies along with a "'healthful' delicacy" such as cake, ice cream, or chocolates. She was a director at the Humane Society; she had attended meetings of the Edmonton Women's Press Club; she had been in on the establishment of the Edmonton Women's Canadian Club. Her singing at teas, musicales, meetings of the Edmonton Ladies' Musical Club, and the Starland had made her a familiar and popular woman. She had a cadre of students at Alberta College, as well as her private pupils. Her vocal students and their parents knew her to be a well-liked and enthusiastic teacher. Her production of *Patience* had widened her already large circle of acquaintance. Without missing a beat she had demonstrated her deft organizational abilities.

Then there were her relatives—Mabel Cautley, Marjorie Pardee and Jessie Dawson—who had welcomed her to the city in 1907 and introduced her to their friends and interests. They could speak for her integrity as a person and her past achievements. Rooming at first with Gertrude Seton-Thompson was fortuitous, for it gave her links to the newspapers and access to advertising.

Yet Jean did not need recommendations or endorsements. She was her own best ambassador. Apart from her indignation with the Winnipeg pound keeper, Hans Jessen, who attracted several complaints for the way in which he kept his hungry, thirsty dogs in filthy surroundings, there is no record of any fallings-out with anyone. It was obvious that she loved being with others. There were hardly any occasions she missed, from the high society balls at which she danced to the athletic competitions for which she sang. Emily Murphy later took a detailed look at her:

She possess[es] a very genius of personality. Had she been given her own way as a young girl and allowed to enter the field of light opera, there is little doubt but that she would have become famous, for apart from her dramatic, well-trained soprano voice, she not only possesses a strong personality but rare gifts as a comedian.

The writer of the article, who also knew her, in which Emily Murphy is quoted, gives a clear picture of Jean:

Anyone who has ever met Miss Forsyth is unlikely to forget her, and probably few women, outside of those occupying public positions, know more people than she throughout the length and breadth of Canada. Hundreds of her pupils are scattered over the country, and many are the people who have enjoyed hearing her sing. Yet without in the least disparaging her musical ability, her greatest contribution to society has been her gift of stimulating and interesting those with whom she comes in contact. To all, whether encountered professionally, socially or casually, she is the same—full of vitality, vivacity and the joy of living. Her smart sayings were liberally quoted in her coterie.

Love of animals is strongly engrained in Miss Forsyth's nature. When she came in to join friends at tea her devoted animals used to follow her in, Berry, a black collie from Dawson, Zip, a tan collie rescued from the street, Mischa, her famous black cat and a tame paraquet. Wherever she goes she creates an atmosphere of spontaneous fun and brightness, pointing undoubtedly to her Celtic ancestry.[7]

Managing the Blue Moon Tea Room took most of Jean's time now. Her name appears fewer and fewer times in the columns of Edmonton social events, especially in accounts of teas. By then bridge parties that required strategy and decision-making had become more popular than teas.

Before she moved into larger quarters at 108 Rice Street, Jean somehow found time to attend the "social event of the season," the Hospital Ball, and joined the "throng" of "flying couples tripping along to the tune of the waltz and two-step."[8] "Peggy" complained of the "viciously draughty" Thistle Rink and the cornmeal spread on the floor to prevent slipping.

Nor could Jean resist taking a minor part in *The Liars*, an 1897 comedy of manners by British dramatist Henry Arthur Jones. It centred on a supposed adultery that could cost a flirtatious wife her husband. Sir Christopher Deering is urged to reason his protégé out of his infatuation with her. Jean played Mrs. Beatrice Ebernoe, a tall dark woman of about thirty who was "very beautiful and spiritual." At one point in the play, she throws herself into Sir Christopher's arms as part of a complicated ruse. Albert Nash, Jean's former student and stage manager for the play, reviewed it. His assessment was tough on most of the actors and actresses from the Edmonton Amateur Dramatic Club. Jean's acting, he thought, "had great charm. She creates a feeling of satisfaction in the audience but she is very absent-minded on the stage and should not laugh when Sir Christopher clasps her to his bosom."[9]

From the outset, the Blue Moon thrived like the city. Jean's newspaper advertisements appeared in the new publication, *The Mirror*, which was based on Gertrude

Balmer Watt's "Peggy" columns. After she settled into her tea rooms next door to her apartment in the Bellamy Block she offered much more than afternoon tea:

BLUE MOON ENGLISH TEA ROOM
Breakfast, Lunch, Afternoon Tea and Supper Served.

Rooms for Dancing, Private Teas

And Bridge Parties.

108 Bellamy Block Rice Street[10]

There was not an occasion for which the Blue Moon was not a desirable place to go. There were the usual teas and bridge parties. And Jean often used the place to entertain her own friends and out-of-town guests. The Templars, Reform Lodge 186, International Order of Good Templars, newly set up in the city, met every Tuesday evening from 8:00 to 10:00 at the Blue Moon and held their elections and ceremonies there.[11] On one occasion they produced a Halloween play, "The Witches Outwitted," to a large gathering in what came to be called "the lodge room." This was followed by a basket social, recitations, and games to the delight of all.[12]

The Edmonton Unitarian Church got its start in the Blue Moon in April 1912.[13] Beginning in April, Reverend Albert J. Pineo rallied "People without comfortable church homes, who are in sympathy with the liberal attitude in theology"[14] to the Blue Moon every Sunday evening from 7:30 to 9:30. He gave lectures on such "liberal" subjects as "The Light of the World,"[15] "Modern Science and the Resurrection,"[16] or "Pioneers of Religious Liberty."[17] He had guests such as Reverend Lewis G. Wilson from Boston (the cradle of Unitarianism), who was the general-secretary of the American Unitarianism, to take a look at "Ancient Buddhism" with the Unitarian Sunday afternoon group, the "Truthseekers."[18] These meetings signalled the increasingly open-minded philosophical and religious views of at least some Edmontonians.

Various patriotic groups used the Blue Moon as the best place to celebrate their special days. The first annual banquet of the Lancastrians of Edmonton, members of which had emigrated from Lancashire in the Northeast of England, was held there. At the end of the event were many toasts to the King, Lancashire County, its commercial savvy, and its "Lasses." Toasts were also made to "Those we left behind us" and the Province of Alberta. Old home songs were sung, and a "vote of thanks was passed to Miss Jean Forsythe of the Blue Moon for the excellent catering."[19] A similar rowdy celebration for the English St. George's Day[20] and the Welsh St. David's Day, with more than 100 attending, were also held there.[21] Even the large gathering of old military veterans (navy, army, military police—even volunteers) met at the Blue Moon for "a good old-fashioned English dinner" after hearing an address by the governor general, HRH the Duke of Connaught, at Queen Anne's School.[22]

Women's groups of various kinds were naturally drawn to the Blue Moon. Jean herself did not belong formally to most of these groups—apart from the Edmonton Humane Society and—for a time—the Edmonton Women's Press Club. Yet she had attended the meetings and receptions of all these groups from their beginnings. Now she was a kind of unofficial hostess at such meetings.

The Edmonton Women's Press Club had originally met at Emily Murphy's home in May 1912. Having seen the Dower Act made law the previous year as a result of her persistent campaign, Emily Murphy was now a major figure in the city. She gathered them to meet Dr. William T. Allison, who wrote a left-wing literary column for the *Winnipeg Telegram* under the pen name "Ivanhoe." He was a professor at the University of Manitoba and had published a book called *Bolshevism in English Literature*.[23] Her other guest was Mr. Franklin Gadsby of Toronto, whose literary work appeared in newspapers and in *Collier's* magazine, to which Emily Murphy also contributed. As before, this tea was informal, her daughters serving, and the focus held fast on ideological questions of the day. The main meeting of the Women's Press Club (Jean had once been their treasurer) was held at the Blue Moon, where the election of officers took place.[24] For the next two years the club met at the Blue Moon Tea Room.

Jean had begun promoting the sale of Ruthenian (Ukrainian) handicrafts at the time of George V's coronation. While Edith was giving her Festival of Empire concert and her solo performance at the Aeolian Hall, Jean opened the Blue Moon for a display of the beautiful embroidered towels from Mundare Ruthenians that Edmonton were sending to Queen Mary as a Coronation gift.[25] The Handicrafts Guild had a library by 1909, started a permanent collection of handicrafts soon after, awarded prizes at annual competitions and ran weaving and other classes for immigrants and children.[26] Jean's support of Ruthenian crafts continued steadily over the next year. She held an exhibition sale of hand-printed china and rugs at her own apartment in February 1912 after the guild's annual meeting in the Blue Moon.[27] A year later she opened a regular salesroom for the Edmonton Branch of the Canadian Handicrafts Guild with assistance from Miss Marion Seymour and, later, Jean Dawson, Jean's cousin's daughter and one of her own vocal students. She saw to it that the papers advertised displays and sales. One write-up in February 1913 claimed that "In most of the best furnished homes of the city the beautiful hand-woven catalogue rugs or portieres are to be found." In September, Miss Steen from Montreal, the agent for the Montreal Handicrafts Guild, was "much astonished" at the Edmonton Ruthenian work. The things sent to Montreal were "much admired" and the Edmonton branch was more successful than most new branches.[28] In November Jean held a fundraising card party for them at the Blue Moon.

The Blue Moon was the place to take important visitors who visited Edmonton. After a packed play, *The Second Mrs. Tanqueray* by Sir Arthur Wing Pinero at the Empire Theatre in July, Jean hosted a tea for the star, Constance Crawley, a famous English actress.[29] The next month the Canadian Club held its meeting, featuring J.S. Williamson, editor of the *Toronto News*, as lecturer, and William John Hanna, provincial secretary of Ontario, as guest of honour at the Blue Moon.[30] And when the touring Casino Company with "the finest cast in America" came to perform Gilbert and Sullivan's *Mikado* they were also entertained there.[31]

As the author of the *Edmonton Journal* profile of her later observed, Jean's courage to be herself was admirable, as was the "utterly frank way she hurls out dynamic statements." Because of this "there are no dull moments in her presence: that is why she attracts young people."[32] Certainly Jean attracted many young people to the Blue Moon. She would have appreciated the tongue-in-cheek humour of two of the young bachelors' clubs: the "Not Outs" (a sly putdown of the British debutante tradition of "coming-out" that was thriving in the East) and the "No-Nam-E-Club" (probably a racial slur). She held many bridge dances, supper dances, and tea dances—with chaperones—for the young men and women in elite British Edmonton to meet each other with the not-so-secret hope of marriage. One "jolly little hop" for more than sixty guests of the "Not Outs" club offered a "delicious *gouter*" and a "Moonlight dance." It was an occasion that "few dances can rival," and compliments were made to Jean Forsyth with "much zest."[33] For another, on St. Valentine's Day 1913, Jean decorated the rooms in red and white and arranged "cozy sitting places for private chats." For these dances there were two small orchestras to choose from: Turner's or the Monarch. Parents of girls in their late teens also held dances there that might as well have been "coming-out" occasions, though neither that term nor the term "debutante" was used. Still, white or ivory dresses were worn by girls for these occasions.

At the same time, Jean had branched out to edit the weekly "Milady's Page" for the *Edmonton Capital*. Like her "Celeste" columns, it was a collection of social and personal columns, entertainments about town (including short silent films), health advice, fashion news, and advertisements for things like tea, cocoa, dandruff and constipation cures, stove polish, and clothes stores. Jean did not write the columns herself, as she had for "Celeste." She used her organizational skill and wide readings to collect and prepare the layout for the page, which ran under Jean's guidance from at least November 25, 1913 to January 31, 1914.[34]

Though she would not have applied this term to herself, Jean was a striking example of the "New Woman." The New Woman was a feminist concept of women that gradually emerged in the late nineteenth century to its zenith in the suffragette movement of the early twentieth century and beyond. The concept is linked to the rebellious, dissatisfied female characters in Norwegian Henrik Ibsen's plays such as *A Doll's House* (1879) and *Hedda Gabler* (1890) as well as to George Bernard Shaw's intelligent argumentative women in such plays as *Mrs. Warren's Profession* (1893) and *Candida* (1898).[35] Such plays had not yet reached Edmonton, where comedies of manners like *The Liars* and Edwardian comic operas like *Patience* prevailed, but there were many women like Emily Murphy, Mabel Cautley, and Dr. Ella Scarlett-Synge who exemplified these very concepts.

Independence (economic and intellectual), intelligence, acute awareness of social ills and a mind to reform them, women's education: these were the key concepts that defined the New Woman. As one writer put it, "The world has tried to move with men for dynamos, and 'clinging' women impeding every step of progress, in arts, science, industry, professions. They [women] have been a thousand years behind men because forced into seclusion."[36]

For married women, the assumed dominance of husbands was an insurmountable object, even though personal liberty to some extent was achievable. For an unmarried woman like Jean Forsyth—especially one who had personified the Western Woman's independence and free spirit—it was much easier to live a life of freedom, making choices independent of others. Her career path from singing to animal advocacy to vocal teaching to journalism to establishing her own business (often overlapping interests) demonstrated clearly the traits of the New Woman. Her flexibility in socializing with the highest ranks at the same time as having harmonious dealings with her staff, her enthusiasm for a wide range of interests from sports events to political or religious meetings to acting allowed her to take every opportunity to profit financially from her various endeavours—especially the Blue Moon Tea Room.

EDITH TRAINS FOR OPERA WITH JEAN DE RESZKE IN PARIS
AND DEBUTS AT COVENT GARDEN, LONDON, 1913

The one thing—perhaps the only thing—Edith Miller had not done was to train seriously for opera. She had been singing arias from operas since she was a student at the Toronto Conservatory of Music, but she had not taken on any sustained roles. Nor had she sought the customary instruction to do so. For this reason, she had never yet appeared at the prestigious Royal Opera House in Covent Garden. She had performed in all the other major London theatres and halls. It is tempting to account for this anomaly by recognizing her Presbyterian roots at Portage la Prairie. At first she had performed in churches and, after graduating with the Gold Medal from the Toronto Conservatory of music, the first instruction she undertook abroad was in religious choral music with Alberto Randegger.

Increasingly, however, she had been moving away from religious music and taking on roles such as Delilah and Lucrezia Borgia that were far from angelic. Most traces of her religious past had disappeared, not only in her material but also in her appearance onstage. She had changed from a shy slim maid to a fulsome and sultry presence. This was at least partly because she was a contralto. Those darker voices were usually cast in dark roles, as foils to the innocent and young girlish sopranos. It was also due to the common polarization of women at the time generally into "angels of the house" and "fallen women."

After her patriotic performances at the time of the Festival of Empire in London she took the plunge into opera with the illustrious Jean de Reszke in Paris. This decision was "a long-held ambition."[1] She began her studies in September 1912, embarking on a three-year course that she intended to complete in thirteen or fourteen months. According to Jean de Reszke and his brother Édouard, "the result more than justified her ambition." At the same time she studied *mise-en-scène* (everything that appears before the camera and its arrangement—composition, sets, props, actors, costumes, and lighting). Her teacher was Mme Weinschenk, a successful actress who had opened her dramatic school at 35 Rue Boissy-d'Anglais.[2] The roles de Reszke had Edith focus on were Delilah in Camille Saint-Saëns's *Samson and Delilah*, Charlotte in Massenet's *Werther*, Amneris in Verdi's *Aida*, and—above all—Carmen in Bizet's *Carmen*. A Paris correspondent wrote, "The 'Manitoba Nightingale' has a confidence in her future which comes from the keen enjoyment she takes in the study of this new branch of her art, and the importance of the work she has already done is another guarantee of the fresh laurels she may expect to gain."[3]

Jean de Reszke was a Polish tenor hailed as "one of the very greatest of all time" who specialized in French and Wagnerian opera.[4] He was noted for his "rounded timbre" and his combination of "a virile singing style with an exceptional degree of gracefulness and vocal refinement."

Pictures show him as a stocky intense balding man (much shorter than his brother Édouard, a bass) assured in the heavy elaborate costumes and wigs he wore for such parts as Romeo, Faust, and Siegfried. He wrote extensively about how he achieved these effects and offered instructions for students to follow.[5] He emphasized the "timbre" for which he was so admired. He advised "drinking in the tone, rather than pushing it out." This would avoid nasal sounds and place the tone so that it resonated right on the hard palate beside the front teeth. "The great idea was to keep the line from the diaphragm through the vocal cords into the mask [of the face]. The whole body was to be as though one was 'settling down' on to the diaphragm, relaxed but ready to spring, as in tennis, boxing, etc., rather than braced up and stiff as if 'on parade.' The effort was to come from the back as if the sound was following 'a line drawn from the small of the back to the bridge of the nose. This invariably added a velvety quality to the voice.'"[6]

Jean de Reszke had visited Winnipeg more than once, where he was remembered for his exorbitant fees. He was in America singing at the New York Metropolitan Opera between 1893 and 1899 and had toured widely outside the

Jean de Reszke as a swordsman, 1896.

Jean de Reszke as
Siegfried in *Götterdämmerung*
at Covent Garden, London, 1898.

Dame Nellie Melba
in *La Traviata*.

Dame Nellie Melba, *Illustrated London News*, June 25, 1904.

opera season. His last visit to Winnipeg, in January 1899, had caused a certain amount of outrage. In earlier performances he had received $1,250 for each appearance and a percentage when receipts exceeded $5,500. On one occasion his pay for a night's work had been $2,200. "This year," a notice in Winnipeg's *Town Topics* said, "the percentage provision does not exist in his contract, but the salary figures are larger."[7] These sums indicate how important Jean de Reszke was in the years before his 1904 retirement. The singer that would replace him was the great Enrico Caruso.

De Reszke had married a countess in 1896, scaled down his appearances after that, and in retirement bred racehorses in Poland and taught singing in Paris and Nice. He attracted students from all over the world.

Edith Miller studied with Jean de Reszke until the summer of 1913. He had prepared her to make her debut—at last—at the Royal Opera House in Covent Garden on July 14. She would play the contralto role of Maddalena in Verdi's *Rigoletto* while Nellie Melba would play the soprano role of Gilda. Melba, whose many lovers and luxurious living caused scandal, lived at gorgeous rooms at the biggest hotel in Paris, where she was waited on by a retinue of servants and ate lavishly (*pêche Melba* and Melba toast were named after her).[8] Irish tenor John McCormack played the Duke of Mantua. Maddalena's role is not a major one. She is used as bait by the villain, her brother Sparafucile, to lure the Duke to his house so he can kill him.

Charles Wheeler reported ecstatically in the *Winnipeg Tribune* on July 16. MISS EDYTH [sic] MILLER MAKES SUCCESSFUL DEBUT ran the heading from a London review, followed by the subheading London Opera Patrons Delighted With Manitoba Nightingale's Appearance at Covent Garden.

> The audience, which was both large and fashionable, gave the Canadian singer the warmest welcome. She and the other leading artists were called seven times before the curtain at the close, amid rapturous applause, Mme Melba generously giving her colonial compatriot the central place in the triumph.[9]

After the performance Colonel George Harvey, the well-known New York publisher, hosted a large and sumptuous supper party in Edith Miller's honour at the top London hotel, Claridge's. It was attended by prominent Canadians in London, such as Lord Strathcona, many Americans, and "leaders in grand opera."

Edith Miller was now launched in an operatic career. She had finally, after intense training with de Reszke, taken the stage with extraordinary success at Covent Garden. It was her first opera.

It would also be her last.

THE BLUE MOON TEA ROOM:
HUB OF EDMONTON'S CULTURAL, POLITICAL, AND SOCIAL LIFE, 1913

The apparently solid and growing city of Edmonton in 1912 began to disintegrate in 1913. This is one of the "unsolved mysteries" explored by professor Paul Voisey in his essay "Unsolved Mysteries of Edmonton's Growth."[1] Among other things the "speculative bubble of rampant real estate speculation burst." Thousands of Edmontonians fled. A widespread "collapse" appeared to be imminent.[2]

This situation would have its effect in the long run, but meanwhile businesses like the Blue Moon Tea Room continued as blithely as before. Sarah Bernhardt, who performed in Edmonton in 1913, was decidedly positive about the city:

> Life in your city is not going to be lived as it is lived elsewhere, and that will be the charm of it. You're being challenged to live free of old notions, and I want to think you'll make the most of it.[3]

If anything, Jean Forsyth's business increased in 1913 and well into 1914. There were several groups that met regularly for meetings there. The Pride of the West Templar Lodge, No. 6, continued to gather there. The *Nordpolen* [North Pole] Sons of Norway Lodge (and soon after the Daughters of Norway) first began meeting there in April 1913. The First Liberal Church (nondenominational), which split off from the Unitarians, who had moved into a temporary site at Third Avenue and Nelson Street, held services there. This "New Thought Temple" had speakers or topics such as R. W. Brown and Edwin Poole's "My Philosophy of Life, or What Life Means to Me";[4] "Love, Laughter and Work," a study of ideal life conditions;[5] George Bradley, editor of the *Castor Advance*, on "The Religion of Socialism, and the Socialism of Religion";[6] a "Health Circle" that discussed healing through mental concentration; or "How to be Young at Eighty."[7] Such topics exemplified the way psychology was infiltrating philosophy and religion once Sigmund Freud's work began to appear in 1900 and Carl Jung's not long after.

Special occasions were still celebrated at the Blue Moon. A dinner for Dan Alton, superintendent of the Street Maintenance Department, was hosted by the department's foreman and office staff and attended by the press and by Frank Oliver, Liberal minister of the Interior. One of the many toasts that evening was made to "The City" by Rev. A. M. McDonald of the South Side. He outlined the rapid growth of Edmonton and maintained that the "enviable position it held today was due to the wisdom of those in charge of our civic affairs, and to the old-timers who had had such unbounded faith in the future greatness of the city."[8] Praise was lavished on Alton as leading "one of the departments which has made a real good showing from a financial point of view during the year in 1913." Music on the violin, piano, and bagpipes ended the gathering.

One highlight was an Edmonton Women's Press Club lunch to honour Lady Van (as in Vancouver). Lady Van wrote for the *Vancouver Sunset* and was eager to share her experience of her recent trip around the world. She admired Monte Carlo,[9] Egypt—especially the Sphinx by moonlight—and Italy. She felt the unrest in China, and thought Japan would soon be Europeanized. She was asked how Canadian scenery compared these "beauty spots."

"The Canadian Rockies are unsurpassed abroad," she said warmly. Then she went on to praise Edmonton, "Your fine broad streets and pretty boulevards, the clean, fresh appearance of Edmonton are delightful."

A meeting of the reeves of Alberta's twenty-five municipalities in January 1914 ended with a luncheon at the Blue Moon.[10] Mrs. Stephen Brown, a former member of the Reform Lodge, No. 12, I.O.G.T. who had moved to California, gave a lecture with more than 100 projected illustrations and other exhibits at the Blue Moon about the state.[11] The Edmonton Choral Union met to celebrate the close of their second session and hear a "bright program."[12] The Reform Lodge Templars hosted a demonstration of Wireless Telegraphy.[13] The groundbreaking United Garment Workers of America, Local 120, held some meetings at the Blue Moon.

The social events that had always been a staple of the Blue Moon's offerings continued, but were far fewer than before. There were instead regular Saturday night "hops" there.

With her usual acuity, Jean introduced *"thés dansantes"* (tea dances) that had become "the vogue in big cities." "The latest ragtime and Tangos" will be played by an orchestra," she promised in her first announcement in October 1913. "The room will be cleared for dancing. The tea tables will be placed in convenient corners, and it is hoped that 'tea and dancing' will catch the society girls and boys, as well as the matrons and old beaux."[14] These *thés dansantes*—always referred to in French with a variety of spellings—caught on at once and soon became a regular Saturday afternoon event at the Blue Moon. At one of these, Jean arranged for a dance instructor, Mrs. A. McDonald, principal of McDonald Academy, an exclusive dance school in Calgary. She was dressed in a dubiously Spanish "Tango gown of mauve brocaded satin trimmed with Irish point lace and pearl garniture" to give a demonstration of the Boston Tango and the new Hesitation Waltz with one of her pupils.[15] These dances were partly the result of new popular American music, such as Scott Joplin's, which incorporated African and Latin American syncopation. They were also connected to the new looser, fluid fashions in two layers for women, which allowed far more ease to perform more athletic dances.

Even with this flurry of activity at the Blue Moon, Jean found time to do other things. In August 1913 she had a Blue Moon booth with a large sign at the Edmonton Exhibition where she served tea, coffee, soft drinks and "wholesome homemade" delicacies.[16]

As a member of the Edmonton Amateur Operatic Society, she played the comic role of Lady Constance Wynne, an elderly English busybody, in Sidney Jones and Harry Greenbank's *The Geisha, a story of a tea house*.[17] In Japan, Lady Constance tells

Jean Forsyth, still the
height of fashion,
Maclean's Magazine,
Jan., 1915.

Royal Navy lieutenant Reginald Fairfax's fiancée back in England to come at once
when she sees him flirting seriously with the chief geisha, O Mimosa San. This
musical operetta also featured a satiric trio of "Gaiety Girls" dressed to the extreme
in London's latest fashions. The light breezy music ensured the great popularity
of *The Geisha* in London and New York when it opened in 1896. The operetta was
part of the Edwardian era's fascination with the Orient in such works as Gilbert
and Sullivan's *The Mikado* (1895) and Puccini's *Madame Butterfly* (1904).[18] Even
fashions were boldly influenced by eastern costume, especially those of Parisian
designer Paul Poiret, including his harem pants.[19] (These harem pants and other exotica were inspired by Vaslav Nijinsky's spectacular performances in Sergei
Diaghilev's *Ballets Russes*.) Turbans decorated with ornate brooches and feathers
were *the* thing to wear in London in 1910. (These Art Nouveau–inspired fashions
would segue into the streamlined Art Deco fashion—with more supple long-line
corsets to allow more fluid movement.)[19]

Jean wrote a long article about Mrs. Mary Sifton, wife of Arthur L. Sifton, premier of Alberta, both originally from Ontario. Jean explains the name of their
"unassuming white-fenced house" of red brick on Sixth Street.[20] Its "soft silken"
name is "Garry Kennaugh," meaning "Come inside and be gay." In her article
Jean takes the point of view of a guest, such as she had often been, arriving at the
house, being greeted by the Siftons; he a *"bon camarade"* and she with her "fascinating gift" of speaking in short staccato sentences, "a relief from the monotones
effected by most society women." Descriptions of the "perfect" English taste of the

interior decor give way to memories of the "interesting people, and pretty clothes, and good-looking cabinet ministers" Jean has met there at receptions. Then she praises her hostess: "no one dresses more elegantly." Even though Mary Sifton is short, "she looks every inch the *grande dame* when entertaining royalties or other distinguished visitors." Jean lists Mary's interests in the local Council of Women, the Canadian Women's Club, arts and crafts organizations, the handicrafts guild, the University of Alberta Club, "and every other club that the flesh is heir to." She concludes with the rumour that the Siftons may winter abroad and possibly reside in England eventually.

At the Blue Moon Jean held a Christmas lunch on Christmas Eve 1913 from 12:00 until 2:00 p.m., for fifty cents, and a Christmas dinner of turkey, vegetables, plum pudding, and mince pies on Christmas Day from 6:00 until 8:00 p.m. After that, on Christmas evening, she also held a Charles Dickens–style Christmas party ("An Old Fashioned Christmas Party"),[21] for about thirty old friends from the south of England who had known each other back home. From 5:00 to 8:00 p.m. the children enjoyed special games. Once they were in bed, a short game of whist was played with prizes donated by the Hudson's Bay Company. From 9:00 p.m. until the early hours of the next morning, the adults played old Christmas games, danced the Sir Roger de Coverley[22] (and others), sang songs and told stories. A wonderful board of Christmas treats was provided by the ladies. At the end of "a very merry evening" a silent toast was proposed "To our own folks at home," and they all clasped hands and sang "Auld Lang Syne" and "God Save the King." Plans were made for more parties in the New Year. Packages of good things were sent from the party to the United Aids in England. Such thoroughly British occasions suggested that the group that had once held sway in the city was now feeling threatened by changes in music, fashion, dance, and politics throughout a more modern world.

Though rumours rarely show up in the newspapers of the time, in Edmonton's social life—as elsewhere—they were rampant. One at the zenith of the Blue Moon's success provoked Jean to write in November 1913 to the *Edmonton Capital*. Earlier that month there had been three simultaneous major attractions at her tea room: a *thé dansante*, a Canadian Women's Club reception, and a matinee.[23] Soon after, there had been a large gathering, the first, of the "old girls" from Whitby Ladies' College near Toronto at which they planned a "Trafalgar Daughters' Society" to raise funds to help girls from Edmonton who could not afford to attend the college. The event was organized by Nettie Berkholder, former principal at Whitby, now principal of Alberta College. Something in one or more of these events must have rankled someone somewhere. The rumour spread that Jean had had financial backing from someone for her Blue Moon Tea Room. She was quick and fierce in her response:

> Owing to a rumor which is going about that the Blue Moon tea room is being financed by certain parties, Miss Forsyth wishes it distinctly understood that no one has ever financed the tea room either in Edmonton or any other place, and that no one has any interest or connection with the Blue Moon tea room except herself.[24]

EDITH MARRIES A BARONET, 1913

Edith Miller was centre stage. All eyes were upon her as she moved through the scene. The setting was an old eighteenth-century church. The lighting was perfect, filtered through a stained glass window in saintly rays to the red carpet on the floor. She was wearing an elaborate white *charmeuse* costume with a court train of gleaming silver brocade falling from the shoulder.[1] If Harold Speed had been there he might have said, "There's my Lady in White." The man beside Edith looked old, very old. His white whiskers jutted out in front of him like a challenge. They walked slowly, step by step.

It was July 23, 1913, exactly a week since Edith's operatic debut as Maddelena in *Rigoletto* at Covent Garden. Yet this was not Covent Garden. This was St. George's Anglican Church in Hanover Square, Mayfair, the most fashionable church in London. Nor was this an opera. Edith Jane Miller was taking a role she might well have thought about for many, many years.

Edith Miller was about to marry.

She was being walked towards the altar where seven bridesmaids waited by the Scottish-born Canadian Donald Smith, 1ˢᵗ Baron Strathcona and Mount Royal. He was still the Canadian high commissioner in London. He was short and bald at age ninety-two. Yet he was proud and meticulously dressed as he assumed the role of Edith's father, to give the bride away. William White Miller had not lived to see his daughter marry. He had died of a stroke at sixty-six only eight months earlier in Portage la Prairie. He was so popular that businesses closed for his large funeral. And Lord Strathcona himself was soon to die, a scant nine months later, his funeral a major event in Westminster Abbey.

Edith's tearful mother, however, had sailed the Atlantic to see her daughter wed. Marriage would mean the end of that stellar career she had wished for Edith. Yet it would also raise the curtain on the prospect of grandchildren and a new role for herself as grandmother.

The bridegroom, tall and thin with pale features like Edith's father, gazed radiantly as Edith approached. He is Max Christian Hamilton Colyer-Fergusson, son of Sir Thomas Colyer Colyer-Fergusson, 3ʳᵈ baronet,[2] from Gravesend, Kent, southeast of London. He is fifteen years younger than his thirty-seven-year-old bride.

It is possible that the couple had met in Paris while Edith was studying opera with Jean de Reszke, for he has arrived for his wedding from that city, and she had returned to her Palace Gardens residence in Kensington, London, only a month before. Or perhaps they had met at one of the many events connected to the Festival of Empire in 1912. Perhaps he had seen her and had responded to that low and lovely voice on the stage in London or Paris. Max's father was educated at

Harrow and Oxford and had become High Sheriff of Kent in 1906, where he was also justice of the peace. Max's late mother (who had died eleven years earlier)[3] was Beatrice Stanley Müller, daughter of Friedrich Max Müller, a German-born Sanskrit scholar at Oxford. He had enjoyed national and international fame for championing Hindu literature and culture.[4] One of Max Colyer-Fergusson's ancestors had been surgeon to Queen Victoria and Prince Albert. Edith was marrying into an old aristocratic and professional family who were wealthy landowners in Kent, where they owned two stately homes, Wombwell Hall and Ightham Mote. They were highly educated and cultured people who would have appreciated fully her career and fame.

Heralded as a generous philanthropist, Lord Strathcona had given Edith "a silver preserve set and a handsome cheque." Sir Thomas had presented a diamond pendant, a diamond ring, and a pearl ring. Her groom, Max, had given her a diamond bracelet with a ring to match.[5] Even in her most lavish costumes, Edith had not seen the like of these jewels.

After the "quiet"[6] ceremony the wedding party returned to 101 Queen's Gate for an elegant reception. Charles Wheeler was there. He had announced the wedding well in advance, and had printed a copy of his invitation in the *Winnipeg Tribune*. Later, he would reprint a copy of the long account of the wedding from "London's leading society newspaper."

"From those who have known Miss Miller since she was in her teens," he wrote on behalf of himself and the staff of the *Winnipeg Daily Tribune*, "I offer their sincere congratulations to bride and bridegroom, with best wishes for a long life of marital felicity."[7] Others at the reception were probably those Canadians who had attended a state ball given by the King and Queen a few days earlier: Sir William Otter, first Canadian-born Chief of the General Staff, head of the Canadian army, and Lady Otter; Sir Clifton Sifton, former minister of the Interior under Sir Wilfrid Laurier; Sir Adam Beck, of Niagara hydro-electric fame, and his wife; and Canadian-born lawyer Hamar Greenwood, who would be knighted two years later and eventually become a viscount,[8] and his wife.[9]

Max and Edith's honeymoon was rumoured to be in America, including a visit to Portage la Prairie.[10]

THE GREAT WAR DERAILS JEAN'S TEA ROOM, 1914

The first sign of trouble for the Blue Moon Tea Room seemed innocuous at the time. Emily Murphy secured a new room for the Edmonton Women's Press Club in the Civic Block, built between 1912 and 1913 to house the city's municipal government. Until November 5, 1913 the club had regularly met at the Blue Moon. On that November day the club met for the first time at its new quarters. The room was "bright, spacious, and well-appointed." Emily Murphy directed the furnishing of the room. She had persuaded the Blowey-Henry Co. to donate a china cabinet. The large room soon had everything from a "comfy couch to dainty cups and saucers."[1] More importantly, the room was now housed in the same building as the City of Edmonton offices and the club was to have the use of the room at all times, not by appointment, as had been the case at the Blue Moon, where any number of trivial or noisy events might take place at the same time as their meetings. The club tendered a "standing vote of thanks" to Emily Murphy for her energy in accomplishing the move and noted "the kindness of the civic authorities." The house committee included Jean's cousin, Mabel Cautley, and the hospitality committee included her friend Gertrude Balmer Watt.

The schedule was to be as follows: each member was to have a tea. Rest hours when no events were scheduled were from 2:00 to 4:00. On club days members could introduce friends. Emily Murphy busied herself writing letters of thanks to the mayor, Lawrence Oliver "Buck" Olsen, and others for their kindness. "The members of the club," ran the notice, "are looking forward to many delightful and hard-working hours in these bright surroundings."

The key word is "hard-working." Doubtless Emily Murphy had in mind a place where their work was as important politically as that taking place in the mayor's office nearby. Nothing is said about leaving the Blue Moon or about Jean Forsyth, who had sat in on the club's meetings as a sort of de facto member by virtue of her hosting the tea rooms. Jean was to some extent qualified as a journalist because of her "Celeste" columns, her editing of the "Milady's Page," and her profile of Mrs. Sifton. But these had not been sustained writings; Jean had not published a book, and so many other aspects of her life and work had nothing to do with writing. Members of the Women's Press Club were serious writers, took their work seriously, and so needed an exclusive and significant address that reflected their intent. It was probably slight consolation to Jean—if she read it—that she had recently been the subject of a small notice in the *Manitoba Free Press*:

> ## TWENTY YEARS AGO TO–DAY – 1893
> Miss Jean Forsyth, of Windsor, Ont., arrived in
> Winnipeg to take the position of leading soprano
> in Grace Church choir.[2]

The official opening of the Edmonton Women's Press Club room took place at a tea in early December. The lieutenant governor, the premier, the mayor, and the city's aldermen and commissioners all attended, along with the press.

Emily Murphy and her followers had successfully campaigned for The Married Women's Relief Act 1910 authorizing the Alberta courts to give a widow part of her husband's estate if he did not provide for her adequately, a precursor to the Dower Act in 1917. This early legislation was the first in many steps towards suffrage for women. The Edmonton Women's Press Club was one of several women's organizations in the city that, in various ways, clamoured for the vote for women and for temperance. Both aspirations were framed as propelling women towards equality with men. That women should vote as men did was clear. The Temperance Movement intended to eradicate the waste of household incomes through men's drinking, curb the mistreatment—even violent treatment—of women and children by intoxicated assaults, and strictly limit the purposes and locations of alcohol sales.

Other women's organizations that shared these goals—directly or indirectly—were the Local Council of Women of Edmonton, the Edmonton Equal Franchise League, the Young Women's Christian Association, the Women's Canadian Club of Edmonton, the Alberta Women's Association: Edmonton Branch, the Women's Christian Temperance Union, the Victorian Order of Nurse, the United Farm Women of Alberta, the United Garment Workers of America, Local 120, as well as the many women's church guilds, ladies' aid associations, and other women's groups.

The event that galvanized these groups to a common purpose, in addition to their desire for universal suffrage and temperance, was the declaration of war in Europe August 4, 1914, in the wake of the June assassination of Archduke Franz Ferdinand, heir to the throne of Austria-Hungary, and his wife Sophie as they rode along the streets of Sarajevo in an open limousine. The assassin was a Serbian nationalist.[3]

Sarah Bernhardt had been right about Edmonton. As she and many others saw it, these western citizens were "being challenged to live free of old notions."[4] The notion of the West as place of vision and efficiency, quickly constructing its own bureaucracies and style, was by now commonplace. It was supported by the rapid acceleration of the city of Edmonton and the equally rapid rise of unions that challenged the status quo. The onset of what would become known as the Great War was less than a decade from the incorporation of the city, and only two years since Strathcona and Edmonton had united—only two years, in fact, from the completion of the city's commanding legislative building.

The idea of the woman of the West was also new: free, strong, untrammelled, independent, and energetic. It was largely women with such qualities who initiated and sustained various organizations dedicated to the improvement of the lives of women and children—even animals. War only accelerated a growing momentum. A motion made by Emily Murphy to the Edmonton Women's Press Club a month after war was declared reflected this:

> Whereas a very large percentage of the people of Alberta will be out of employment owing to the war;
>
> And whereas this province is sending thousands of bread-winners to the front leaving their families to be largely provided for by the public;
>
> And whereas the laborers on railway construction who come into Edmonton, Calgary and other points in the province, or lose much of their year's wages during their first week in town, owing to intemperance;
>
> And whereas it is the manifest duty of the government to provide against such contingencies and their resultant distress, especially when the country is in a state of war;
>
> Be it resolved that we, the Edmonton Women's Press Club earnestly pray the government of this province to suspend all liquor licenses until next May, or until such time as peace is declared, thus leaving free an enormous amount of cash for the maintenance of the households of Alberta and to the general strengthening of the financial situation.[5]

The *Edmonton Capital* reported that the motion was unanimously adopted and forwarded to Premier Sifton, asking him to use his influence in "putting it into force" in anticipation of the suffering that would come as an "aftermath to the outbreak of war."

The club also decided to compile a weekly newsletter for the men at the front to inform them of the "doings of the homeland." The Edmonton Industrial Association would "multigraph" (rotary typesetting and printing machine, commonly used in making many copies) the newsletter to be sent to army headquarters and hospital committees for distribution to the ranks. They would circulate this idea to other Canadian Women's Press Clubs in other provinces.

One illustration of the changes coming to the city: At the Blue Moon Tea Room in late December 1913—seven months before war became a fact of life—a young man celebrated his twenty-first birthday, his "coming of age." The "jolly little party" given for Lionel Gillman and his "girl and boy friends" by his mother was noted in the next day's *Edmonton Capital*. "Congratulations were showered upon" Lionel and a list of the pretty dresses—many including the sash-like "girdles" and soft over-tunics now fashionable—of his sister May, his girl friends, and the three chaperones were duly described.[6] Such gaieties would soon give way to the enlistments of young men eager to be sent abroad.

Eight months after his jolly coming-of-age party, Lionel Gillman signed up as a lieutenant with the 9th Battalion, the first infantry battalion, which was authorized and recruited in Edmonton. He and his fellow recruits took the train to Valcartier, Quebec, where the battalion mobilized its twenty-seven officers and 527 other ranks and sailed for England on October 3, 1914.[7] Other battalions and regiments soon followed. Of the 45,000 men from Alberta who enlisted, 43,000 were volunteers.[8]

Three months before the war began Jean offered free tea to the officers and men of the 3rd contingent stationed for a month in Edmonton.[9] In November, over a year after war had been declared, she held a well-advertised Patriotic Tea at the Blue Moon with a musical program from 4:00 p.m. to 6:00 p.m. Proceeds went to the Patriotic Fund or the Red Cross.[10] Although a few of the usual pre-war events—meetings of the Theosophical Society and the Sons of Norway in particular—took place at the Blue Moon, they dwindled in number as the months, then the years of war passed. Jean made an attempt to adapt her business to wartime conditions, but she must have known that luxuries like tea rooms and cafes were doomed. Women had more important things to do.

It could be said that the women of Edmonton turned their attention almost as one to do whatever they could do for their men overseas. Dances, artists on tour, theatrical performances—even the silent movie theatres that now numbered seven in the city—seemed increasingly trivial when dreaded news told of death, injury, and privation.

Some organizations already engaged in alleviating suffering at home, such as the hospital Ladies' Aid, the Victorian Order of Nurses, and church groups that fed and clothed the poor found their tasks expanded by war. Now they were helping soldiers overseas or those returned from active service or prisoner-of-war camps wounded and shell-shocked.

Meanwhile, other women's groups such as the Edmonton Women's Press Club, the Edmonton Equal Franchise League, the Women's Canadian Club, the Alberta Women's Association and the Women's Christian Temperance Union of Edmonton pushed on towards their political goals.

Several new women's organizations sprang up in direct response to the war. The Women's Volunteer Reserve, modelled on the Women's Volunteer Reserve of Great Britain, organized women to train in target shooting, marching drills, and signalling as well as in first aid. The St. John Ambulance Association organized women for a special branch in August 1914. The Edmonton branch of the Canadian Red Cross, set up five months after war was declared, began work in January 1915. The Great Western Garment Company and the Emery Manufacturing Company cut garments and bandages for them free of charge. In November 1915 the Westward Ho! chapter of the Imperial Order Daughters of the Empire turned its attention to "assist patriotic work" and "care for widows and children of soldiers." They set up a soldiers' club with reading rooms and a cafeteria for social events. Several new branches of the IODE sprang up with war-related enterprises. Even the women's art and musical clubs turned their attention to the war by focusing on works inspired by war.

Edmonton branch, Women's Canadian Club, 111912.
Back row from left: Mme Cauchon, Mrs. F. C. Jamieson, Mrs. J. H. (Florence) Riddell,
Mrs. A. F. Ewing, Mrs. Duncan Marshall, Mrs. H. M. Tory, Mrs. G. S. Armstrong, and
Mrs. W. A. Greisbach. Front row from left: Mrs. D. G. McQueen, Mrs. G. H. V. Bulyea,
Mrs. (Emily) Murphy (president), Mrs. A. L. (Mary) Sifton, and Mrs. Gray.

Of great importance was the foundation in 1915 of the United Farm Women of Alberta. In 1913 the constitution of the United Farmers was amended to admit women into the organization with the same privileges as men. "Wide-awake women realized that back of their social problems lay the economic problem."[11] "The farmer's problem was his wife's problem also" because household machines, good health care, and better schools at all levels were "directly connected with better markets, co-operative buying and selling, and better agricultural credit."[12] In 1914 farm women assembled with the men at the United Farmers' annual meeting. The following year, they outnumbered the men, and formed their own association with a separate annual meeting.

The founding was timely. Edmonton's 1913 real estate collapse had threatened to close down the city. Yet the Great War kept the city afloat. As Paul Voisey explains, "With rising wheat prices in Europe and good yields at home, agriculture boomed. Farmers acquired more land and machinery, almost doubling the acreage under production, and prairie cities and towns, including Edmonton, recovered by meeting renewed demands."[13] At the end of its first year the United Farm

Women of Alberta had twenty-three clubs with about 500 members. The causes they advocated included: "Banish the Bar [Temperance]," "Woman's Franchise," and "Rural Education."

Like the United Farm Women of Alberta, many of the women's organizations in Edmonton had overlapping aims and, sometimes, overlapping representation in memberships. This interlacing was empowering. Everywhere there were sewing and knitting circles, not because these were ladylike arts but because socks, mitten, scarves, toques, vests, and other garments and items made for the soldiers were directly useful to the war effort. Fundraising events such as rummage sales, musical gatherings, educational institution drives, and religious meetings were unceasing. "Comforts" such as cigarettes, toffee, chocolate, gum, cocoa, soap, pencils, and local newspapers were packaged and sent to military hospitals, Red Cross stations, and army camps overseas. One group collected women's kid gloves (an expensive social fashion) to send to England to make leather vests for Italian soldiers. One former commander of the Red Cross knit 128 pairs of socks.[14] Dr. Ella Scarlett-Synge, who had been appointed medical health officer by the Serbian government, singlehandedly appealed to Vancouver, where she had once lived, for funds to purchase drugs and medical supplies for a base hospital in Serbia, to help "the suffering Serbians, whose men and women are in the ranks fighting for their rights."[15]

Some idea of the magnitude of the war efforts of Edmonton's volunteer women's clubs can be seen in the statistics for 1915–1916. The total raised, plus the value of goods shipped, came to $94,276—a sum equivalent to more than 2 million dollars in 2016 currency.

As for items donated, there were 14,408 pairs of socks, 500 shirts, 6,752 other items of clothing (such as pajamas, bags, and service uniforms), two sets of communion vessels and one private pocket communion set.[16]

Jean Forsyth did not belong to any of the city's women's organizations, old or new, during the Great War. Age sixty-three when war was declared, her thoughts might have been turning to retirement from what had been a surprisingly prosperous business at the Blue Moon Tea Room, which had been the centre of her life for four years as well as the centre of many aspects of Edmonton's life. Yet the events that had once made the Blue Moon the hub of so many of the city's activities now seemed off-centre as the men left to serve their city, their country, and the British Empire.

JEAN SELLS THE BLUE MOON TEA ROOM, 1916

Two years into the Great War Jean Forsyth sold the Blue Moon Tea Room. This was not surprising. She was sixty-five and the feverish activity of the Blue Moon had diminished to a trickle. Women, long the mainstay of the Blue Moon, were now not only throwing themselves wholeheartedly into supporting the soldiers overseas, they were filling the jobs previously held by the city's young men. At the Bank of Montreal, for instance, 80 percent of the (male) staff had gone off to war.[1]

In 1916 Jean sold her business to Ada Caley, a former a cook at the University of Alberta, who would continue as proprietor of the Blue Moon until 1921, but with none of Jean's panache. Jean herself moved out of her room next to the Blue Moon and into the LeMarchand Mansion, an elegant apartment building then the "envy of all Edmonton."[2] Built between 1909 and 1912 at the corner of 110th Street and 100th Avenue, it was the last word in luxury and style. René LeMarchand, a former valet to a French nobleman, had emigrated from France to join his brother, a priest, in 1905. His dream was to combine North America's mechanical conveniences with grand living Parisian-style to create "the finest and most modern apartment block west of Toronto."[3] At first he operated a luxury goods store in Edmonton, but he entered the booming real estate market by raising investment capital from the Paris Union Garçons de Café (Paris Union of Waiters).

The LeMarchand Mansion was designed in the classically inspired French Beaux Arts style. Four storeys high, it was H-shaped, the pillared entrance set back behind a circular drive that swept around a fountain and flowerbeds. The red brick walls with sandstone trim were embellished with columns, pediments, arches, and *voussoirs* (wedge-shaped stones or brick used to construct an arch or vault). It was built with typically Parisian wrought-iron balconies and windows that, adapted to Edmonton's climate, had special ledges to store storm windows in the summer. The lobby featured a grand fireplace surrounded by marble flooring and there were two elevators, a first for an apartment building in Edmonton.

There were forty-three suites of varying sizes, from four to nine rooms, none of them windowless. Each had a brass-hooded fireplace; some had two. Each had a dumb waiter, a mail chute, and a gas range. The gas supply for heating and cooking was in a separate building buried on the property for safety. The woodwork and decorations in halls and apartments were beautifully crafted of the finest materials. Each apartment had its own fire escape—a feature that must have reassured Jean after her experience in the fire at the Cauchon Block in Winnipeg. The brick-and-mortar walls were specially designed to "deafen" sound and contain fire. The apartments attracted some of the city's best: lawyers, doctors, businessmen, and politicians.

That Jean Forsyth could take one of the apartments in the LeMarchand Mansion on retiring bears witness to the financial success she had achieved—without help—after a varied career culminating in her final business venture: the Blue Moon Tea Room.

That year, 1916, was a stellar year for the women of the Canadian West, with the Prairie provinces among the first in the country to grant women the vote: Manitoba in the lead on January 28, with Saskatchewan on March 14, and Alberta on April 19. (The federal vote for women became law in 1919.)

Given the stridently vocal and ardently political nature of so many women's organizations in Edmonton it is not surprising that Alberta was among the leading provinces granting votes for women. Edmonton was home to Emily Murphy, who in 1916 was appointed the first woman magistrate in the British Empire, and to Nellie McClung, who had moved to Edmonton in 1915 from Winnipeg. They were two members of the Famous Five, who fought for women to be legally declared "persons" under the constitution, which was granted by the British Privy Council in 1929.

McClung was popular for her many effective speeches urging suffrage and other reforms. She was also a dynamic member of the Edmonton Equal Franchise League. She published her fourth book, *In Times like These*, in 1915: "This tour de force, a mixture of wit, satire, good humour, and common sense, assembled Political Equity League speeches, wartime addresses, and feminist and temperance arguments. Suffrage was firmly linked to Prohibition."[4] Nellie McClung was too late to enjoy the Blue Moon, but her path and Jean Forsyth's crossed from time to time.

Though she was no longer involved in the politics of her city and no longer arranged and hosted gatherings at the Blue Moon Tea Room, Jean continued to teach vocal pupils and hold recitals for them. No doubt she continued to have friends and visiting ladies in for tea at the LeMarchand Mansion and no doubt attended cultural and social events, but now, instead of performing on stage or directing shows or being singled out for her stylish clothes and hats, she was simply "noticed" in news columns as being "in the audience."

A FINAL CONCERT, 1919

Jean Forsyth was ready to receive her guests. She shook her sleek black tunic so that it fell gracefully over the fluid black skirt underneath. The skirt was the new fashionable length. It fell to just below mid-calf. This shorter length was part of the war effort. Using less material saved more money and more cloth for the soldiers. Jean welcomed it. The slim lines free of bustles and drapery were a great boon when she took a walk. Turning to young Gene Secord and straightening the lace collar that sat so well over her black tunic with the V-neck, she said, "Here they are. Our first guests. It will probably be my cousins Reg and Mabel Cautley. They're always early! Sometimes I tell them a later time so they'll arrive with the others." She laughed her chiming laugh and Gene joined in.

Gene's parents, Richard and Anna Secord, opened the front door of their home. In blew an April chill dampened by the cold rain. "It is not the Cautleys after all," whispered Jean. "It's my cousin's daughter, Jean Dawson. She used to help me at the Blue Moon, and I've no doubt she'll lend a hand with the tea before my recital today. She's such a lovely, kind girl."

Anna Secord took Jean Dawson's wet coat, umbrella, and gloves and handed them to Richard—a fatherly, round-faced, heavily-moustached man—who put the umbrella into a brass umbrella stand and hung the coat in the cloak cupboard. Richard Secord had come to Edmonton by way of Chicago and Winnipeg in 1881 and had made great wealth with his partner, Alexander McDougall, in fur trading, land scrips, and outfitting. In 1907 the two men started McDougall & Secord, a financial house and mortgage corporation. Richard had been remarkably civic-minded, arranging financing for the Low Level Bridge in 1900, and also providing financial support for Misericordia Hospital the same year. Two years later he helped fund the Thistle Rink. He had also backed the *Edmonton Journal* (the Conservative alternative to Frank Oliver's Liberal *Edmonton Bulletin*), where Jean had written her "Celeste" columns.

Tonight, April 4, 1919, the Secords had generously opened their large house on 105th Street for Jean Forsyth's spring recital of vocal students.

Jean Dawson walked quickly away from the door as others arrived and right up to Jean and Gene Secord, who were formally receiving the guests in the hall. "My word!" she said to her cousin. "I'm so sorry about the disagreeable weather. There probably won't be the turnout you deserve. And this is your last recital. Such a shame!"

Jean simply smiled and welcomed her cousin warmly. "It can't be helped," she said. Then, turning to Gene, added, "I think there are altogether too many 'Jeans' in this hallway!" The three laughed as one of Jean's students approached. "Oh no!" she said, sparking another round of laughter. "Here's another!"

It was Jean Turnbull, the effervescent daughter of Thomas Turnbull, manager of the Canadian Bank of Commerce and a director of the hospital board. She arrived with her parents, but her mother stayed behind to chat with Anna Secord. "I'm simply full of jitters," Jean Turnbull said to her teacher. She held out her hand to show how it shook.

"Never mind, my dear," Jean said in a reassuring voice. "Once you get up there just think about your song—what it means, how you feel about it, what you want to tell the audience by singing it. You'll see." She patted Jean on the back. Then she called someone over and asked her to take the girl into the parlour to show her to her seat and check that she had her music with her.

Several more guests came in with exclamations of "Brrr! What an evening!" and "Winter's a mite early, isn't it?" Some of the men wore fashionable Burberry trench coats, modelled on those the soldiers wore in the muddy trenches, and stylish fedora hats.

Jean and Gene directed them to the dining room where hot tea and baked dainties awaited them. The young students gathered together as if to boost their confidence for what was to come. Host Richard was chatting with Henry McKenney. Henry, too, had profited from dealing in furs and land. A Liberal and Roman Catholic, he was MLA for a succession of constituencies from 1905 to 1917. No doubt the two men were talking business or politics, not music. Their heads were leaning in towards each other.

Eventually a bell rang to summon them into the parlour where a grate fire was flickering nicely, spreading warmth into the room. Comfortable chairs had been arranged in front of a place next the piano where the performers were to stand. The seven performers were seated in the front row, clutching their music.

Before the recital proper began, Jean Forsyth announced that Mrs. George H. Van Allen, wife of the Liberal lawyer, would perform two numbers at the piano. Everyone quieted and the cold drizzly night outside was forgotten. Next, by way of offering a buffer between the social part of the evening and her jittery pupils, she announced that the popular soprano Mrs. Robert Cockburn, who performed around the city, would sing two songs. At the end of these—beautifully rendered, as her listeners expected—a "storm of applause" resounded through the room. Now the audience was relaxed, "tuned in" to the recital that was to follow.[1]

This student recital was unlike those Jean had presented before. There were fewer students; there was no need any longer for larger venues like the Empire Theatre. The audience was small—even for a home performance like this, she noted. Jean herself was sixty-seven. She had retired from the Blue Moon and from the women's clubs she took part in. Her writing days were over. And certainly she was no longer to be seen on stage in concerts or plays. She knew in her heart that it was time to give up teaching too, aside from helping out the occasional student. Certainly there would be no more recitals.

The music is not what it used to be, she thought with regret. Tonight there will be no lullabies, no arias from popular opera, no songs in foreign languages, no religious hymns. Because of the war, times have changed and music with it. So many more songs now are based on short-lived loves, on the heart-rending distance between families and their sons, on the silence of the grave, and on the girls in England and France who have loved and lost their North American soldiers.

Jean's eyes were shiny as she called forward each of her students in turn, before sitting down at the piano to accompany them. She knew she must not cry. First came Miss Judy Pace to sing, "She Is Far from the Land (where her young hero sleeps)." It is about a girl who sings to mask her despair at the death of her young soldier's love.

> She sings the wild songs of her dear native plains.
> Every note which he lov'd awaking—
> Ah! little they think, who delight in her strains
> How the heart of the minstrel is breaking!

He has died for his country, and it will not be long before she follows, suicide from grief.[2] Judy's mother, a member of the University of Alberta University Women's Club, was clearly moved. She was a fundraiser for the Royal Alexandra Hospital and a member of the First Canadian Contingent Corps.

For comic relief Jean placed Miss Dorothy Donley next. She was an avid curler and daughter of A. B. Donley, who dealt in wholesale lumber. Dorothy was dressed in a simple white dress with a ruffled yoke and the neat ankle-high black lace-up boots popular for girls at the time. She wore a pink ribbon hairband. Her song "The Little Brown Owl" was a cheery American song about a lonely bachelor owl that finds a mate after years of asking "To-woo-oo!" His mate replies, "I do-oo!" He finds it "a thousand times comfier when you're "Two-oo!"[3]

The recital proceeded with a mixed program that spoke of Jean Forsyth's long experience. She knew how to vary the music, both in its rhythms and its content. Miss Chappelle sang a spirited waltz translated into English from the French called—despite the April weather outside—"April Smiles." Miss Edith Buchanan sang "Crimson Roses" about the loss of love.

> We, too, smile away all sadness,
> Bathing in the sunshine free,
> Blest indeed that summer's promise
> Writes itself in melody.[4]

Jean looked sideways at Edith. She was moved in an unusual way. Normally she focused fully on the singer. Now something tugged at her. She straightened up, turned back to the music and the duty that was such a pleasure as Edith finished the song, "Roses white, and roses crimson, have no charm for me today." Edith blushed to the applause and scuttled back to her seat.

Eileen Drummond—another popular soprano in the city, as Jean once had been—launched merrily into a smart whimsical upbeat foxtrot from the Broadway hit musical *Listen Lester* that had appeared the year before. "Waiting" was a comedy of situation about a couple. Each one waits in a different place impatiently for the other to arrive.

Jean gave a nod to Jean Turnbull, the final performer. She caught her eye as if to say, "I'm with you. You'll be wonderful." Young Jean looked round the room and found her mother seated at one side. They smiled. Jean started in on what would become one of the most famous songs of the Great War: "Roses of Picardy." Ah! Such a lovely melody, Jean thought. It says so much about loss and love and distance. And the roses in Picardy *are* beautiful. I've seen them myself. Now I shall be free to travel wherever I want. Until I no longer can.

> And the roses will die with the summertime,
> and our roads may be far apart,
> But there's one rose that dies not in Picardy!
> 'Tis the rose that I keep in my heart![5]

So many sad songs now, Jean thought as she accompanied her pupil on the piano. Her playing was neither too fast nor too slow, neither too loud nor too soft. The piano and song were as one. Like the woman in "She Is Far from the Land" I must mask my melancholy, Jean thought. I must hide—not my love—but my sense that so much in my life is over. I must "smile away my sorrow." I have acquitted myself well. I know that. Yet how I have loved the balls, the dramas, the world-shaking meetings, the work for animals, the writing, the comings and goings at the Blue Moon. And this...this...these young people so full of life and laughter and joy! How I shall miss them! They have been *my* children too. I wonder how long I shall have? My energy is failing. My summertime is passed. I can feel it. But I still love to attend everything I can. I want to die in my bed in the LeMarchand Mansion when the time comes. As it surely must. Jean felt a chill. The thought passed through her like a fine thread or the single clear high note that Jean Turnbull was now singing. "*roses will die...*"

"Death," Jean thought, "Death...when...." She was drifting.

Jean had been playing the accompaniment for young Jean's second song, "Love's Dawning." Again that chill. What could it mean? *roses will die... death...* ? The girl *had* dropped her nervousness once she began to sing, as Jean had predicted. Now she curtsied, gave a smile to her mother, then to Jean.

Jean closed the music, stood up and bowed to the hearty applause. She could see Vernon Barford's wife. How lovely it had been to work with him on *The Geisha*. How apropos! They had contributed so much to music in Edmonton. And over there was the druggist Arthur Archibald's wife. She was a "teacup reader" at the IODE teas. Maybe I should test my premonition against my tea leaves, Jean thought. Mrs. Archibald was sitting beside Mrs. J. R. Brown, another IODE member. Oh! And Mrs. McMillan from the Edmonton Ladies' Musical Club was behind them. How lovely that she had come out tonight, even though Jean hadn't gone to their gatherings in years. She turned her head. And there was Aloysia McKenney with her father. Who is that beside her? Oh, yes, of course, her friend Marion Ross, daughter of the province's railway engineer. And Dr. D. J. Harrison's wife. That *was* a fright—his removal of bones from a foot, and at a *home* operation! Who was it now that endured that horror?

What was Eileen Drummond doing moving to the centre of the stage like that? Jean could see the green silk dress swaying as she moved. She was holding something in both hands. What was it? There were no awards for this evening. The recital had ended. Her teaching had ended. She bit her lip.

Eileen Drummond turned towards Jean and began to speak. Jean found she could not grasp what was being said. Eileen waved a green sleeve to tell Jean to come forward. When she arrived at Eileen's side, she was greeted by applause such as she did not remember during her whole career. Eileen handed her a "purse of gold of substantial denominations." At once Jean's students "crowded about their much-loved teacher to thank her, to congratulate her, to offer all good wishes to her, and offer their *bon voyages* for the "extended visit" she was about to make to the East.

Jean Forsyth and Edith Miller died within three years of each other—Jean, on New Year's Day 1933, at age eighty-two; Edith, on June 24, 1936, at age sixty-one.

Jean's retirement from running the Blue Moon Tea Room in 1916 was followed by visits to friends across Canada. In between these visits, she attended the social events, concerts, plays, and recitals she had enjoyed all her life.

After her last student recital in the spring of 1919 she no longer sang, played as an accompanist, or taught. There was a new gathering of young music students, and teachers much younger than she to train them. She remained a member of the Edmonton Women's Press Club, attending their luncheons with out-of-town guest speakers, though she no longer wrote herself. She never lost her *joie de vivre*. At age seventy-two she was one of the older people gamely dancing "the notorious foxtrot" at an IODE dance at Edmonton's Memorial Hall held in aid of the Japanese.[1] Now and then she was remembered in news columns about the past as a prominent local singer. Many of her students went on to careers in various aspects of music.

It was the invention of a record-playing machine, the Victrola, and the advent of radio, in the first decades of the twentieth century, which set the enjoyment of music on a path that would relegate to the sidelines live concerts such as those in which Jean took part. Jean lived to hear recordings of orchestras and star singers, such as Enrico Caruso, on the radio and on Victrolas, which featured the logo of a white dog, Nipper, cocking his ear to the horn that curled from the turntable to hear "His Master's Voice." She must have realized that she could not have had her musical career in this new era.

When Jean died in her bed at LeMarchand Mansion after a short illness, a wave of obituaries followed. Some, such as the *Edmonton Bulletin* and the *Winnipeg Tribune*, highlighted her organization of the first Winnipeg Humane Society. Even her "beautiful dogs" were praised as "the marvel and joy of Edmonton."[2] Others said she was "a brilliant member of Winnipeg's society set."[3] "Pussy" Forsyth's Blue Moon Tea Room was hailed as the "gay centre around which the social life of the city revolved; no musical event, no social function, no dramatic or musical comedy presentation was complete without her delightful spirit."[4] Jean's "Celeste" columns drew accolades as "probably the gayest and most charming account of social and musical doings that has ever been written here."[5] All wrote of her enormous musical contributions to the communities of Winnipeg and Edmonton. The *Tribune* pointed out that she had taught Edith Miller.

Edith ended what seemed to be the blossoming of an operatic career with her marriage in 1913. Unlike Jean, she had long since moved from Winnipeg to an international career abroad. By 1929 she was the subject of a "Do You Remember" column in the *Winnipeg Tribune* remarking on her "rare charm of manner" and her "luscious"[6] voice. Her honeymoon visit to Portage la Prairie was the last time she saw Canada. Soon after the honeymoon, she moved into her husband Max Colyer-Fergusson's estate Wombwell Hall near Gravesend in Kent, her mother joining her.

On January 10, 1917 Edith gave birth to her first and only child: James, who became the fourth baronet on the death of his grandfather in 1951. Her death preceded her husband's by only four years. Max died in action as a lieutenant in the Royal Army Service Corps during the Second World War. (An Oxford graduate, James Colyer- Fergusson served as a captain in the East Kent Regiment during the war, returning from five years in a prisoner-of-war camp to work for British Rail. He would later become a much-hailed philanthropist in Kent.)

Although Edith had not been in Canada for twenty-three years, her death did not go unnoticed in the western press. She was still described as the "Manitoba Nightingale" and summaries of her remarkable career were accompanied by superlatives. She was "better known to tens of thousands of Canadians as Edith J. Miller...and was justly heralded as an artist among supreme artists on the concert stage of Canada...her smile set many a young heart throbbing a bit faster."[7] Her success abroad was summarized as if it were part of a goddess's life.

*

Edith's grave is a large, simple monument with three sections, each marked with an elegant cross—one for her husband Max, one for her, and one for their son James, who died in 2004. The monument stands in St. Margaret Churchyard, Gravesham Borough, Kent, England.

Jean Forsyth was buried in an unmarked grave—section 01, block 0004, plot 0008—in the Edmonton Cemetery where the city's oldest monuments stand. She is not among the "Some Notables" listed in the cemetery's website.[8]

ACKNOWLEDGMENTS

This book owes its existence to Gail Kreutzer. On October 25, 2013, I received an email from her suggesting that I write a book about Jean Forsyth. She had just finished reading my book *Aunt Winnie*, in which I had briefly mentioned Jean. Gail had been a volunteer at the Winnipeg Humane Society for fourteen years by then and had been on its board for ten years. She was deeply impressed that Jean Forsyth had been the organization's founder in 1893. She was even more impressed that no one at WHS had heard of Jean Forsyth. I emailed back a lukewarm response because I thought of *Aunt Winnie* as my last book. Gail persisted, and she began sending me packages of materials she had researched on Jean Forsyth—all at her own expense. Fast forward a year or so and a large stack of these packages was piled on my floor. One day I decided to open one of them. What I read drew me like a magnet. What was this? Onstage performances by Jean? Dealings with Emily Murphy and Nellie McClung? A teashop where a dizzying variety of events occurred? That was it. In January 2015, I sent an email to Gail, who lived in Arnes, Manitoba—a place I'd never heard of—to say I very much wanted to write this book.

Over the next ten months we developed a working partnership on email. Gail continued to research and send me packages of materials about Jean. I filed them chronologically, directed Gail to find materials I needed for the context to Jean's story, and began to write. I soon noticed that news clips about Jean Forsyth also mentioned a singer called Edith Miller. I set Gail to including her in our research. Edith turned out to be just as compelling as Jean, and the working title became "A Tale of Two Voices." Gail was my first editor, responding within a day or two to each chapter I sent. She also looked after the endnotes. We would not meet in person until July 2015 when I visited her and her partner Joanne Arbez in Arnes. By that time I had finished about half of the manuscript. We had much to discuss. I cannot thank Gail enough. We remain friends.

Don Foley at St. David's, Niagara-on-the-Lake is a one-of-a-kind photographer. His grasp of computer photography is excellent, and he used this talent to restore many photographs—some taken from grainy, folded, old newspapers, and brought some of them to life. I thank him warmly for all the work he did for this book at his studio, Foley's Photographic Services.

Other individuals have helped with this book. To each of them I am grateful. Vicki Burns, retired executive director of the Winnipeg Humane Society, responded promptly to requests for information. Alison Stover in Chatham went to the Chatham archives to check Forsyth family files and took photos of Forsyth monuments in Chatham's Maple Leaf Cemetery. I thank Moira Eyjolfsson for research assistance, and Val Klym, Jo-Anne Pollock, and Linda M. Goodman for their suggestions. A special thank you goes to Joanne Arbez, Gail's partner, for freeing up so much of Gail's time to work on this book.

Librarians are the lifeblood of research. All the librarians who contributed to this project were cheerful, helpful, and prompt. I sincerely thank: Stuart Hay, Reference Services, the Manitoba Legislative Library; Jennifer Claybourne, University of Minnesota Digital Library Services, Minneapolis; Karine Sarant-Hawkins and Andrew Potter, research assistants, Collections Department, and Jennifer Camilleri, Picture Library administrator, the Royal Academy of Arts Library, London, England; and Lori Jackson, the Kenora Public Library.

I am grateful to the large number of archivists who assisted so professionally with this project. They were indispensable. I thank Allan Rowe, research officer, Alberta Historical Places, Archives of Manitoba staff; Erin Strouth, archivist, Archives of Ontario; Melissa McCarthy, Tim O'Grady, and Lorraine Butchart at the reference desk, City of Edmonton Archives; Sarah Rathjen, archives assistant, City of Victoria Legislative and Regulatory Services; Julia McIntosh, Reference Services Division, Library and Archives Canada; Carol Ranson, archivist, Minnedosa Regional Archives; Tania Sharpe, CEO/chief librarian, Cassey Beauvais, manager, Public Services, and Heidi Wyman, manager, Support Services, the Chatham Public Library; Robin Francis, head of Archives and Library and Gudrun Muller, intellectual property officer, the National Portrait Gallery Archives; Karen Simonson, reference archivist, and Angie Friesen, reference archivist intern, the Provincial Archives of Alberta; Jamie L. Hoehn, archivist, University of Minnesota Immigration History Research Centre Archives, Elmer L. Anderson Library, Minneapolis; Kathy McGregor, administrative assistant, City of Portage la Prairie records; staff at the Government of Alberta (Alberta Connects); staff at Carberry Plains Archives; staff at MacEwen University; and staff at the University of Manitoba Archives Reference Library.

As might be expected, humane societies responded to this project. Heartfelt thanks go to volunteer Mary Timonin at the Winnipeg Humane Society, who digitally copied all the WHS minutes in the Manitoba Archives that mentioned Jean Forsyth. Aileen White, Christine Boult, and Briette Steinke, also of the WHS, assisted. Louis Borassa and Jocelyn Wady at the Edmonton Humane Society were very helpful.

Educational institutions responded helpfully to requests. I thank Susan Dutton, Bishop Strachan School; Tanya Pimenoff, assistant director of Alumnae Relations, Branksome Hall; Susan Pink, communications associate, Havergal College; Kim Arnold, archivist, Presbyterian Ladies' College; Dr. Dana Medoro, associate professor, American Literature, and Dr. Pam Perkins, professor, Department of English, Film and Theatre, University of Manitoba; Jodi MacDonald, Access and Privacy coordinator, Business Continuity coordinator, records officer at the Education and Advanced Learning Department of the Manitoba Government.

Thank you to the following genealogical societies: Norma Wolowyk, the Alberta Genealogical Society; Judi Bouchard, chair, and Valerie Butterfield, queries coordinator, the Kent branch of the Ontario Genealogical Society; and staff at the Oxford branch of the same society.

Church organizations provided valuable information. My thanks to: Erin Acland, the Manitoba and Northwestern Ontario United Church Archives; Elizabeth Mathew, reference assistant, the United Church of Canada Archives; and Jacquie Bennet, Trinity United Church, Portage la Prairie; Diane Haglund, archivist, the United Church of Canada Winnipeg Archives; Knox Church, the First Presbyterian church in Portage la Prairie; and Holy Trinity Anglican Church, Winnipeg.

Music organizations also contributed to this book, and I'd like to thank: Emily Worthington, curator and administrative assistant, the Royal College of Music, London, England; Sarah Farrell, receptionist and administrator, the London Academy of Music; Lezlie Bouza, student services representative, the Royal Conservatory School, and staff at Massey Hall, Toronto.

Newspaper staff and journalists answered questions: Tyler Stephens, the *Brandon Sun*; Nicholas Wilkins, the *New York Times*; and John Rhodes, *Chatham This Week*.

Kristi Sam, Bonnie Dribnenki, and the cemetery ground/maintenance crew, Municipal Cemeteries, City of Edmonton, helped locate Jean Forsyth's grave.

I must end on a sad note. Marc Côté, my former editor at Cormorant Books, Toronto, suggested both J. Gordon Shillingford Publishing and Signature Editions, each in Winnipeg, as possible publishers of this book. I am very grateful to Marc. Both publishers were interested in the book. At that time, I had no idea that Karen Haughian, proprietor of Signature Editions, had been married to Gord Shillingford for many years. Gord responded enthusiastically to my manuscript proposal within two weeks of getting it in September 2015. He had just emailed me that he was looking forward greatly to reading it in early January 2016, when Gail discovered online that he had died suddenly at age fifty-five on January 26. Such a terrible tragedy. Praises for Gord flowed in from everywhere. Eventually, once she got back on her feet, Karen emailed me (very kindly, under the circumstances) to say that my manuscript would be delayed, but would be published either under J. Gordon Shillingford Publishing or her own Signature Editions. Marc in Toronto and my old friend John Pearce, a literary agent at Westwood Creative Artists/Literary Agency living in Esquimault, offered me sage advice during the limbo following Gord's shocking death.

Karen assigned freelance editor Douglas Whiteway, Winnipeg writer and journalist, to edit the manuscript. Doug has worked for two of the Winnipeg newspapers (the *Tribune* and the *Free Press*) that are quoted liberally in this book. In addition he was an editor of the well-known historical magazine *The Beaver* from 1998 to 2007. He has also written numerous mysteries under the pen name C. C. Benison. Doug has proven to be a gifted and thorough editor both for the fictional and nonfictional chapters of this book. His professionalism—highlighted with dashes of wit—have made this book what it finally is. Thank you, Doug!

Elspeth Cameron
September 2016

ELSPETH CAMERON pioneered the first major biography of a Canadian literary figure with Nova Scotian *Hugh MacLennan: a Writer's Life* in 1981. This book won the Canadian Biography Award for that year and was shortlisted for the Governor General's Award. It was Montrealer Irving Layton's explosive reaction to her next biography, *Irving Layton: A Portrait*, in 1985 that brought her work to a wide Canadian public. She continued with a biography of BC poet Earle Birney (1994), which won the City of Vancouver Book Award. At the same time, she began writing journalistic profiles of Canadian cultural celebrities such as Veronica Tennant, Timothy Findley, Anne Murray, Peter Newman, and Jack McClelland. These won a number of awards. Her biography of Toronto sculptors Francis Loring and Florence Wyle (*And Beauty Answers*, 2007) was shortlisted for the City of Toronto Book Award. In 2013 Cameron published a hybrid biography/memoir, *Aunt Winnie*. Her memoir *No Previous Experience: A Memoir of Love and Change* (1997) won the City of Calgary Book Award.

Elspeth Cameron taught Canadian literature and Canadian Studies from 1970 until 2010 at Concordia University (Loyola College), the University of Toronto, Brock University, and the Institute for the Study of Canada, McGill University.

GAIL KREUTZER cares a great deal about animal welfare issues. She has volunteered with The Winnipeg Humane Society for fourteen years, eleven of which were as a board member (2003–2014). For a time during her tenure she served as a co-host with Vicki Burns on the weekly CJOB radio show "All About Animals." She has contributed articles about animal welfare issues for *H2O Gimli* and *Beaches Adventure Guide* and The Winnipeg Humane Society newsletter and the article "A Tribute to Jean Forsyth" for the Humane Society website. As an avid reader with a particular interest in Canadian culture, she is familiar with and has enjoyed Elspeth Cameron's biographies over the years. Gail is employed as an educator with Evergreen School Division where she began her career in 1984. She currently resides in Arnes, Manitoba and has a cat called Jean after Jean Forsyth.

EPIGRAPH

1. Jean Forsyth, "West to East," *Club Women's Records* (Canadian Women's Press Club Edmonton Branch, 1916), 23. http://peel.library.ualberta.ca/bibliography/4201.html

ONE

1. Lennox Browne and Emil Behnke, *Voice, Song, and Speech* (London: William Clowes and Sons, Limited, 1884).

2. Emma Seiler, *The Voice in Singing* (Philadelphia: J. B. Lippincott Company, 1900).

3. Jean Forsyth, "A Singing Student in London," *Harper's New Monthly Magazine* (February 1892): 385–91.
   The short story from which much of this information and dialogue is taken is actually by Jean N. McIlwraith (1858–1938), who used the pen name "Jean Forsyth." She was born in Hamilton, Ontario, and educated at Hamilton Ladies' College. This was not far from Chatham where the real Jean Forsyth was born and grew up. In London, Jean McIlwraith took cookery lessons and vocal lessons. "A Singing Student" was her first short story and was based on personal experience. It is possible that she and the real Jean Forsyth knew each other and discussed their vocal classes with William Shakespeare. It is also possible, instead, that Jean McIlwraith, who travelled widely and was involved in several of the arts, had read newspaper accounts of, or attended concerts that Jean Forsyth gave in eastern Ontario and thus choose her pen name. It seems unlikely—given the number of similarities and the geographical closeness of the two women

contemporaries—that the choice of pen name was accidental. Jean McIlwraith later worked as a reader for Doubleday Page, New York, and was a prize-winning author of historical romances for juvenile readers. Her complex and varied career is worthy of a book in itself.

TWO

1. H. H. Godfrey, *A Souvenir of Musical Toronto* (Second Annual Issue 1898–99), 40. https://archive.org/stream/1898souvenirofmu00godfuoft/1898souvenirofmu00godfuoft_djvu.txt

2. "A Portage Musician in Toronto," *Manitoba Free Press*, July 2, 1892.

THREE

1. Silas Farmer, *The History of Detroit and Michigan or the Metropolis Illustrated* (Detroit: S. Farmer and Co., 1889), 355. "Acquisition To College," *Edmonton Bulletin*, August 30, 1907, and Richard Bak, *Detroit: A Postcard History* (Charleston SC: Arcadia Publishing, 1998), 47.

2. "1840 to 1880," *Virtual Jewish World: Detroit, Michigan*, http://www.jewishvirtuallibrary.org/jsource/vjw/Detroit.html

3. "Schumann Society," *Detroit Free Press*, January 28, 1884; "Amusements," *Detroit Free Press*, May 7, 1887; "The Baron at Whites," *Detroit Free Press*, May 17, 1888; "Church Services," *Detroit Free Press*, December 31, 1888; and "Epworth League," *Detroit Free Press*, January 15, 1891.

4. "The Reportorial Round," *Winnipeg Tribune*, October 5, 1893.

5. Chicagogreys, "Exploring Chicago's History, Places, and People," http://chicagogreys.com/tag/kinzie-mansion/ "John Kinzie Silversmith (1763–1828): his early career as Shaneeawkee 'The Silver Man'," http://www.er.uqam.ca/nobel/r14310/Kinzie/ "John Kinzie," *Wikipedia*, last modified November 7, 2015. https://en.wikipedia.org/wiki/John_Kinzie

6. Anna Jameson, as cited by Victor Lauriston, *Romantic Kent: The Story of a County 1626–1952* (Chatham: The Corporation of County Kent and the Corporation of the City of Chatham, 1952), 151.

7. John Rhodes, "Daniel Forsyth Built Chatham's First Frame Home," *Chatham This Week*, May 23, 2012. Victor Lauriston, *op cit.*, 6.

8. Victor Lauriston, *op. cit.*, 2–63.

9. *Ibid.*, 166.

10. *Ibid.*

11. Rev. Canon Howard, *Notes on the History of the Church of England in Chatham, Ontario*, 1917. http://kentanglican.awardspace.com/3.htm

12. *Ibid.*, 180–81.

13. *Ibid.*, 172.

14. *Ibid.*, 171.

15. *Ibid.*, 180.

16. *Ibid.*, 153.

17. *Ibid.*, 169.

18. *Ibid.*, 167–68.

19. *Ibid.*, 168.

20. N. B., "Jean Forsyth of Edmonton," *Canadian Women in the Public Eye, Saturday Edmonton Journal*, September 22, 1923.

21. Details are taken variously from John Rhodes, *Chatham This Week*, May 23, 2012; Rev. Canon Howard, *Establishing the Church in Chatham, Ontario*, http://kentanglican.awardspace.com/4.htm and Victor Lauriston, *op. cit.*

22. Charles H. Wheeler, "Musical and Dramatic," *Winnipeg Tribune*, December 12, 1896.

23. James B. Hartman, "The Growth of Music in Early Winnipeg to 1920," *Manitoba History*, No. 40 (December 2000).

FOUR

1. Alan F. J. Artibise, ed. and Intro., *Gateway City: Documents on the City of Winnipeg 1873–1913*, A. B. McKillop, Gen. Ed., *Volume V: The Manitoba Record Society Publications* (Winnipeg: The Manitoba Record Society in assoc. with The University of Manitoba Press, 1979).

2. James B. Hartman, "The Growth of Music in Early Winnipeg to 1920," *Manitoba History*, No. 40 (December 2000).

3. "Great Success of the Rowing Club Ball Last Night," Written for the Women, *Winnipeg Tribune*, October 21, 1893.

FIVE

1. "The Apollo Club: Their First Concert This Season at the Bijou Last Night," *Manitoba Free Press*, November 30, 1893; C. H. Wheeler, *Winnipeg Tribune*, November 30, 1893; and "Nervousness of Singers," *Town Topics*, May 13, 1899.

SIX

1. Madge Macbeth, "Canadian Women in Business," *Maclean's Magazine*, vol. XXVIII no. 3 (Toronto: MacLean Hunter, January, 1915), 43.

2. "For Suffering Animals," *Winnipeg Tribune*, April 18, 1928.

3. "The Humane Society: Record of Work Done Since Organization," *Manitoba Free Press*, January 10, 1895.

4. N. B., "Jean Forsyth of Edmonton," *Canadian Women in the Public Eye, Saturday Edmonton Journal*, September 22, 1923.

5. "Minutes," The Winnipeg Humane Society, June 22, 1894, (MG10 B36).

6. *Ibid.*

7. "A Consulting Veterinarian to be Appointed," *Winnipeg Tribune*, April 26, 1894; "Official Inspection of Dairies Commenced," *Winnipeg Tribune*, July 6, 1894; *Manitoba Morning Free Press*, January 14, 1895; and "Dr. Hinman's Denial," *Winnipeg Tribune*, June 11, 1895. Dr. Hinman was opposed by some farmers who resented the trouble caused by Dr. Hinman's advice that "when they found an animal they knew to be tubercular they should not allow it to run amongst the herd." Some asked for his removal.

8. "The Colonel's Court: Man Fined for Cruelty to Animals," *Manitoba Morning Free Press*, May 31, 1897.

SEVEN

1. Giles Bugailiski, "Wheeler, Charles Henry," *Dictionary of Canadian Biography*, vol. 14, University of Toronto/Université Laval, 2003–, Accessed June 29, 2015. http://www.biographi.ca/en/bio/wheeler_charles_henry_14E.html

2. "*Romeo And Juliet* Performed at the Bijou—Mr. Cautley 'Faints' in the Last Act," *Winnipeg Tribune*, September 15, 1892; "Cautley, The Alleged Actor: He is Sent Back to England—His Fare Was Paid," *Tribune*, October 18, 1892.

3. Charles Wheeler, "Matinee Musicale," *Manitoba Free Press*, January 22, 1894.

EIGHT

1. "The Reportorial Round," *Winnipeg Tribune*, September 26, 1892.

2. "Musical and Dramatic Altogether Likely That Miss Edith Miller Will Take Up Her Residence Here," *Tribune*, June 2, 1894.

3. "Portage Paragraphs," *Manitoba Free Press*, January 17, 1891 and "Neepawa Church Enterprise," January 27, 1891.

4. "St. Mary's Church Entertainment," *Tribune*, February 9, 1891.

5. Charles H. Wheeler, "Musical and Dramatic The Mendelssohns' Visit—Miss Edith Miller's Progress," *Tribune*, December 5, 1891.

6. "Musical and Dramatic Miss Edith Miller's Progress," *Tribune*, December 5, 1891.

7. "Concert In The Evening," *Tribune*, August 24, 1892.

8. "Mr. Henneberg's Concert," *Tribune*, June 23, 1894.

9. "Written For The Women A Number of Successful Afternoon Teas," *Tribune*, October 21, 1893.

10. "Something About the Lenten Season—Mrs. Mathewson's Tea," Written for the Women, *Tribune*, February 17, 1894.

11. "Written for the Women," *Tribune*, January 27, 1894.

12. "Written for the Women," *Tribune*, May 19, 1894.

13. "Written for the Women," *Tribune*, January 20 1894 and July 28, 1894.

14. "Written for the Women," *Tribune*, February 3, 1894.

15. "Musical and Dramatic," *Tribune*, March 17, 1894.

16. "Two Parlor Concerts," *Manitoba Morning Free Press*, March 30, 1894.

17. "Musical and Dramatic," *Tribune*, March 17, 1894.

18. "Budget of Personal News," *Tribune*, August 11, 1894.

19. "Boys' Brigade Concert," *Tribune*, November 21, 1894.

20. "A Peep Into Society Circles," *Tribune*, November 24, 1894.

21. "A Peep Into Society Circles," *Tribune*, December 1, 1894 and "The Week in Society," *Tribune*, February 9, 1895.

22. *Manitoba Morning Free Press*, May 6, 1895, 5.

23. "A Peep Into Society Circles," *Tribune*, December 1, 1894; "This Week in Society," *Tribune*, February 9, 1895.

NINE

1. Wheeler, "Musical and Dramatic," *Winnipeg Tribune*, August 25, 1894.

2. Wheeler, "Preliminary Proceedings for the Incorporation of a Conservatory of Music," Musical and Dramatic, *Tribune*, June 23, 1894.

3. Wheeler, "Musical and Dramatic," *Tribune*, August 18, 1894.

4. Wheeler, "Musical and Dramatic," *Tribune*, August 25, 1894.

5. Wheeler, "Musical and Dramatic," *Tribune*, August 18, 1894.

6. Wheeler, "Musical and Dramatic," *Tribune*, August 25, 1894.

7. Wheeler, "Musical and Dramatic," *Tribune*, September 8, 1894.

8. "Conservatory Concert: A Brilliant Assemblage and a Programme of Rare Merit," *Tribune*, September 14, 1894.

9. Wheeler, "Winnipeg Conservatory of Music and established Fact," Musical and Dramatic, *Tribune*, August 18, 1894.

10. Wheeler, "The Conservatory Staff," Musical and Dramatic, *Tribune*, August 25, 1894.

11. "Conservatory Concert: A Brilliant Assemblage and a Programme of Rare Merit," *Tribune*, September 14, 1894.

12. S. Roy Maley, "Women's Musical Club of Winnipeg," *The Canadian Encyclopedia* last edited July 24, 2014. http://www.thecanadianencyclopedia.ca/en/article/womens-musical-club-of-winnipeg-emc/

TEN

1. "The Rowing Club Ball Last Night Proved a Brilliant Success: Description of Dresses," A Peep Into Society, *Tribune*, December 8, 1894.

ELEVEN

1. "Humane Society: Important Reports and Election of Officers for the Ensuing Year," *Winnipeg Tribune*, January 10, 1895, March 14, 1895, and "The Humane Society," *Manitoba Morning Free Press*, April 12, 1895.

2. "The Humane Society," *Manitoba Morning Free Press*, April 12, 1895.

3. George T. Angell, *Twelve Lessons on Kindness to Animals* (Boston: American Humane Education Society and Massachusetts Society for the Prevention of Cruelty to Animals, 1891).

4. George T. Angell and Reverend Thomas Timmins, *Band of Mercy Melodies*, (Boston: American Humane Education Society and Massachusetts Society for the Prevention of Cruelty to Animals, between 1882 and 1920).

TWELVE

1. "Local Brevities," *Manitoba Morning Free Press*, May 15, 1895.

2. "St. Andrew's Opening Concert: An Artistic Program Enjoyed by a Large Audience," *Manitoba Free Press*, February 6, 1895.

3. Wheeler, "Musical and Dramatic, *Winnipeg Tribune*, September 14, 1895.

4. "Concerts at Regina," The Reportorial Round, *Tribune*, July 29, 1895.

5. "Portage La Prairie: Club Quarters Opened With a Ball," *Manitoba Morning Free Press*, January 2, 1895.

6. "St. Andrew's Opening Concert: An Artistic Program Enjoyed by a Large Audience," *Manitoba Morning Free Press*, February 6, 1895.

7. "At Holy Trinity: '*Athalie*' Sung Last Night With Great Acceptability to Those Present," *Tribune*, April 24, 1895.

8. Wheeler, "Musical and Dramatic," *Tribune*, April 20, 1895.

9. "Music and the Drama," *Manitoba Morning Free Press*, October 14, 1895.

10. Wheeler, "Musical and Dramatic," *Tribune*, August 31, 1895.

11. Wheeler, "Musical and Dramatic," *Tribune*, October 5, 1895.

12. "Music and the Drama," *Manitoba Morning Free Press*, October 14, 1895.

13. Wheeler, "Musical and Dramatic," *Tribune*, November 23, 1895.

14. Wheeler, "Musical and Dramatic," *Tribune*, November 30, 1895.

15. Jim Davidson, "Melba, Dame Nellie (1861–1931), *Australian Dictionary of Biography*, vol. 10 (MUP), 1986; and "Nellie Melba, *Wikipedia*, last modified November 27, 1915, https://en.wikipedia.org/wiki/Nellie_Melba

THIRTEEN

1. "Cauchon Block on Fire," *The Winnipeg Tribune*, December 16, 1895.

2. Randy R. Rostecki, "The Early History of the Cauchon Block, Later the Empire Hotel," *Manitoba Pageant* (Spring 1976) Vol. 21, No. 3. http://www.mhs.mb.ca/docs/pageant/21/cauchonblock.shtml

FIFTEEN

1. "Portage Paragraphs," *Manitoba Morning Free Press*, May 11, 1896.

2. "Music and Drama," *Manitoba Morning Free Press*, May 9, 1896.

3. Malcolm Sterling Mackinlay, *Garcia the Centenarian and His Times* (New York: De Capo Press, 1976), 99.

4. Mackinlay, 204–05.

5. "Truths for Singing Teachers and Students," Étude *Magazine*, October 1913. http://etudemagazine.com/etude/1913/10/truths-for-singing-teachers-and-students.html

6. "Madam Marchesi and Her Singing School," *The Queenslander (Brisbane, Qld: 1866–1939)*, (March 24, 1894): 549.

SIXTEEN

1. Wheeler, "Musical and Dramatic," *Winnipeg Tribune*, June 6, 1896.

SEVENTEEN

1. "Music and Drama," *Manitoba Morning Free Press*, April 17, 1897.

2. "Emma Albani," *Wikipedia*, last modified May 31, 2015, last accessed July 4, 2015. http://en.wikipedia.org/wiki/Emma_Albani

3. "The Albani Concert," *Winnipeg Tribune*, January 23, 1897.

4. *Ibid.*

EIGHTEEN

1. Charles H. Wheeler, "Musical and Dramatic," *Winnipeg Tribune*, February 1, 1896 and February 15, 1896.

2. "The Albani Concert," *Tribune*, January 23, 1897.

3. "Music and Drama," *Manitoba Morning Free Press*, April 17, 1897.

4. "Music and Drama," *Tribune*, April 9, 1897.

5. "A Concert At Portage," *Manitoba Free Press*, April 9, 1897.

6. "City of the Plains," *Tribune*, August 9, 1897.

7. *Ibid.*

8. "Amusements," *The New York Times*, February 27, 1882.

9. George Sweet, "Professional Cards," *The Musical Courier*, vol. 23 no. 2, (July 8, 1891): 54.

10. Giovanni Battista Lamperti, *The Techniques of Bel Canto* (New York: G. Schirmier), 1905, Trans. from German by Dr. Theodore Baker.

11. Details taken from *The Musical Record and Review*, 1883; *The American Magazine*, vol. 21, 1886, 11; *The Grove Dictionary of American Music*; *The Musical Courier*, vol. 23, 574; *Werner's Magazine: A Magazine of Expression*, 1894; *The Musical*

Record and Review, 1881; *The Musical Courier*, n.d., 1891; *The Monthly Musical Record*, 1881; *The Evening World* (New York, New York: January 22, 1891 and March 5, 1891), 2.

12. "Bel Canto: The Old Italian Vocal Technique and its Golden Age," academia.edu.

13. Charles H. Wheeler, "Musical and Dramatic," *Tribune*, September 17, 1898.

TWENTY

1. *Town Topics*, June 18, 1898.

2. Major Key, "Music Observations," *Winnipeg Tribune*, July 28, 1934.

3. *Manitoba Free Press*, May 27, 1899.

4. "Music and Drama," *Daily Nor'Wester*, February 25, 1898.

5. *Manitoba Morning Free Press*, April 2, 1898.

TWENTY-ONE

1. "Manitoba and Northwest: A Happy Contralto," *Victoria Daily Colonist*, February 22, 1898.

2. "Famous Choirs of New York," *The New York Times*, May 1, 1898 and October 22, 1898.

3. Wheeler, "Music and Dramatic," *Winnipeg Tribune*, February 5, 1898.

4. "James Henry Mapleson," *Wikipedia*, last modified May 5, 2015, https://en.wikipedia.org/wiki/James_Henry_Mapleson; Emma Nevada, "Col. J. H. Mapleson Dead," https://www.msu.edu/~graye/emma/mapleson_obit.html; "Miss Hauk Explains," *The New York Times*, December 10, 1878; *The Fort Wayne Sentinel*, February 24, 1879; "Mapleson's Pile," *The Saint Paul Globe*, April 14, 1879; "Minnie Herself Again," *The New York Times*, February 18, 1882; "Col. Mapleson's Plans," *The New York Times*, April 17, 1882; "Battle of the Managers," *The New York Times*, April 24, 1883; "Mapleson vs. Abbey," *The*

Courier-Journal (Kentucky), November 6 and 14, 1883 and January 26, 1884; "Col. Mapleson Lying Low," *The New York Times*, November 29, 1885; "Fighting over Mapleson," *The New York Times*, May 2, 1884; "Col. Mapleson's Overdrafts," *The New York Times*, May 5, 1884; "Opera Singers in Court," *The New York Times*, February 17, 1885; "Col. Mapleson's Desire," *The New York Times*, August 12, 1885; "A Tenor's Big Demand," *The New York Times*," December 10, 1885; "Singer Come High," *The Saint Paul Globe*," November 8, 1896; and "Singers Reply to Mapleson," *The New York Times*, November 18, 1896.

5. "Famous Choirs of New York," *The New York Times*, October 23, 1898.

6. "Music and the Drama," *Manitoba Free Press*, June 3, 1898.

7. "Music," *Town Topics*, July 30, 1898.

8. "The Social Round," *The Ottawa Journal*, December 20, 1898.

9. "Music," *Town Topics*, November 19, 1898.

10. "Mr. Vanderbilt's Funeral," *New York Times*, September 16, 1899.

TWENTY-TWO

1. Wheeler, "Musical and Dramatic," *Winnipeg Tribune*, November 23, 1895.

2. *Town Topics*, May 11, 1901, 3.

3. "Music," *Town Topics*, June 18, 1898.

4. Wheeler, "Musical and Dramatic," *Tribune*, February 4, 1899; and "The New Indian," *Town Topics*, March 11, 1899.

5. "Singers Come High De Reszke Fixed The Price," *The Saint Paul Globe*, November 8, 1896.

6. "Music and the Drama," *Manitoba Free Press*, September 3, 1898.

7. "Music and Drama," *Manitoba Morning Free Press*, May 27, 1899.

8. "Music," *Town Topics*, July 2, 1898.

9. "Albertans in the Public Eye: Mr. Jackson Hanby," *Saturday News*, March 2, 1907.

10. Wheeler, "Musical and Dramatic," *Tribune*, July 27, 1895.

11. "Celebration at Portage," *Tribune*, May 17, 1895; and "Portage La Prairie," *Manitoba Morning Free Press*, May 27, 1895.

12. Wheeler, "Musical and Dramatic," *Tribune*, July 27, 1895.

13. Wheeler, "Musical and Dramatic," *Tribune*, November 16, 1895.

14. "Music," *Town Topics*, July 23, 1898.

15. *Town Topics*, October 15, 1898.

16. *Ibid.*

17. Wheeler, "Musical and Dramatic," *Tribune*, May 27, 1899.

18. "Music and Drama," *Winnipeg Free Press*, May 27, 1899.

TWENTY-THREE

1. Details from Henry Trachtenberg, "El Politico on the Urban Frontier: 'Fighting Joe' Martin and the Jews of Winnipeg, 1893–96," *Manitoba History*, no. 31 Spring/Summer 1998; Jim Silver, "Winnipeg's North End: Yesterday and Today," *Culture*, January 2010; and Moses Finkelstein, "Personal Reminiscences of an Early Jewish Settler in Western Canada," *The Reform Advocate* (Chicago: Bloch and Newman), 1914.

2. "Tribune Trumps," *Winnipeg Tribune*, October 21, 1905; "Rosa's Remarks: the Entertaining Chatter of a Matinee Girl," *Town Topics*, March 11, 1899; "A Good Indian Gone," *Tribune*, October 18, 1902; "Tribune Trumps," *Tribune*, August 5, 1907; and "Murderer to Hang: A Bad Indian Will Swing Tomorrow," *Tribune*, October 23, 1902.

3. Details taken from "1880s in Western Fashion," *Wikipedia* https://en.m.wikipedia.org/wiki/1880s_in_Western_fashion ; "1890s in Western Fashion," *Wikipedia* http://en.wikipedia.org/wiki/1890s_in_Western_fashion ; "1880s in Women's Fashions," *Wikipedia*, last modified April 8, 2015, https://en.wikipedia.org/wiki/1880s_in_Western_fashion

4. "Winnipeg MB Manitoba Hotel Fire February 1899," http://www3.gendisasters.com/ and "File: Manitoba Hotel, pre-1899.jpg," *Wikipedia*, last modified September 7, 2015. https://commons.wikimedia.org/wiki/File:Manitoba_Hotel,_pre_1899.jpg

5. "Society," *Town Topics*, June 16, 1900.

6. *Town Topics*, November 24, 1900 and "James Tees (1854–1906)," *Memorable Manitobans*, last modified August 5, 2015 http://www.mhs.mb.ca/docs/people/tees_j.shtml

7. Wheeler, "Musical and Dramatic," *Tribune*, November 15, 1900.

8. *Town Topics*, October 20, 1900.

9. "Music," *Town Topics*, September 2, 1899.

10. "Music," *Town Topics*, September 23, 1899.

11. *Town Topics*, September 3, 1899.

12. *Town Topics*, March 17, 1900.

TWENTY-FOUR

1. "Advance Notices," *Town Topics*, July 28, 1900.

2. "City and General," *Brandon Daily Sun*, July 24, 1900.

3. "City and General," *Brandon Daily Sun*, August 21, 1900.

4. "The Miller Concert," *Brandon Western Sun*, August 30, 1900.

5. "Music and Drama," *Town Topics*, August 30, 1900.

6. John Buchan, *Lord Minto: A Memoir* (London: Thomas Nelson and Sons, Ltd., 1924), 118.

7. "Advertisement," *Calgary Weekly Herald*, August 23, 1900, 4.

8. Edmund H. Garrett (editor), *Victorian Songs; Lyrics of the Affections and Nature*, (New York: Little, Brown and Co., 1895).

9. "A Successful Concert by Miss Edith Miller and Company at the Opera House," *Calgary Weekly Herald*, August 30, 1900.

10. "Music and Drama," *Town Topics*, September 6, 1900.

11. "Edith J. Miller Company," *Vancouver Daily World*, September 11, 1900.

12. "Music and Drama," *Saturday News*, June 29, 1912.

13. "A Coming Treat: Early Appearance of the Edith J. Miller Grand Concert Company," *Victoria Daily Colonist*, August 30, 1900.

14. "Edith Miller Engagement," *Victoria Daily Colonist*, September 7, 1900.

15. "Edith J. Miller Company," *Vancouver Daily World*, September 11, 1900.

16. "City and General," *Winnipeg Free Press*, September 13, 1900.

17. "Music and Drama," *Town Topics*, October 6, 1900.

18. "Music and Drama: Edith J. Miller Concert Company," *Town Topics*, October 13, 1900.

TWENTY-FIVE

1. "Reportorial Round," *Winnipeg Tribune*, December 12, 1900.

2. "City and General," *Winnipeg Free Press*, January 30, 1901.

3. Wheeler, "Musical and Dramatic," *Tribune*, January 25, 1901.

4. "Music and Drama," *Winnipeg Free Press*, February 2, 1901.

5. Wheeler, "Musical and Dramatic," *Tribune*, March 7, 1901.

6. "Society," *Town Topics*, March 30, 1901.

7. "Fancy Portraits," *Punch*, September 17, 1881, no. 49.

8. "Singing at Westminster Church," *Tribune*, March 4, 1901; "Foresters Reception," *Tribune*, February 23, 1901; and "Old Maid's Convention," *Tribune*, February 22, 1901.

9. "Music and Drama," *Town Topics*, December 1, 1900.

10. "Music and Drama," *Town Topics*, November 24, 1900.

11. "Music and Drama," *Town Topics*, December 1, 1900.

12. "Music and Drama," *Town Topics* December 15, 1900.

TWENTY-SIX

1. "Reportorial Round," *Winnipeg Tribune*, January 11, 1901 and *Town Topics*, November 17, 1900.

2. *Tribune*, February 27, 1901.

3. "Mrs. Galt Musicale," *Tribune*, December 1, 1900.

4. *Town Topics*, February 2, 1901.

5. "Society," *Town Topics*, March 16, 1901.

6. *Tribune*, July 27, 1895.

7. *Town Topics*, May 18, 1908.

8. Wheeler, "Musical and Dramatic," *Tribune*, May 23, 1902.

9. "Music and Drama," *Manitoba Morning Free Press*, November 7, 1902.

10. "Music and Drama," *Tribune*, May 12, 1904.

11. "Annual Meeting of Humane Society," *Manitoba Free Press*, January 26, 1904.

12. "Minutes," Winnipeg Humane Society, December 17, 1900.

13. "Minutes," Winnipeg Humane Society, December 14, 1899.

14. Madge Macbeth, "Canadian Women in Business," *Maclean's Magazine*, vol. XXVIII no. 3, (Toronto: Maclean-Hunter, January, 1915), 43.

15. "Annual Meeting of Humane Society," *Manitoba Free Press*, January 26, 1904.

16. *Manitoba Free Press*, April 22, 1902.

17. "Music," *Town Topics*, June 1, 1901.

18. "French Literary Club," *Tribune*, March 13, 1902.

19. "Society," *Town Topics*, June 8, 1901.

20. *Town Topics*, August 31, 1901.

21. "Society," *Town Topics*, July 13, 1901.

22. "Society," *Town Topics*, April 13, 1901.

23. "Society," *Town Topics*, November 2, 1901.

TWENTY-SEVEN

1. "Presbyterian," *Yukon World*, February 26, 1905.

2. Details taken from "Show Is Success," *Dawson Daily News*, July 29, 1905.

3. Charles H. Wheeler, "Music and Drama," *Winnipeg Tribune*, February 5, 1902.

4. "For the Sake of Music," *Vancouver Daily World*, May 4, 1903.

5. *Tribune*, February 20, 1895.

6. James B. Hartman, "Manitoba History: The Growth of Music in Early Winnipeg," *The Manitoba Historical Society*, no. 40, Autumn/Winter 2000–2001; and "Music in Winnipeg," *The Canadian Encyclopedia*, http://www.thecanadianencyclopedia.ca/en/article/winnipeg-man-emc/

7. C. L. G., "Music," *The Guardian* (London), February 20, 1895.

8. Wheeler, "Musical and Dramatic," *Tribune*, May 2, 1903.

9. This proved to be true. The next year Mrs. Verner had indeed taken Jean's place touring Manitoba. In late May at Killarney, southern Manitoba, she sang what was a relatively secular lyric for her, "With Verdure Clad," and was presented with a bouquet, according to the *Winnipeg Tribune*, May 26, 1906.

10. Wheeler, "Musical and Dramatic," *Tribune*, April 30, 1904; and Wheeler, "Musical and Dramatic," *Tribune*, January 18, 1904.

11. *The Dawson Mall*, September 22, 1905, as quoted by Charles Wheeler, *Tribune*, October 6, 1905.

12. Jean Forsyth did direct a production of Gilbert and Sullivan's *Patience* in Dawson City before she returned to Winnipeg.

TWENTY-EIGHT

1. "Early Tent Communities," *City of Edmonton Archives online*, http://www.edmonton.ca/city_government/edmonton_archives/early-tent-communities.aspx

TWENTY-NINE

1. "Edmonton—A City Called Home," *Historic Timelines 1904–1906*, http://www.epl.ca/edmontonacitycalledhome/EPLEdmontonCityCalledTimeline.cfm . And see a detailed account of Indian treaty history in Greg Poelzer & Ken S. Coates, *From Treaty Peoples to Treaty Nation* (Vancouver/Toronto: UBC Press, 2015)—on English contracts and property ownership.

2. Alan F. J. Artibise, ed., *Gateway City: Documents in the City of Winnipeg 1873–1913* (Winnipeg: The Manitoba Record Society and The University of Winnipeg Press, 1979), 118. The nineteen were: J. A. M. Aikins, K.C., W. F. Alloway, J. H. Ashdown, N. Bawlf, Edward Brown, D. C. Cameron, D. S. Currie, E. L. Drewery, C. Enderton, Rev. C. W. Gordon (a.k.a. Ralph Connor), E. F. Hutchings, W. C. Leistikow, J. D. McArthur, Rod McKenzie, Sir Daniel McMillan, A. M. McNichol, Alex Macdonald, A. M. Nanton, and Capt. W. Robinson.) But it was not to be in Edmonton. And ("Edmonton Historic Timeline," http://www.epl.ca/edmontonacitycalledhome/EPLEdmontonCityCalledTimeline.cfm) and J. G. MacGregor, *Edmonton: A History* (Edmonton: Hurtig Publishers, 1967.)

3. William C. Wonders, "Edmonton in the Klondike Gold Rush," *Edmonton: The Life of A City*, ed. Bob Hesketh and Frances Swyripa (Edmonton: NeWest Press, 1995), 63 and 69.

4. John P. Day, "Edmonton Civic Politics, 1891–1913," *Urban History Review/Revue d'histoire urbaine* (No. 3-77, 1978): 42–68.

5. Mary Markwell, "The Northwest Girl," *Town Topics*, January 25, 1902.

6. Gilbert A. Stelter, "What Kind of a City is Edmonton?" *Edmonton: The Life of a City*, ed. Bob Hesketh and Frances Swyripa (Edmonton: NeWest Press, 1995), 5.

7. See photo of the *Revillon Frères* shop interior in Paul Voisey, "Unsolved Mysteries of Edmonton's Growth," op. cit., 320.

8. John P. Day, "Edmonton Civic Politics 1891–1913," *Urban History Review/Revue d'histoire urbaine* (No. 3-77, 1978): 64.

9. "The Early Days of Edmonton Theatre," http://www.yegishome.ca/news/2002/05/02/the-early-days-of-edmonton-theatre and http://www.lastlinkon theleft.com/e006movie.html

10. Jars Balan, "Ukrainian Theatre: Showtime on the North Saskatchewan," *Edmonton: The Life of a City*, op. cit., 88–95.

11. "Early Tent Communities," *City of Edmonton Archives online*, http://www.edmonton.ca/city_government/edmonton_archives/early-tent-communities.aspx

12. N. B., "Jean Forsyth of Edmonton," *Canadian Women in the Public Eye*, *Saturday Edmonton Journal*, September 22, 1923.

THIRTY

1. Details taken from Harold D. Speed, *The Practice and Science of Drawing* (London: Seeley, Service & Co., Ltd., 38 Great Russell Street; and Harold D. Speed, *Oil Painting Techniques and Materials* (U.S.: Dover Publications, 1987); and "Harold Speed," *Wikipedia* https://en.wikipedia.org/wiki/Harold_Speed. Speed's books are still available and are used in many art classes.

THIRTY-ONE

1. "SPECIAL SERVICES," *Vancouver Daily News*, October 6, 1906.

2. "Local Notes," *Manitoba Free Press*, April 7, 1905, p. 13.

3. "Concerts, Recitals, &c.," *London Standard*, May 4, 1906, 1.

4. *Belfast Newsletter*, as quoted by Charles H. Wheeler, "Musical and Dramatic: Splendid Programme Prepared—Miss Edith J. Miller's Success in Ireland—'Happyland Attractions,'" *Winnipeg Tribune*, May 26, 1906.

5. *The Irish Times*, as quoted by Charles H. Wheeler, "Musical and Dramatic: Splendid Programme Prepared—Miss Edith J. Miller's Success in Ireland—'Happyland Attractions,'" *Tribune*, May 26, 1906.

6. "London Notes," *New York Musical Courier*, (February 6, 1907), as quoted in *Manitoba Free Press*, February 23, 1907.

7. Charles A. Hooey, "Ones Who Got Away: Muriel Foster," *MusicWeb International*, www.musicweb-international.com/hooey/foster_away.htm

8. "London Notes," *New York Musical Courier*, (6 February 1917), as quoted in *Manitoba Free Press*, February 23, 1907.

9. *London Standard*, February 12, 1907.

10. "London Notes," *New York Musical Courier*, (February 6, 1917), as quoted in *Manitoba Free Press*, February 23, 1907.

11. Details of the exhibit at its first showing in Rome, "Keats-Shelly [sic] Pleases," *The New York Times*, February 15, 1907.

12. "London Notes," *New York Musical Courier*, February 6, 1917, as quoted in *Manitoba Free Press*, February 23, 1907.

13. Ffrangcon-Davies, *The Singing of the Future* (New York: John Lane), 1907.

14. "King Hears American Musicians," *The New York Times*, February 15, 1907.

15. Wheeler, "Musical and Dramatic: Congratulated by King Edward," *Tribune*, March 9, 1907.

THIRTY-TWO

1. "Personal," *Edmonton Bulletin*, April 3 and 5, 1907.

2. "Alberta Past and Present: Historical and Biographical," http://www.mocavo.com/Alberta-Past-and-Present-Historical-and-Biographical-Volume-3/124831/337

3. "Musical Miss Jean Forsyth," *Edmonton Bulletin*, May 9, 1907.

4. Much later, in 1932, Gertrude Seton-Thompson would publish a 447-page handbook on good manners under a pseudonym, Gertrude Pringle: *Etiquette in Canada: the Blue Book of Canadian Social Usage.* (Toronto: McClelland and Stewart, 1932).

5. "Note and Comment," *Saturday News*, May 4, 1907.

6. Gertrude E. Seton-Thompson, "The Women of Edmonton," *Canada West*, volume VII, no. 1 (London: Vanderhoof-Gunn Company Ltd., Publishers, November 1909), 25.

7. "Dr. Riddell," *Winnipeg Tribune*, June 6, 1898.

8. "From One Day to the Other: Miss Forsyth's Opinion," *Edmonton Bulletin*, May 10, 1907.

THIRTY-THREE

1. "Alberta's First Annual Music Festival," *Saturday News*, May 9, 1908.

2. Details from *Edmonton Bulletin*, May 17, 1907; Charles H. Wheeler, "Musical and Dramatic Jackson Hanby Writes of the Town's Taste," *Winnipeg Tribune*, July 29, 1905; and "Reminiscences:

Some Recollections, Humorous and Otherwise, of Jackson Hanby," *Tribune*, December 28, 1918; and "Do You Remember Jackson Hanby?," *Tribune*, July 3, 1929.

THIRTY-FOUR

1. Gertrude Balmer Watt (Peggy), "The Mirror," *Saturday News*, September 28, 1907.

2. "Humane Society Meets," *Edmonton Bulletin*, March 20, 1908.

3. "Fort Saskatchewan," *Edmonton Bulletin*, July 2, 1907.

4. *Ibid.*

5. "Edna Sutherland (1869–1956)," *Memorable Manitobans*, revised August 17, 1910. http://www.mhs.mb.ca/docs/people/sutherland_e.shtml

6. "From Day to Day: Acquisition to College," *Edmonton Bulletin*, August 30, 1907.

7. "The Alberta College, Pioneer of Higher Education in the Province," *Edmonton Bulletin*, May 4, 1907.

8. "Fort Saskatchewan," *Bulletin*, December 18, 1907.

9. "Ladies' Musical Club," *Bulletin*, October 4, 1907.

10. Gertrude Balmer Watt (Peggy), "The Mirror," *Saturday* News, November 16, 1907.

THIRTY-FIVE

1. "Arthur Shattuck," *Neenah Historical Society*, http://www.focol.org/neenahhistorical/Historical%20Photos/Notables%20Images/Notable%20Text/Shattuck.html

2. "Blanche Marchesi," *Wikipedia*, last modified October 25, 2015, https://en.wikipedia.org/wiki/Blanche_Marchesi; "Marie Brema," *Wikipedia*, last modified December 31, 2015, https://en.wikipedia.org/wiki/Marie_Brema; "Landon Ronald," *Wikipedia*, last modified October 16, 2015,

https://en.wikipedia.org/wiki/Landon_ Ronald; "Ben Davies (tenor)," *Wikipedia*, last modified July 6, 2015, https:// en.wikipedia.org/wiki/Ben_Davies_(tenor); "Efrem Zimbalist," *Wikipedia*, last modified December 16, 2015, https:// en.wikipedia.org/wiki/Efrem_Zimbalist; "George Grossmith," *Wikipedia*, last modified December 31, 2015, https://en.wikipedia.org/wiki/George_Grossmith; "Natalia Janotha," *Wikipedia*, last modified June 1, 2015, https://en.wikipedia.org/ wiki/Natalia_Janotha.

3. Charles H. Wheeler, "Musical News of the Day," *Winnipeg Tribune*, June 20, 1908.

4. *Ibid.*

THIRTY-SIX

1. "Note and Comment," *Saturday News*, March 28, 1908 and "Humane Society Meets," *Edmonton Bulletin*, March 20, 1908.

2. "Social," *Edmonton Bulletin*, September 19, 1908.

3. John W. Leonard, *Woman's Who's Who of America: A Biographical Dictionary of Contemporary Women of the United States and Canada* (American Commonwealth Company, 1914), 168. Gertrude E. Seton-Thompson, "The Women of Edmonton," *Canada West*, volume VII, no. 1 (London: Vanderhoof-Gunn Company Ltd., Publishers, November 1909), 29. For a thorough treatment of Emily Murphy's full career in Edmonton, see Faye Reineberg Holt, "Magistrate Emily Ferguson Murphy," *Edmonton: The Life of a City*, ed. Bob Hesketh and Frances Swyripa (Edmonton, NeWest Press, 1995), 143–49. For a thorough treatment of Katherine Hughes's full career in Edmonton, see Pádraig Ó Siadhail, "Katherine Hughes, Irish Political Activist," *Edmonton: The Life of a City*, ed. Bob Hesketh and Frances Swyripa (Edmonton: NeWest Press, 1995), 78–87.

4. John W. Leonard, *Woman's Who's Who of America: A Biographical Dictionary of Contemporary Women of the United States and Canada* (American Commonwealth Company, 1914), 168.

5. "Lecture Course on Nursing," *Edmonton Bulletin*, March 12, 1907.

6. "Music and Drama," *Saturday News*, August 1, 1908.

7. Arthur Balmer Watt, "A Scattering of Seeds: The Creation of Canada, A Land as Green as the Sea," *Scottish Immigration*, http://www.whitepinepictures.com/ seeds/i/13/history1.html

8. Gertrude Balmer Watt (Peggy), "The Mirror," *Saturday News*, August 8, 1908.

9. *Ibid.*

10. "Entertained at Luncheon," *Edmonton Bulletin*, August 5, 1908.

THIRTY-SEVEN

1. Gertrude E. Seton-Thompson, "The Women of Edmonton," *Canada West*, volume VII, no. 1 (London: Vanderhoof-Gunn Company Ltd., Publishers, November 1909), 31 and "First Annual Session Of Council Of Women," *Edmonton Bulletin*, January 8, 1909.

2. Gertrude E. Seton-Thompson, "The Women of Edmonton," 25–34.

3. Gertrude E. Seton-Thompson, "The Women of Edmonton," 28.

4. Gertrude E. Seton-Thompson, "The Women of Edmonton," 26.

5. Gertrude E. Seton-Thompson, "The Women of Edmonton," 25.

6. Gertrude Balmer Watt, "A City of Contrasts," A *Woman in the West* (Edmonton: The News Publishing Company, 1907), 15.

THIRTY-EIGHT

1. "Music and Drama," *Town Topics*, May 15, 1909.

2. "Miss Edith Miller," *Edmonton Bulletin*, May 17, 1909.

3. Personal, *Manitoba Morning Free Press*, July 30, 1904.

4. "Miss Edith Miller," *Edmonton Bulletin*, May 17, 1909.

5. Charles H. Wheeler, "Tour For Miss Miller: Noted Canadian Singer is Coming to Canada in April—Will be Heard in Winnipeg," *Winnipeg Tribune*, February 22, 1909.

6. CLEF, "Music," *The Ottawa Journal*, March 6, 1909, p. 17.

7. Charles H. Wheeler, "Music and Drama," *Tribune*, April 12, 1909.

8. "Coming Amusements—Edith Miller," *The Ottawa Journal*, April 26, 1909.

9. *Town Topics*, May 1, 1909.

10. Charles H. Wheeler, "Musical Review of the Week," *Tribune*, May 1, 1909.

11. Charles H. Wheeler, "Veritable Triumph For Miss Edith Miller," *Tribune*, May 10, 1909.

12. Cheryl MacDonald, *Emma Albani: Victorian Diva*, (Dundurn Press, 1984).

13. Music and Drama, *Town Topics*, May 15, 1909.

14. Charles H. Wheeler, "Veritable Triumph for Miss Edith Miller," *Tribune*, May 10, 1909.

THIRTY-NINE

1. *Brandon Weekly Sun*, May 13, 1909.

2. "The Opera *Patience*," *Edmonton Bulletin*, May 17, 1909.

3. "The Opera *Patience*," *Bulletin*, May 18, 1909.

4. "Miss Edith Miller," *Bulletin*, May 17, 1909.

5. "Miss Edith Miller is Coming," *Saturday News*, May 15, 1909, including an extract from her agent N. Vert, London.

6. "*Patience*," *Bulletin*, May 26, 1909.

7. "The Opera *Patience*," *Bulletin*, May 27, 1909.

8. "Home and Society," *Saturday News*, May 29, 1909.

9. "Here and There," *Saturday News*, May 29, 1909.

10. "The Mirror," *Saturday News*, May 29, 1909.

11. "Lloydminster in Gala Attire," *Bulletin*, July 6, 1909.

12. "Music and Drama," *Saturday News*, July 24, 1909.

FORTY

1. Jean Forsyth (Celeste), "The Journals Page for Women," *Edmonton Journal*, October 22, 1910.

FORTY-ONE

1. "Prominent Women Here," *Bulletin*, August 4, 1909.

2. "Social Jottings," *Bulletin*, September 10, 1909.

3. "Home and Society," *Saturday News*, January 15, 1910.

4. Gertrude Seton Thompson, "Society in the Capital," *Bulletin*, May 28, 1910.

5. "Social Jottings," *Bulletin*, January 22, 1910.

6. "Home and Society," *Saturday News*, July 16, 1910.

7. *Ibid.*

8. "Home and Society," *Saturday News*, October 30, 1909.

9. "The Mirror," *Saturday News*, August 28, 1909.

10. "Social Jottings," *Bulletin*, December 31, 1909.

11. "The Curling Tea," *Bulletin*, March 12, 1910.

12. "Social Jottings," *Bulletin*, January 14, 1910.

13. "Home and Society," *Saturday News*, January 15, 1910.

14. "The Hambourg Recital," *Bulletin*, March 18, 1910.

15. "Musical and Dramatic Review of Week," *Winnipeg Tribune*, April 9, 1910.

16. "Around the City: The Festival Chorus," *Bulletin*, May 6, 1910.

17. "Social Jottings," *Bulletin*, December 31, 1909.

18. "Home and Society," *Saturday News*, February 5, 1910.

19. "Home and Society," *Saturday News*, February 19, 1910.

20. "Joseph Morris (Alberta Politician)," *Wikipedia*, last modified August 20, 2015. https://en.wikipedia.org/wiki/Joseph_Morris_(Alberta_politician)

21. "Home and Society," *Saturday News*, April 23, 1910.

FORTY-TWO

1. "Empire," *Edmonton Capital*, April 25, 1910.

2. "Home and Society," *Saturday News*, November 27, 1909.

3. "Miss Forsyth to Sing," *Edmonton Bulletin*, October 4, 1909.

4. "At the Starland," *Bulletin*, October 12, 1909.

5. "Starland the Popular Family Theatre," *Bulletin*, October 14, 1909 and "Starland the Popular Family Theatre," *Bulletin*, October 16, 1909.

6. Hilary Russell, "All That Glitters: A Memorial to Ottawa's Capitol Theatre and its Predecessors," *Canadian Historical Sites: Occasional Papers in Archives and History*, No. 13. Last updated September 15, 2006. www.parkscanadahistory.com/series/chs/13/chs13-1a.htm

FORTY-THREE

1. Details taken from "Home and Society," *Saturday News*, October 22, 1910; Penelope, "Society in the Capital," *Bulletin*, October 22, 1910; "Home and Society," *Saturday News*, October 29, 1910; Penelope, "Society in the Capital," *Bulletin*, October 29, 1910; Gertrude E. Seton-Thompson, "The Women of Edmonton," *Canada West*, volume VII, no. 1, (London: Vanderhoof-Gunn Company Ltd., Publishers, November 1909) p. 32; and "Business Women in Canada," *Maclean's*, January 1915.

FORTY-FOUR

1. Peggy, "The Mirror," *Saturday News*, November 18, 1911.

FORTY-FIVE

1. Barbara Tuchman, *The Guns of August*, as quoted in Jane Ridley, *Bertie: A Life of Edward VII* (London: Chattus & Windus, 1962), 568.

2. "The Imperial Roof Tree," *Papers Past*, vol. LXVII, issue 14076 (June 22, 1911): 10.

3. "The Great Exhibition," last updated August 29, 2015, https://en.wikipedia.org/wiki/The_Great_Exhibition.

4. "Festival of the Empire," *Making Britain*, 1911. http://www.open.ac.uk/researchprojects/makingbritain/

5. The medal seems to depict Britannia standing on the waves. This is a peaceful goddess holding a trumpet, not the typical martial Britannia holding a trident and wearing a plumed helmet.

6. "The Imperial Roof Tree," *op. cit.*

7. "Empire Concerts," *London Standard*, May 29, 1911.

8. "Orchestrated by Sir Alexander Mackenzie," *London Evening Standard*, May 27, 1911, and "Canada Ever," by Laura Lehman, the young Canadian singer Edith Miller was encouraging in Britain.

9. Rupert Christiansen, *The Victorian Visitors: Culture Shock in Nineteenth-Century Britain* (NY: Atlantic Monthly Press, 2000), 192–93.

FORTY-SIX

1. Madge MacBeth, "Canadian Women in Business," *Maclean's Magazine*, January 2015.

2. *Ibid.*

3. Jars Balan, "Ukrainian Theatre: Showtime on the North Saskatchewan," *Edmonton: The Life of a City*, ed. Bob Hesketh and Frances Swyripa (Edmonton: NeWest Press, 1995).

4. John P. Day, "Edmonton Civic Politics, 1891–1913," *Urban History Review/Revue d'histoire urbaine* (no. 3-77, 1978): 184; and Paul Hjartson, "'Now Then, All Together!' Assimilation, the Book, and the Educations of new Canadians 1896–1918," "History of the Book in Canada Conference," for *History of the Book in Canada/Histoire du livre et de l'imprimé au Canada*, vol. II (1840–1918).

5. Catherine Cole, "Garment Manufacturing in Edmonton," *Edmonton: Life of a City*, (Edmonton: NeWest Press), 161–69; and "Edmonton: A City Called Home," *Edmonton Historic Timeline*, http://www2.epl.ca/EdmontonACityCalledHome/EPLEdmontonCityCalledTimeline.cfm

6. John P. Day, *op. cit.*, 66.

7. N. B., "Jean Forsyth of Edmonton," *Canadian Women in the Public Eye, Saturday Edmonton Journal*, September 22, 1923.

8. "Home and Society," *Saturday News*, October 7, 1911.

9. "Music and Drama," *Saturday News*, December 24, 1910.

10. *The Mirror*, October 25, 1912.

11. "Good Templars Meet," *Bulletin*, February 13, 1912.

12. "Good Templars Meeting," *Bulletin*, November 2, 1912.

13. Susan Ruttan, "Historical Timeline of the Unitarian Church of Edmonton," *The Unitarian Church of Edmonton: The History Project: A Century of Achievement*, http://www.ucehistory.org/history_TIMELINE.html

14. "Church Services," *Bulletin*, January 25, 1913.

15. "Church Services," *Bulletin*, April 26, 1912.

16. "Church Services," *Bulletin*, December 14, 1912.

17. "Church Services," *Bulletin*, October 7, 1912.

18. "Noted Unitarian Coming," *Bulletin*, November 16, 1912.

19. "Lancastrian Dinner a Splendid Success," *Bulletin*, February 12, 1912.

20. "Celebrate England's Day," *Bulletin*, April 26, 1912.

21. "Anniversary of St. David Celebrated: Welshmen Honor Patron Saint of Their Country by Banquet in Blue Moon," *Bulletin*, March 1, 1913.

22. "To the Veterans," *Bulletin*, August 31, 1912.

23. William Talbot Allison, *Bolshevism in English Literature* (London: Kessinger Publishing, 1921).

24. "Vanity Fair," *The Mirror*, October 18, 1912.

25. "Ladies Send Coronation Gift," *Bulletin*, May 9, 1911.

26. "Canadian Handicrafts Guild," *Wikipedia*, last modified July 23, 2014, https://en.wikipedia.org/wiki/Canadian_Handicrafts_Guild

27. "Home and Society," *Saturday News*, February 24, 1912.

28. "Secretary's Report of Edmonton Branch of Canadian Handicrafts Guild," *Bulletin*, February 25, 1913.

29. "Home and Society," *Saturday News*, July 13, 1912.

30. "Toronto Editor Coming," *Bulletin*, August 15, 1912.

31. "Musical and Dramatic," *The Mirror*, October 4, 1912.

32. N. B., "Jean Forsyth of Edmonton," *op cit.*

33. Penelope, "In the Realm of Women," *Bulletin*, February 26, 1912.

34. Previous to November 25, 1913 no editor was named for these "Pages." Jean Forsyth might have written all or some of those as well.

35. Shaw marched in the suffragette protests in London, England.

36. "New Woman," *Wikipedia*, last modified August 23, 2015. https://en.wikipedia.org/wiki/New_Woman.

FORTY-SEVEN

1. *Winnipeg Free Press*, June 15, 1912.

2. Madame Weinshenk, "Professor de Mise en Scene," *American Students Census*, Paris (1903), 209.

3. *Winnipeg Free Press*, June 15, 1912.

4. "Jean de Reszke," *Wikipedia*, last updated September 11, 2015, pp. 1–11. https://en.wikipedia.org/wiki/Jean_de_Reszke; P. G. Hurst, *The Operatic Age of Jean de Reszke: Forty Years of Opera, 1974–1914*, (New York: Robert M. McBride Co., 1959).

5. Daniel James Shigo, "The Teaching of Jean de Reszke," *Voice Talk Historical Perspectives on the Art of Singing*, http://www.voice-talk.net/2011/03/

teach-of-jean-de-reszke.html-l#uds-search-results This source includes several references to materials about de Reszke as a teacher.

6. Walter Johnstone-Douglas (de Reszke's assistant), "Jean de Reszke's Principles of Singing," *Music & Letters*, 6 (1925): 202–9.

7. "Music," *Town Topics*, January 14, 1899.

8. *Town Topics*, July 7, 1900; "Dame Nellie Melba," *Encyclopaedia Britannica*, online, http://www.britannica.com/biography/Nellie-Melba/images-videos/Nellie-Melba/157043 and "Dame Nellie Melba," *Melba Opera Trust*.

9. Charles H. Wheeler, "Edith Miller Makes Successful Debut: London Opera Patrons delighted With Manitoba Nightingale's Appearance at Covent Garden," *Winnipeg Tribune*, July 16, 1913.

FORTY-EIGHT

1. Paul Voisey, "Unsolved Mysteries of Edmonton's Growth," *Edmonton: The Life of a City*, ed. Bob Hesketh and Frances Swyripa, (Edmonton: NeWest Press, 1995), 324–25.

2. *Ibid.*, p. 324.

3. Sarah Bernhardt, as quoted in a review of Stewart Lemoine's *At the Zenith of Empire* (Edmonton: NeWest Press, 2007); "In Pursuit of Potential," *Canadian Literature*, issue 223 (Winter 2014).

4. "New Thought Temple," *Edmonton Capital*, February 14, 1914.

5. *Ibid.*, April 18, 1914.

6. "Religion-Socialism Lecture," *Edmonton Capital*, May 7, 1914.

7. "Church Services," *Bulletin*, May 16, 1914.

8. "Dinner Tendered To Supt. Alton," *Bulletin*, January 7, 1914.

9. "Circled the World Entirely By C.P.R.," *Bulletin*, October 10, 1913.

10. "Visiting Reeves Arrive In City," *Bulletin*, January 29, 1914.

11. "Paper on California," *Edmonton Capital*, February 23, 1914.

12. "Choral Union to Meet," *Bulletin*, May 16, 1914.

13. "Demonstration of Wireless Telegraphy," *Edmonton Capital*, May 19, 1914.

14. "The Gay World," *Edmonton Capital*, October 20, 1913.

15. "Boston Tango Demonstrated," *Bulletin*, February 19, 1914.

16. Penelope, "In the Realm of Women," *Bulletin*, August 9, 1913.

17. "Next Week's Attractions," *Bulletin*, February 4, 1914.

18. "Geisha," *Wikipedia*, last modified October 21, 2015. https://en.wikipedia.org/wiki/Geisha

19. "Women's Dress & Style from 1900 to 1919," *History of Women's Fashion—1900–1919, Glamourdaze*. http://glamourdaze.com/history-of-womens-fashion/1900-to-1919

20. "The Gay World: Mrs. Sifton," *Edmonton Capital*, October 25, 1913.

21. "An Old Fashioned Christmas Party," *Edmonton Bulletin*, December 29, 1913.

22. A simple English/Scottish country dance with four couples lined up facing each other.

23. "The Gay World," *Edmonton Capital*, November 10, 1913.

24. *Ibid.*, November 24, 1913.

FORTY-NINE

1. "Personal and Social," *Manitoba Free Press*, July 30, 1913.

2. The rank of baronet was passed down from father to son. Max's father was the 3rd baronet in the family, but Max never succeeded to the title, as he predeceased his father.

3. Sir Thomas had not yet remarried, though he would marry Freda, daughter of the Rt. Hon. Arthur Cohen, K.C. in 1914.

4. "Sir Thomas Colyer Colyer-Fergusson, 3rd Bt.," *The Peerage, last edited July 27, 2015, http://thepeerage.com/p8014.htm#i80140* and "Max Christian Hamilton Colyer-Fergusson," *The Peerage*, last edited February 17, 2011, http://thepeerage.com/p24656.htm#i246560

5. "Personal and Social," *Manitoba Free Press*, July 30, 1913.

6. "Miss Edith J. Miller's Wedding Announced," *Manitoba Free Press*, May 23, 1913.

7. "Sidelights on Shows Billed for the Coming Week," *Winnipeg Tribune*, July 12, 1913.

8. "Hamar Greenwood, 1st Viscount Greenwood," *Wikipedia*, last modified August 5, 2015, https://en.wikipedia.org/wiki/Hamar_Greenwood,_1st_Viscount_Greenwood

9. *Medicine Hat News*, July 21, 1913.

10. *Manitoba Free Press*, July 30, 1913.

FIFTY

1. "To Open Women's Press Club Room," *Bulletin*, November 6, 1913.

2. "Twenty Years Ago To-Day—1893," *Winnipeg Tribune*, August 29, 1913.

3. "This Day In History," www.history.com/this-day-in-history/archduke-franz-ferdinand-assassination

4. As quoted in Stewart Lemoine, *At the Zenith of Empire* (Edmonton: NeWest Press, 1913); "In Pursuit of Potential," (winter 2014), *Canadian Literature* Issue 223.

5. "Press Club will ask Province to Suspend Licenses," *Edmonton Capital*, August 21, 1914.

6. "Coming of Age Party," *Edmonton Capital*, December 30, 1913.

7. "Lieutenant Henry Charles Lionel Gillman," *Canadian Great War Project*, http://canadiangreatwarproject.com/searches/soldierDetail.asp?ID=116189

8. "Alberta in the Great War," *Alberta, Past and Present, Historical and Biographical*, https://archive.org/stream/albertapast-preseo3blue/albertapastpreseo3blue_djvu.txt

9. "Patriotic Tea in Blue Moon Tea Rooms Ad," *Bulletin*, November 9, 23 and 24, 1915.

10. "Personal and Social," *Manitoba Free Press*, April 12, 1915.

11. "United Farm Women of Alberta," *Club Women's Records*, 1916 Report, 52.

12. *Ibid.*, 112.

13. Paul Voisey, "Unsolved Mysteries of Edmonton's Growth," *Edmonton: The Life of a City* (Edmonton: NeWest Press, 1995), 324.

14. *Ibid.*

15. "To Help Serbians," *Medicine Hat Daily News*, December 1, 1915. Dr. Synge spells Serbian "Servian.

16. "Club Women's Records," *Canadian Women's Press Club Edmonton Branch*, 1916. http://peel.library.ualberta.ca/bibliography/4201.html

FIFTY-ONE

1. "Bank of Montreal," *Bulletin*, June 17, 1916.

2. Sharon Adams, "Stately Mansion Maintains Beauty, Dignity in Old Age," *Edmonton Journal*, January 26, 1977.

3. "LeMarchand Mansion, " http://www.edmontonmapsheritage.ca/location/lemarchand-mansion/

4. Michelle Swann and Veronica Strong-Boag, "Mooney, Helen Letitia (Mcclung)," in *Dictionary of Canadian Biography*, vol. 18, University of Toronto/Université Laval, 2003–, accessed August 28, 2016, http://www.biographi.ca/en/bio/mooney_helen_letitia_18E.html.

FIFTY-TWO

1. Details taken from "Miss Forsyth is Presented With Gold Purse," *Bulletin*, April 5, 1919.

2. "American Old-time Song Lyrics," www.traditionalmusic.co.uk

3. Ada L. Harris (lyrics) and Wilfrid Sanderson (music), "The Little Brown Owl," (NY: Boosey & Co., Inc.,), MCMXVII.

4. Caroline D. Hall (lyrics) and William H. Doane (music), "Crimson Roses Gem in the Heather" (Cincinnati: John Church & Co.), 1874.

5. Frederick Weatherly (lyrics) and Haydn Wood (music), "Roses of Picardy" (London: Chappell & Co.), 1916.

AFTERWORD

1. "Dance to Aid Japanese Held by D[uke] of Y[ork] Chapter of I.O.D.E. Was Tremendous Success," *Edmonton Bulletin*, October 6, 1923.

2. "Jean Forsythe, Former Local Woman Dies," *Winnipeg Tribune*, January 4, 1933.

3. *Ibid.*

4. "Passing of Jean Forsythe Is Great Loss to Edmonton," *Edmonton Bulletin*, January 3, 1933.

5. *Ibid.*

6. "Do You Remember," *Winnipeg Tribune*, July 11, 1929.

7. "One of Canada's Noted Artists," *Winnipeg Tribune*, July 4, 1936.

8. "Cemetery Search," *The City of Edmonton*, http://www.edmonton.ca/programs_services/service-cemetery-search.aspx